He Delivered
EVEN ME,
He Will Deliver
EVEN YOU

MISTI STEVENSON

Printed in the United States of America

10 9 8 7 6 5 4 3 2 1

ISBN-13   978-0-9894268-0-0

Dedication

~

TO MY HUSBAND AND CHILDREN, thank you for supporting me through the many long hours it took to bring forth this book.

Acknowledgements

~

M Y JOURNEY AND this book could not have happened without all of my angels. I first want to express my gratitude to my agency-loving grandparents. They showed me by their example that there was another way to live. To my husband, who came into my life as a knight in shining armor, thank you for never leaving my side and for continuing to give me strength, love, and laughter. I love you. And to my five angel children, who came into my life as the dews of heaven, thank you for your innocence and joy. I look forward to seeing all that you will become.

To my friend Amanda, thank you for being my first friend to know all about me and love me anyway. You gave me courage to go forward in sharing my story with others. I also want to thank my morning walking group for inspiring me daily, and for being the best sound board a girl could ask for.

I give a heartfelt thanks to all of my bishops whose guidance and revelation both put me on the right path and kept me traveling ever upward. To my trusted counselors, Marilyn and Janice, I owe more than I am able to give. Thank you for using your God-given gifts to bless my life.

I also want to acknowledge all of those who helped in the production of this book: Chris and Evie Stewart, Jennifer Griffith, and KayLynn Flanders. I am so grateful for your advice and insight. Thank you for letting me lean on your experience. This book would not have happened without you.

Contents

Preface

～

THIS BOOK, IN no way, is meant to dishonor my parents or my extended family. They loved me 100 percent. They did the best they knew how. It seems that my pain might have been more understandable had they purposely mistreated me. But, the opposite is true. They always did and still do everything in their power to make my physical life comfortable. I love and honor them for that. I don't know if I would have ever written my story had I not felt that it was a calling from Heavenly Father. My hope in doing so is this: that others might renew their strength to keep fighting, to keep praying, and to keep doing until they feel the Savior's Atonement working out the kinks in their lives too. I know that He will. If He could heal *Even Me*...I know He can heal *Even You!*

Introduction

~

THIS IS AN adventure I never thought I would take. A secret I thought would only be disclosed in the next life. Part of me even thought I would be somewhat of a hero there for putting on such a great show here. In heaven, people would know of all the pain I felt and they would be so amazed at how I kept it all together. They would pat me on the back and would be in awe. I really thought that pain would be my lifelong constant companion and only in the next life would it all be resolved.

Obviously, I was wrong about that since I am about to figuratively shout from the rooftops all of my deepest, scariest, darkest secrets and how the Atonement healed them.

And, you know what? Being wrong feels good.

I guess it is not the "being wrong" that feels good, but knowing the truth. The scriptures say, "The truth shall make you free" (John 8:32), and I know that now more than ever. In fact, I now know that almost everything I thought to be true was only an illusion. I will be forever grateful to my parents who faithfully took me to church, because that was the only road I could have been on to find the truths I have found. It was there that the Spirit testified to me that the gospel was true and that I had a Heavenly Father that loves us all. This carried me. Literally.

So here I am. Writing a book. I have been reminded that this is what I am supposed to do. It feels right. I am excited about it. Writing a book is new territory for me, but I am going forward anyway.

I feel somewhat like Nephi of old might have felt when he was commanded to build a ship. The Lord wanted him to do something he had never done before. It had to have been just a bit enticing to stay in the beautiful land Bountiful for a while and just enjoy a break from their long trek in the wilderness. But he knew that as good as Bountiful was, there was still a greater mission for him and there was a promised land out their waiting, not only for him but for a whole nation that would follow.

Now, I'm not saying there is a whole nation waiting for me, but there may be at least a few who will benefit from the telling of my story. And if that is what the Lord wants me to do, well...I've always been that sort of a girl.

CHAPTER 1

Ancient Rocks

~

MY JOURNEY, LIKE all of ours, began before I was born. I'm not talking about the pre-mortal existence. No, the journey that I am referring to is the journey that began in the lives of my ancestors before me. Their decisions, sins, and experiences were passed down to me in the womb. I may have come out with ten fingers and ten toes, but I also came with some rocks in my little unseen backpack. Yes, I was innocent like all babies are, yet I was still laden with what would be future challenges because of the choices of those that came before me. We all are. We pass much more down to our children than just our good looks. Truly, we are all connected.

We often hear the metaphor of "rocks in our backpacks" and how the rocks that weigh us down represent sin. It is a common belief that we, ourselves, put the rocks in there. It is not common, however, to hear of how often our parents, grandparents, and even great-great-grandparents unknowingly place rocks in our backpacks well before we even understand that they are there.

Jesus teaches us in Exodus that sin can affect the children, grandchildren, and great-grandchildren of the sinner: "For I the Lord thy God am a jealous God, visiting the iniquity of the fathers upon the children unto the third and fourth generation of them that hate me;

And shewing mercy unto thousands of them that love me, and keep my commandments." (Exodus 20:5–6)

Of course, this knowledge—that we receive the consequences of our fathers' sins—is not a prison sentence. The Savior's Atonement has provided a way out of any and all dysfunction that we may inherit. Preach My Gospel teaches us, "All that is unfair about life can be made right through the Atonement of Jesus Christ." He says that He will show mercy to those that love Him and keep His commandments.

We not only get rocks from the sins of those who came before us, but we also get rocks from the false traditions that we are taught as truth from the time that we are little babies. Doctrine and Covenants 93:38–40 teaches, "Every Spirit of man was innocent in the beginning; and God having redeemed man from the fall, men became again, in their infant state, innocent before God. And that wicked one cometh and taketh away light and truth through disobedience, from the children of men, and because of the tradition of their fathers. But I have commanded you to bring up your children in light and truth."

This passage of scripture explains that although we were innocent in our infant state, Satan comes to take away that light through our own disobedience and because of the traditions of our fathers. Certainly this is one of Satan's favorite tools. He knows he can weigh down generations through the disobedience of one. The sins and false beliefs of our parents (as well as ourselves) can affect generations.

You may not be taught a blatant falsehood like there is no God or that the Church isn't true. Instead, they may be more subtle falsehoods such as, "You are only as good as you are beautiful," or "You are only honoring your parents if you relinquish your agency to be under their complete control."

It is obvious that those two statements are completely false, yet if we learn them from the time we are infants we can be led away from true freedom and happiness by the false traditions of our parents. Maybe our parents created those traditions and maybe they are just mirroring what they were taught. It doesn't matter. What does matter is that we recognize this as a tool of Satan to destroy families as well as individual souls.

My parents aren't to blame for my misery any more than their parents were to blame for theirs. It is what we do with the rocks that we have been given that is the true test of this life. My parents had many rocks in their own backpacks, yet in one critical way, they heeded the counsel to bring up their "children in light and truth." They weren't perfect at following many of the commandments but they did, however, give me truth. They did this by simply taking my siblings and me to church, where our testimonies were born.

However, "that wicked one," even Satan, tried to confuse me, and this he did very well. He made it very clear that something was missing. There was a wide gap between what I was learning at church and what I observed in my home. I was taught that both places were right, yet they didn't congeal. That caused much hidden havoc and dysfunction within me.

We learn that deliverance from all the weaknesses that we inherit is found in His love. It is found in His truth. It is the only key to personal freedom. However, a seeker of truth can only really have freedom if truth is actively and painfully applied. In other words, one must turn the key of truth in order to open the door to peace and real freedom—freedom from the falsehoods we take on as truth as children.

Fortunately for me, I had enough pain in my life that I sought for truth like a pirate seeks for treasure. Once I found it, I actively and painfully turned the key to freedom. I want my children to know their mother's path to peace: this is one of the reasons I am writing my story. Although I will have had different stones in my path than theirs will, ultimately it is the same path. Jesus Christ paved the way, and when we are ready, He throws our rocks off our paths for us. Only He is strong enough to do it.

From where I was then to where I am now is the journey that I am about to define. That journey took me across the wide gap of confusion and brought me to truth and ultimately to healing. Our loving Savior made a humanly impossible journey divinely possible.

CHAPTER 2

Rocks in My Mother's Backpack

~

MY MOTHER WAS born into a family where the parents were sealed in the temple, but, as we all know, that doesn't mean "happily ever after." There are nine kids in her family. She was number four. She was born in 1952. She says she has a lot of fond memories growing up. She loved their vacations (especially Disneyland), holidays, and just the summer-day freedoms she and her siblings had in running around the neighborhood endlessly.

From what I understand, her biggest rock was thrown in her path, unknowingly, by her father, when she was in the seventh grade. Her sister took the family car for a drive. She was not 16 yet and she did not ask permission. While on the freeway, she got a flat tire. A nice man stopped to help her change it. She was standing in between the two cars when a drunk driver hit her car and smashed her legs between them. The two bumpers were overlapping. They put my aunt in the back of the station wagon while waiting for help. Days later, she had to get one of her legs amputated on what would've been one of the happiest days of her young life—her 16th birthday.

The back of the station wagon was a mess from my aunt's injuries. My grandpa made my mom clean it up—blood, veins, and all. My mom would sometimes tell us of the horror that that was to her to have to clean off the back of the station wagon. My mom got so sick afterwards, she developed what we now know as Obsessive-Compulsive Disorder. She washed her hands until they bled and she got clear down to 70 pounds in the seventh grade! She was in need of help but no one took care of her; no one knew how. She says it was her own ability to tell herself that she wouldn't die if she didn't wash her hands all the time that got her past it.

She got over the hand washing, but the OCD never went away, it just manifested itself in other ways. It manifested in the obsessive way she had to keep her house clean, as well as other nonchemical addictions. My grandma said that at dinnertime at their house, my mom would be the first one done with her food. She would clean up even before everyone else was done. A mother's dream, but not super healthy for a 13-year-old girl.

Sometime thereafter, my mother's father bought a farm a couple hours from their home and was gone a lot. From what I understand, living a bachelor life instead of being home with his nine kids resulted in a few bad habits that he didn't have before. He also got caught in a semi-affair. I say "semi" because I don't know all the details. I do know that it caused a strain on their marriage and things were never quite the same again.

My mom's mother, on the other hand, had her own rocks or false beliefs that she was carrying around. She was more interested in money, worldly possessions, and what was on the outside of her children than what was on the inside. Thus, many of her children were left with a huge internal void. They tried to fill that void with various addictions. The problem was that it only made the emptiness more tangible.

Was she an awful, horrible mom? Of course not! She loved her children fiercely but acted more on her false beliefs than on actual truth. God teaches us truth. He teaches that although we tend to look on the outward appearance of man, He looks at our hearts (see 1 Samuel 16:7). If Heavenly Father pays more attention to the hearts of His children than their worldly appearances, we would be wise to do the same.

Through it all, my mom learned to be what we now know as co-dependent. One definition of co-dependence is this: "Relating to a relationship in which one person is psychologically dependent in an unhealthy way on someone who is addicted to a drug or self-destructive behavior..." (Codependent, n.d.).

An example of this was in my parents' relationship. My mom fell in love with my dad—a man that was obviously not the best choice at the time. Her first memory of my dad was feeling sorry for him because in her high school math class he smelled like smoke. Without the baggage of imperfect parents and an imperfect childhood (in other words, a pretty normal "earthly" upbringing), she, a good Mormon girl, might have run the other way. I say, "might," because maybe the Lord would have wanted them together anyway. I like to believe that is true. However, even though my mom could smell smoke on him and she was known as the Molly Mormon who would never do such a thing, she was still attracted to him. She thought she could save him. She thought she could change him. Thus, the codependence won out.

They had a passionate and volatile dating relationship that was on and off. They ended up getting married when they were only 19. Her lifelong dream of a temple marriage was gone and forever haunted her. That was a huge rock in her backpack! She didn't know how to use the Atonement and truly forgive herself. That rock was then placed unknowingly into my backpack as well. Even down to the time that I was dating my husband, she still cried when she talked about not marrying in the temple when they first wed.

11

I never really understood the scripture I quoted earlier in Exodus, "For I the Lord thy God am a jealous God, visiting the iniquity of the fathers upon the children unto the third and fourth generation of them that hate me; And shewing mercy unto thousands of them that love me and keep my commandments" (Exodus 20:5–6). I understand a bit more now. I can see how our parents' sins affected them and thus affect us. Likewise, what we do, does and will affect our children.

My story is about rocks in my backpack and how they were removed. My backpack was filled with rocks from mostly my mother's side, but I'm sure there were some from my father's side as well. No one gave them to me intentionally. In fact, my ancestors dealt with the same problem. They had their own rocks to deal with. If there is blame to give then I also share in that blame because I, too, added rocks to my own backpack.

I was in the fifth grade when I first began to notice that it was a bit harder to move forward in life than I thought it would be. My rocks were really weighing me down, and that was the first time I even knew they were there. I recognized them at first, but when no one else saw the rocks, I was forced (or felt forced) to pretend they didn't exist. I was too scared to do anything else. I was scared to face the rocks. Especially as a child, I had no idea what to do with them. I was scared of breaking the rule in our family that at all costs we do everything we can to look perfect on the outside. My mom believed that if all looked perfect on the outside, then life was good and all else should work out fine. After years of that motto not working for me, I took a quantum leap of faith and acknowledged those scary rocks again. I followed the Spirit's guidance until ultimately the Savior lifted them off of my back.

CHAPTER 3

Breaking Chains

~

REAKING THE CHAINS of multigenerational dysfunction is not an easy task, but I am here to testify that it can be done. I am not sure how far back the dysfunction goes in my family lines, but it is obvious that my mom's family bathed in it. Out of nine kids there was one alcoholic, three pregnancies out of wedlock, two addicted to pain medicine to the point of brain alteration, two with Obsessive-Compulsive Disorder, one of those with psychiatric help, one whose children were taken from her and her husband for a while because of anger and domestic disputes, 7 divorces (2 siblings had 2 divorces each), one in and out of jail his whole adult life, and one attempted suicide.

It makes me so sad to look at all the pain that they carry. They aren't bad people. I believe for the most part people do the best they can. The knowledge they gain is really their only weapon to escape. Otherwise, they play the part that they have been given. The pain in my mom's family is obviously great, yet when they are together, it is all about the superficial. How they look, whose kids are looking better or doing better, etc. Basically, whoever "looks" like they have it all together wins. Even though they still love one another, they have a hard time seeing through to what really matters. It is hard for me to write this. I know that if they ever read it, I will be ostracized from the family, at least for a while. The worst thing you can do is make the family look bad.

Whenever I am with that side of the family or ponder on the dysfunction there, I feel troubled and find myself wishing I could somehow make it all right. I feel like Alma, "Oh, that I were an angel, and could have the wish of mine heart, that I might go forth and speak with the trump of God, with a voice to shake the earth, and cry repentance unto every people! Yea, I would declare unto every soul, as with the voice of thunder, repentance and the plan of redemption, that they should repent and come unto our God, that there might not be more sorrow upon all the face of the earth" (Alma 29: 1–2).

I am not saying that they have major sins to repent of. I understand more now than ever before what repentance means. The totality of the word is so much more than turning away from sin. It is also turning away from anything, even the traditions of our fathers that keep us from Christ. Turning to Christ means turning away from whatever culture we come from and turning to the culture of Christ. It is not always easy. It can be a bit like trying to pull away from a life-size magnet at times. Heavenly Father allows us to fight to pull away and then, when on His omniscient time-table He says, "It's enough," He gently and powerfully pulls us far enough away that the magnet of family dysfunction can no longer pull us in. The key is to keep doing our part in trying to change until He steps in. God loves our agency and our growth enough that unless we are showing that we are earnestly doing everything in our power to change, He won't step in and save us (see 2 Nephi 25:23). If we aren't trying, what we are saying is that we are choosing to stay in the chains of dysfunction.

Alma explains the power of agency in these next verses. "But behold, I am a man, and do sin in my wish; for I ought to be content with the things which the Lord hath allotted unto me. I ought not to harrow up in my desires, the firm decree of a just God, for I know that he granteth unto men according to their desire, whether it be unto death or unto life; yea, I know that he allotteth unto men, yea, decreeth unto them decrees which are unalterable, according to their wills, whether they be unto salvation or unto destruction. Yea, and I know that good and evil have come before all men; he that knoweth not good from evil is blameless; but he that knoweth good and evil, to him it is given according to his desires, whether he desireth good or evil, life or death, joy or remorse of conscience. Now, seeing that I know these things, why should I desire more than to perform the work to which I have been called? Why should I desire that I were an angel, that I could speak unto all the ends of the earth?" (Alma 29:3–7).

I love the Book of Mormon. It truly is the iron rod. It keeps us from veering off the path even if it is something seemingly as benign as grief over not being able to change your family for the better. These verses of scripture teach me that the Lord is over all and I should be content with what the Lord has allotted me. Verse 8 further explains the Lord's ways: "For behold, the Lord doth grant unto all nations, of their own nation and tongue, to teach his word, yea, in wisdom, all that he seeth fit that they should have; therefore we see that the Lord doth counsel in wisdom, according to that which is just and true."

All flesh is truly in God's hands and what a relief that knowledge can be to us! Too often we feel that all flesh is in *our* hands and unduly give ourselves grief over those in our family that we feel it is our duty to change. Only the Lord, through his Holy Spirit can truly teach and change others. We are really only here to be the best example we can be and to listen to the Spirit when he wants us to step in and do more. I guess that is why He teaches us to be a light on a hill.

Still, our brains can know it isn't our responsibility to change all the dysfunction in our families, but our hearts often don't. We may not be able to change whole families but maybe we can, by example, and with Spirit-led teaching help one person in our family to change, and thus change the generations after them. It helps to remember that the second commandment says "love your neighbor as yourself" and not "change your neighbor as yourself." That is God's territory. The only chains we have power to break are the ones within ourselves. Everything else is by example only. What a relief!

My dad's family, like every other family, had rocks of their own. And I received some of those rocks, too. However, I didn't spend as much time with them and when I did, their rocks weren't as apparent or as detrimental to me personally. They may have been harder to deal with for others in my dad's family. Everyone reacts differently to the same rocks. Some personalities can easily overlook dysfunction and not be affected in the least. That's how I was with my dad's family. In general his family, or at least my grandparents, provided me with a shining example that I loved and tried to follow. Their lives were lived in agreement with what I had learned at church. They were at peace and I wanted to follow them.

My mom's family, though "fun," was not at peace. I didn't understand it but somehow I knew that it was affecting me negatively. I knew the pain and confusion I was feeling was somehow connected to them.

Before you begin to read about my early life, it is important to remember that things aren't always as they look. Dysfunctional families come in all shapes and sizes. Like the various presents at a bridal shower, my family's present would have had the biggest bow and the shiniest paper. It would've made you think that it had the very best present inside, yet when you opened it, you would've found it void of any real content. Too much time had been spent in its presentation—so much so, that there was no time left for the real reason it was wrapped in the first place: for its contents. Instead, all that would be left when the present was opened would be the torn and useless wrapping paper.

In many ways I felt like that beautiful present. Great care was taken by my mother to create a beautiful-looking "Misti life." In her mind there was a false belief that she lived by: if it *looked* good, it *was* good. Like decorating a beautiful present, what she did wasn't necessarily wrong; it just wasn't enough. Without any purposeful harm, she raised me to be a beautiful but helpless and never-ending daughter.

I say "never-ending" because she needed me to need her forever. Co-dependence is a tricky thing to recognize unless you know the symptoms. That is why children of co-dependent parents often feel like something is inherently wrong with themselves. They can't pinpoint exactly what it was that went wrong in their upbringing. They feel guilty when they have negative feelings towards their parents because their parents sacrificed and did so much for them. However, what they don't know is that over-caretaking might have been the problem.

Another definition of co-dependence is this, "Codependency describes behavior, thoughts and feelings that go beyond normal kinds of self-sacrifice or caretaking. For example, parenting is a role that requires a certain amount of self-sacrifice... although a parent could nevertheless still be codependent towards their own children if the caretaking or parental sacrifice reached unhealthy or destructive levels." (Codependency, n.d.)

You have probably heard the comment that so-and-so "lives through their child." Co-dependent people often do that, and doing so gravely handicaps their child. They don't get to live a life of their own because the parent needs them too much.

At a seminar about Codependency, Dr. Leon Blake (Ph.d, director of LDS Family Services) said, "When there is an extreme reliance on another person, there becomes a need to control that person."

In a nutshell, that is what happened to me. It confused me. It was like being trapped in a funhouse at a carnival; it looked like fun on the outside but for some reason it felt wrong and a bit creepy. Had it not been for my extreme pain, I probably would've been on my deathbed still confused, and more than likely I would've perpetuated the "funhouse effect" to my children.

Pain is a great motivator and thus, I made it my life's quest to not only figure it out, but to escape it for myself and the generations after me. Yes, the sins of the parents are on the heads of the children, but I chose to focus on the "mercy" part of that scripture. If God is perfectly fair then He would have to provide a way out. I didn't know how He could do it but I trusted He would. I was a believer in mercy. It took much longer than I would've chosen had I been in charge. However, He didn't disappoint. His power and His mercy healed all my wounds, specifically those that were unknowingly placed upon me by those that loved me the most.

CHAPTER 4

Before I Noticed Rocks

~

I WAS BORN ON April 5, 1975. My mom was very excited to get another girl. My dad was disappointed I wasn't a boy. My mom said that I was her easiest pregnancy, her easiest delivery, her easiest baby, and her easiest one to raise. After she took one look at me out of the womb and I looked like her side of the family, she must have decided then and there that I would be the one that could drown all of her sorrows. I would be the one she could mold into who she wished she were. I would be the one she could live vicariously through. Tag and I was it. Did she mean to hurt me? Absolutely not. She had no idea that this baby—me—who she loved so much would hurt so terribly year after year because she would glean the joy right out of me by unknowingly overriding my agency. Knowledge is power. Had she known better, she would have done better. I believe this with all of my heart.

At first there was joy. Babies just come that way. They are so clean. No resentments, things to forgive, or bad memories; just love. I had an older sister, who was my elder by three and a half years. I remember my yellow room and the big yellow mouth toy box. When my brother came four years later, I was moved to the blue room with my sister. We had a blue canopy bed. My mom was always good at making our home beautiful and clean.

My first bad memory was seeing my parents fight so badly that my dad punched a hole through the wall. Yes, he was strong but, having a cast on his wrist helped immensely, I'm sure. I remember it like the cinematography in some movies—like the camera was off balance to create a feeling of commotion. I knew what happened wasn't right. I'm not sure if I was scared.

The first house I lived in was in a neighborhood with a lot of tiny, one-story homes. Some had an upstairs, and from my perspective they were huge. Any home with stairs seemed magical.

My dad worked at Thiokol and since money was tight, my mom weighed sugar beets during the night. She did this because she loved Christmas and wanted to keep the tradition that she grew up with. Her family was wealthy and they had always received a lot for Christmas. We were also spoiled at Christmas. In some strange way, I blamed some of my pain on my mom's Christmas spending habits. There was too much pretending that life was perfect. It didn't match how I felt and was very confusing.

I met my first best friend while living in Sandalwood. Her name was Marcy. Her older sister, was my older sister's best friend too. That was really convenient for play dates and sleepovers. Marcy was a year older than me. My first memories of her were playing outside and finding what we called "cheesies" and eating them. We would gather cups full before we would feast. I'm assuming they were edible. I never got sick from them.

Marcy lived around the corner on the other street. I got my first sidewalk knee scrape on my way over there. That must have been traumatic for a 3-year-old to remember that. I also remember the carpet in Marcy's house was a shaggy red. Funny what random details a young mind remembers.

Our tiny little house had a backyard that I loved. We had a cool boat-like teeter-totter. My dad always had a dog. This first dog was huge! It was a Heinz 57 (a mix of a few kinds of dogs). My sister called it Bear because it was black and hairy.

There was a car dealership by our home. Sometimes before dinner, Mom would send my sister and me over there with a few quarters to buy some soda pop.

I have a few insignificant memories from inside our home. Mom used to wash our hair in the kitchen sink. We would lie down on the bar and tilt our head back and under the faucet. Then, we would dry our hair by leaning over the heater vents. I also remember climbing on the bar to get in the cupboard and sneakily eat the butter. Thankfully I grew out of that desire.

My mom and her sister started teaching dance when I was only two. Thirty-five years later, they are still teaching dance. I was three when I started taking dance. I was in class with my best friend, Marcy. From what I hear, I was pretty good from the beginning. Dancing quickly became my identity. It was who my mom's family was. I was no exception. Pretty much all of my growing up memories are infused with dance in some way or another.

When I was just over 4 years old, we moved to a little old white house just east of town. We lived there for several months while our new house was being built. My dad built most of our new home himself. My dad's brother sold us the property. It was beautiful. It overlooked a river. The house seemed huge when we moved in. My sister and I loved the stairs!

One of my favorite memories happened right after we moved in. *The Wizard of Oz* was playing on TV. We were in the basement on our new rust-colored carpet. My mom sat cross-legged and held me on her lap while we watched the movie. My dad was asleep on the couch in back of us. It makes me want to cry when I think of this memory. So sweet. So simple. So full of love.

Soon after our move I met my second best friend, Heather. She lived right behind my house up a small, weedy hill. We had kindergarten together with Mr. Manning. We hit it off right away. We had so much fun together because no matter what we did, there was laughing to go along with it—lots and lots of laughing. My nickname in elementary school wasn't "laughing hyena" for nothing.

Our homes were built in an old apple orchard so there were always plenty of apples. Heather and I loved to pick green apples and eat them in her playhouse (I called it a Taco Time playhouse because it looked like the wooden playhouses at all the Taco Time restaurants). Heather liked her green apples with salt. I liked them plain.

Heather and I had tons of fun having sleepovers. We loved sleeping outside either on my trampoline or in her playhouse. We got the biggest kick out of toilet papering our neighbors. One time, while sleeping in the Taco Time playhouse, we toilet papered her next-door neighbor. Her dad woke us up at 5:00 in the morning to clean it up.

We also loved to create our own "tree houses," or more appropriately named, "club houses," since they weren't up in trees. There were lots of wild, tightly grown trees to the east of my house. Some of them were plum trees. We loved to eat the fruit. Within the woods by my house we cleared out a spot and stacked up the debris for our outside walls. We rolled big tree logs for our couch, somehow made a table, and even laid carpet out that Heather's dad wasn't using. We had an "official" clubhouse and so we held "official" meetings. We wrote up an agenda and nailed it to a tree. I asked the only nonreligious person in our group say the opening prayer. If I remember right, he said it anyway. What funny and good memories! Those are priceless.

Heather and I also loved to play in our sandbox. We mostly made rivers and dams with the hose water. Another thing we did with the hose was make a circle with it on the side patio and fill it with water (a whole inch deep). It was our makeshift pool. Then we would get peas from my garden and sprinkle the "pool" with peas. Then came the real luxury—we laid down in the water and lazily ate the floating peas as if we were queens getting fed grapes.

We loved any activity with water. We jumped on the trampoline with the sprinklers, ran through the sprinklers, and one or two times we even made our own waterslide down the back hill. It quickly became a mudslide that we slid down while sitting in plastic garbage sacks. What a fun mess!

Some memories from each grade in school:

Kindergarten: Mr. Manning—A chubby, nice man. He tied my shoes for me once and they were too tight. I think I learned to tie my own after that.

1st grade: Mrs. Fisher—A skinny, short, blonde-haired woman who was not smiley and very serious. I remember being so excited for first grade that I woke up around five o'clock that morning. I was excited to wear my new knickers and vest. It was a maroon velvet vest with black and white knickers. My sister and I were dressed the same that day. At recess one day a boy in my class named Brandon had a new puffy coat on with a high collar. He had it sticking straight up to look like a vampire. He claimed he was a vampire. I told him, "No you aren't." He and I went back and forth a bit until he told me to give him my thumb and he would prove it to me. Unfortunately, I did. He bit my thumb so hard that I went in crying to the teacher. He got in trouble. My kids love that story.

2nd grade: Ms. Cullimore—A big, tall, dark-haired lady. I had a crush on a boy named Tom in my class. Unfortunately, he liked Heather. One day at recess, I fell hard on the asphalt while being chased by a boy. I had the worst puss-filled scab that I can remember. Also in 2nd grade I had the classic nightmare—I dreamed I went to school naked and was in front of my class performing or singing something. Pretty traumatic, yet I think I thought it was funny.

3rd grade: Mr. Firth—A tall, bald man. A couple of weeks before 3rd grade, my mom took my sister and I to the hairdresser to get our hair cut. The new style was to cut your bangs clear back to almost the crown of your head. She cut my hair that way. I hated it. The very next day I started growing my bangs out, so my picture on the first day of school is of me in my turquoise green jumpsuit with crimpy long hair in the back and two little ponytail balls on the top of my head. To make matters worse, although at the time I liked it, I had two silver braces on my two front teeth. It was quite the look.

4th grade: Mrs. Maughan—She had light brown hair and was more of a grandma figure. Every day a girl in my class, Susan, would tell me the same joke: "How many skinny people can you fit in a shower? I don't know—they keep slipping down the drain." Then she'd follow up with: "How many people fat people can you fit in a shower? None, they won't fit through the door." I would laugh and laugh—every day. I thought she was the funniest girl ever. She even had a funny look because she, herself, was so skinny. I began to notice that year that all the boys seemed to like all the other girls and not me. They liked Tami. I thought it was because she had really thin lips. I began wishing my lips were thin like hers. I would practice making my lips look thinner while smiling. That year during recess, we loved to hang upside down on this long silver bar. We made up all sorts of stories as well as all sorts of choreography on that bar.

5th grade: Mr. Pierson—A tall, strong, dark-haired man that was also a farmer. I loved him the very most. He was strong and stern but had a sly smile that was almost always there. I knew he liked me. Looking back I think he was my favorite because he was confident, happy, and had good boundaries. He did not override agency. He was fun to please as well as to tease. He also loved to tease us. My best friend, Heather, and I finally had a class together again. Fifth grade was our last year of elementary school. What a great year that was!

(Unfortunately, it was my last great year.) A lot of us girls would run outside the second the recess bell rang. We had handstand contests on the grass. We realized that if you arched your back like a "C" you could win easier because it seemed to help you stay up longer. That was the year I got my name on the board for the first time (a kid put it there, not Mr. Pierson). I cried. I wasn't very good at getting in trouble.

My elementary years were obliviously happy. I had no pain yet, so I didn't notice what was indeed already beginning to make me sick under the surface. I was still childlike and went along, as children often do, with blinders on to the bad and only looking for the next spot of fun. "Fun" was easy to see in my life at the time because that was what my mom was all about.

Holidays in my early years were so much fun. The Halloween carnival at my elementary school was a blast! My favorite thing was the cakewalk. I won a cake almost every year. I loved the days in the fall when I would stay home from school for no reason at all. My brother and I especially loved staying home from school if there was a fresh layer of frost on the ground. We would run outside, get on the trampoline, lay down with our faces pressing on the black material so that we could see the frost on the ground through it. We often brought blankets out with us. We would talk about Jack Frost and get all excited because frost meant Christmas was coming. Mom talked up the Christmas fantasy so much from the time we were little that we bought into it. It was as if we believed Heaven would be here come December 25th. She began getting us revved up about Christmas the second Halloween was over, and often before.

My favorite Christmas was when I was 5 years old. We woke up Christmas morning when it was still dark. It seemed magical as I came down the stairs to the most perfect little kitchen set that I could've imagined. It had cupboards and a fridge that had pictures of all the goods a fridge should have in it. It came with a table and chairs to eat all the pretend food on. I remember literally shivering with excitement.

During Christmas break, we would do a lot of playing out in the snow. I loved the snow. Whenever I knew it was supposed to snow, I would open the back door (which was really the side door) and flip on the patio light to see how much snow had fallen. I loved the way the light glistened on the snowflakes. My favorite color has always been white. Maybe it has its roots in snow. The sun reflecting off freshly fallen snow reminded me of Heaven. It was so white and pure. Heaven was a symbol of the peace and of the place I wanted to one day be with my family. Thus, the color white has always been my favorite color.

Christmas memories were wonderful, at least during my elementary school years. After that, they were the antithesis of how I was really feeling and I silently resented it all, even as I was playing the part of the happy excited girl.

Mom practically worshiped Christmas, so she worked really hard to make it perfect, or at least what she thought was perfect. I only liked it until about the fifth grade. It was then that I began to notice that it was too much. It all seemed fake—like she was playing house from the months of October through December. The perfection of her Christmases, I noticed, weren't worth all the stress, money, and let-down that she had afterwards when it was over. I knew that money was tight and could then sense the post-Christmas crunch. My parents fought a lot over money, which added to my anxiousness when we received so much Christmas morning. I began to dislike getting presents because I realized it wasn't worth it; however, I couldn't tell my mom that so I just pretended to be more excited than I was. I liked getting new things, but I hated how I felt afterwards. I felt like a bad girl; like if I didn't get so much everyone would be happier.

I began to realize that the true meaning of the holiday was being overlooked. I learned at church that Christmas was meant to rejoice in Christ. It just didn't match up with how our family lived or more specifically, how we celebrated Christmas. It didn't match up with how I was beginning to feel. That discrepancy, coupled with the rule in our family to never hurt mom's feelings, made for a lot of years of pretending so that Mom could continue to play house in her make-believe world of Christmas each fall.

I lived in such a confusing world. During my early years, I was quite oblivious to the dysfunction in my family. I could go back and write of some of the problems that I remember now that I can look back through the lens of an educated adult, but although a reality, it wasn't in the forefront of my reality at the time. I do remember my parents fighting a lot, especially about my dad's Word of Wisdom habits. I remember my mom taking me for a drive past the café to see if my dad's truck was there. I prayed it wasn't there because if it were, my mom would assume my dad was in there drinking coffee. They would have a big fight about it later. From what I know now, I can clearly see that my dad was the addict and my mom was the co-dependent whose worth was dependent on whether or not she could change my dad. Nevertheless, I wasn't old enough to comprehend it, and so as children often do, I thought my family was normal. With childlike faith, I accepted it and all of its falsehoods as truth.

In so many ways from the outside looking in, my parents were the perfect parents. We were well taken care of physically. Our house was clean. We were clean and well dressed. We had plenty of after school activities. Mom almost always had a home-cooked meal ready for us after school. Dad would take us hunting and fishing with him. I especially loved how he wrestled with us. He is still heard today threatening the grandkids with, "I'm going to check your oil." That means he is going to pretend to stick his finger in that soft part on

27

your neck in between your collarbone. We loved it then and my kids love it now. We had a garden and loved going out to help plant it. Mom and Dad took care of our every need physically. If we needed anything, they did it.

That sounds good doesn't it? Unfortunately, they also made every decision for us. In order to deserve love, we had to cooperate and do and be whatever they decided was best for us. Some parents unwisely believe that they always know what is best for their children. Instead of parents, they become puppeteers.

Elder Larry Y. Wilson of the Seventy said in the April 2012 general conference, "Compulsion builds resentment…and it makes people feel incompetent…. If parents hold on to all decision-making power…they severely limit the growth and development of their children…. Such children often either rebel against this compulsion or are crippled by an inability to make any decisions on their own" (Wilson, 2012).

When I was young and needed a lot of care, I couldn't have asked for better parents, as far as my physical needs went. However, as I grew and they continued to over-parent, it caused confusion and extreme havoc inside of me. I didn't know how to get out of the pretend world that they had created. I was the puppet. I lived and moved as they decided. Living a controlled life eventually brings a lot of pain. Your spirit knows you aren't alive and it sends pain as its warning signal. Eventually my pain became like a constant fire alarm. I could hear it and feel it; however, I didn't know what to do. I tried to pretend it wasn't there until I could take no more.

I guess for that I should be thankful. I could have never learned all that I have learned had I not gone through what I did. The Lord truly consecrates all our afflictions for our gain, and in the end helps us love those who caused the affliction in the first place. What a loving and merciful creator we have!

CHAPTER 5

The Imperfect Beauty of Agency

~

MY MOM'S PARENTS and my dad's parents couldn't have been more different. I favored my mom's side before I got sick, but afterwards I glorified my dad's side. I began to see that somehow my mom's side was the cause of my sickness. I began to really notice the differences between the families. Right or wrong, I began judging everyone because I needed peace and I was trying to figure out who had peace and why they did.

I noticed that when I was with my mom's side of the family, everything that was important to them seemed superficial. In mighty contrast with that, when I was with my dad's parents, everything had purpose. I felt free and I felt capable there. It is interesting to note that when with my mom's side, I had every comfort and pleasure possible. I had every physical need met for me. Yet, I didn't when with my paternal grandparents. It didn't make sense to me. I was more physically at ease with my mom's side, yet I was more happy and peaceful with my dad's side. I tried to figure that out. Looking back it's easy to see. While with my mom or her side of the family, I was more of a doll or a figurine to dress and move how and where my mom wanted. But at my dad's parents' house, I was a person, capable of moving and learning myself. Although less instantly gratifying, life felt exciting with them.

The main difference was that I was in control of my life when with my dad's side. When with my mom's side, my mom and grandma were in control. I was feeling the exhilaration of agency with the one verses the nothingness of being controlled with the other.

My mom didn't feel as comfortable with my dad's family, so we didn't go there nearly as often as we went to her parents' house. Even though both sets of grandparents were within ten minutes of our house, we didn't share equal time. From my mom's comments and reactions when we talked about my dad's parents, I knew that she didn't think they were as good as her family. She helped us notice that they weren't as clean and that their food wasn't as good as her family's food. I knew that another unspoken rule in my family was to never disagree with Mom as to whose family was better. I just did as I was told. I didn't ruffle her feathers about it.

We did, however, go up to my dad's parents' house for hunting endeavors, family reunions, and once in a while for a sleepover. It was there that I gained a desire to be righteous, as well as an appetite for healthy food. We often stayed at their house in the summer for a few days while my parents celebrated their anniversary. I remember feeling a bit homesick at first, and then after a while not wanting to go home.

I have wonderful memories of reading scriptures, eating home-made fresh, cracked-wheat cereal with honey, picking fresh carrots out of their garden, going for a walk with Grandma to see Grandpa out milking the cows, and then walking along the high cement fence in front of all the cows while Grandma held my hand. I loved to sleep on their tiny exercise trampoline that was in their family room. Grandma stayed up late and was always up early making break-fast. She loved to can all kinds of fruit. I loved to eat her frozen cherries. She and Grandpa made good caramel popcorn. Grandpa would often go downstairs to the freezer to get the huge bucket of

Farr Better ice cream to make us "a cone." It felt so homey there. Grandma was, in my point of view, the perfect wife and homemaker. They served in the temple, Grandpa as a bishop, and together as missionaries among the Native Americans in Arizona. When my dad was a boy, they took in at least one orphan Native American boy who became what my dad fondly called his "Indian brother."

Grandma also did a lot of genealogy work. She co-created at least one genealogy book with thousands of dates and names, as well as old pictures and journal entries. I can't imagine the time and energy that took. I am blessed to have one of those books. It is priceless to me.

She had a room dedicated to just genealogy work. I loved going in there and getting one of those big sheets of genealogy papers to turn over and paint on. Grandma would make us homemade paint to use. She always made it pink. She hung our art on her walls. I noticed that she didn't care about how things looked, she cared more about us, her grandchildren. Several pieces of my "artwork" were still on display in their home clear until they both passed on. I was seventeen when they died. Grandma died in July and Grandpa died three months later from a broken heart. I took my art pieces down as we emptied their house. What a gift of unconditional love that was to me to see my "artwork" hung up all of those years. And it's important to note that they weren't professional looking in any sense of the word. One of them was made out of empty paper towel rolls!

My grandparents loved each other, and as far as I could see, they never fought like my parents did. I wanted to be just like them some-day. I learned from them that money doesn't make someone happy. I learned that being obedient does. I am so grateful that I had their example. Although now, as an adult, I can now look at their lives more objectively and see that even they had trials, imperfections, and wayward children. They were dysfunctional in ways as well, yet I still see their examples to me as absolutely priceless! What I still see when I look back at my paternal grandparents is that they were trying to please the Lord, and no matter the rocks in their way, they were continually trying to stay on the path. Their example of doing the basics like reading their scriptures daily, going to the temple, serving a mission, and doing good to the homeless is priceless to me. I love them dearly for that. As I was going through my hard times, I often imagined that my grandma was my guardian angel. I believe she was and still is my heavenly helper.

CHAPTER 6

Noticing and Ignoring My Rocks

~

WHEN I LOOK back on my life, fifth grade was when the pressure in my physical volcano began to really build. My schedule was pretty tight. I took tumbling, ballet, and jazz on Monday for two and a half hours, Tuesdays and Thursdays I was in Logan for four hours including driving time. On Wednesdays and Fridays I had more dance classes. I didn't have a lot of playtime. Although I loved to dance, I remember being jealous of those kids who could come home from school each day and watch cartoons.

On top of my crazy 5th grade school and dance schedule, I had other, more weighing stresses. The list was long. My dad hadn't taken home a paycheck for a whole year. My parents were borrowing money from my dad's parents. My best friend, Heather, told me that she was moving to Arizona in just one year. I was going to junior high in a few months. My parents were fighting a lot. They had even sat us down to tell us that they were going to get a divorce. My other best friend, Marcy, had just moved with her mom to another house because her dad had an affair with my uncle's wife. On top of all that, I was beginning to be aware of the uncertainties of life and how unsafe I was. I was going to go to a junior high where I was told that the older girls might beat you up if they didn't like you, my best friend was going to leave me, and my parents might be splitting up. Life was just beginning to lose its magic. My childlike belief was being shattered that all you had to do was not drink and smoke and get married in the temple and then life would be perfect.

I may have been able to handle all of that pressure and stress that was on me at the time had my mom had good boundaries. However, she didn't. She looked at me more as an extension of herself and she shared with me, her child, information I was not old enough, nor secure enough, to handle. I remember being in the car with my mom one day when she told me that my aunt couldn't control her thoughts. She said she went to an R-rated movie where there was killing of children and now my aunt had repeated thoughts in her head of killing children. I learned she was diagnosed with Obsessive-Compulsive Disorder (or OCD).

Wow! What? I didn't know that could even happen! That was the absolute scariest thing that I had ever heard of! I had in my 11-year-old mind that she couldn't quit thinking of stabbing children, but it could've been by some other means. My mom told me that she "had to" go see a psychologist. The world was no longer a safe place for me to be in. If a person could actually not quit tormenting themselves with their own thoughts, I knew, without question, that I did not want to ever be that person! OCD seemed like the plague. I felt uncomfortable being around my aunt after that.

I couldn't forget what my mom told me, not only because it was scary, but also because my aunt was one of my dance teachers. Every time I saw her, I tried to forget what I knew.

I am not sure how many months went by between the time I knew about my aunt's problems and the time my own volcano erupted. The pressure mounted inside of me until finally about a month after fifth grade my brain said it was enough.

When a soul can't take any more, the brain says, "Let me figure out a solution. I know! We can cause all kinds of havoc in her brain so that she no longer has to face what is too overwhelming."

This is how it happened. We practiced every June at least twice a week to get ready for the Osmond Show. There was a Fourth of July celebration that was held every year at the BYU football stadium. There were famous celebrities that always came and performed, and we, the Star dance companies from all over the state (and some from out of state), would cover the field and perform either with the celebrities or just do a patriotic number. We often had big props or flags that would look great visually to even the highest seat in the stadium. Needless to say, it was a big production with countless hours of practice.

We always went to Provo a few days early to practice with all the other teams on the football field. It was hot and sweaty. We would start early in the morning, have a lunch break and then go back and practice again until late. We felt so special to be performing with real celebrities. I got to dance on stage when I was in 2nd grade with just twelve or so dancers behind the newly crowned Miss America, Vanessa Williams. I practically felt like a star myself sometimes.

We always stayed at "The Royal Inn," which wasn't "royal" at all. Unlike the celebrities that we performed with, our motel was pretty dumpy. This motel was so gross that one time I remember sleeping in the car. The reason I bring up the motel is because it is the setting of the actual place that my volcano exploded and I became sick with an illness that seemed like I would never fully get rid of in this life. Ironically, it was the exact illness that I feared the most—OCD.

One night while staying at this motel, my aunt asked a few of my cousins and me to stay in her room. She and her husband could not have any children (thus the reason her OCD planted on thoughts of killing kids). We stayed up late that night talking. I mentioned that I played a game with myself as I folded towels. I can't even remember what it was exactly but I will never forget what my aunt said next. She said, "You remind me of myself."

Wow! If that statement had been a knife, I would have bled to death right then and there! In my young 11-year-old mind, she told me that I was exactly like her and that I was doomed to be crazy like she was.

The next day, after we had spent the morning practicing for the Osmond show, we came back to the hotel for lunch and a nap. I lay down by my dad to take a quick nap but my eyes would not relax. I began to feel a ton of what I now know as anxiety. *Why couldn't I relax my eyes? Why was I even thinking of my eyes? No normal person does this. My aunt is right. I must be like her.* I was scared. Frightened might be a better word. I did not want to be crazy like I thought my aunt was. It was like someone had placed me in the center of a dark maze and told me to find my way out or I would die. Right away Satan was on my shoulder telling me to not tell anyone else about this. "It's our little dark secret. No one else can know how crazy you are," he said.

For two weeks after that every day became a bit worse. I hated to go to sleep. I hated to even close my eyes to pray. However, I knew I needed Heavenly Father's help, so I would kneel by my bed and put pressure on my eyelids to help distract me from it while I prayed. And pray I did. "Please Heavenly Father, help me to forget my eyes. Help me to forget that it bothers me to close them. Please help me to not be crazy like my aunt. Please make this go away today."

When my regular prayers by my bed didn't seem to be working, I went to a quiet place that I could plead for heaven's help. I went outside and sat on the swing so I could face the river that was below our house. I looked at the field of grain on the other side of the river and the beautiful, tall mountain that was well north of the wheat fields. That view became my temple. It was my peaceful place that I went to think. It didn't matter if I was enjoying it from the living room window or from the swing outside. That view caused me to ponder on my faith in God and how He created the beautiful scene that I was so fortunate to have just outside my home.

This particular day I remember going out to the swing set after church. I didn't swing. I just sat on it and mindlessly swayed as I pled with my Heavenly Father to make things like they were, to make me forget. I didn't even know how it could be possible. How could a person forget? But if God made me, then He could fix me. That was my initial childlike reaction. That was the belief of my untested faith. But like Nephi said in 2 Nephi 5: 1–2, I found that even faithful prayers are sometimes not answered in the way that we want.

Nephi said, "I Nephi, did cry much unto the Lord my God, because of the anger of my brethren. But behold, their anger did increase against me, insomuch that they did seek to take away my life."

I, too, experienced an increase in my trial instead of a decrease. I couldn't understand why God wasn't answering my prayers. Why was it getting worse if I was praying so hard?

Church was particularly hard for me. Have you ever counted how many times you pray in one three-hour block of church? Each time I prayed, I experienced what I now know as a ton of anxiety. Why? Because I had to close my eyes to pray! It would be like someone who has claustrophobia having to get in a small elevator over and over again every time they went to church. It was such a confusing thing. I didn't understand it but I did know that something was very wrong with me.

After two or so weeks I finally got the courage to tell my mom. I went in her room on a hot summer day. I passed the swamp cooler in the hall on my way to my mom's room. It was loud and ever so humid. She had one leg bent on her bed, her right leg hanging down to the floor as she flipped through the newspaper. I didn't even sit down. I just stood at the end of the bed and told her my problem. I don't remember exactly what I said and to this day my mom can't even remember the conversation. Funny how she can't remember it but I couldn't forget it. After I told her my problem, she said in a non-sympathetic and "you're interrupting my newspaper reading" tone, "Well don't dwell on it because I don't have the money to take you to a psychologist."

I stood there dumbfounded. Not knowing what else to say, I just walked out.

That solidified it for me. Even my mom thought that if I didn't quit thinking about it (ironically, that was the problem), that I would be just like my aunt. I would be crazy like her. People would talk about me like I'm crazy just like her, and my own mom and dad would think I am weak-minded just like they thought she was. I knew that I could tell no one ever again. I felt so alone. Even my prayers seemed like they were not being heard. I had a secret that if I ever divulged again, I would be labeled and doomed. I felt my only choice was to pretend. That was the only thing that I thought could keep me safe. So, I went on and went on with a smile, though hidden was the tainted thought that I was irreparably flawed.

Thankfully, my naturally happy disposition somehow stayed with me underneath it all. I laughed when things were funny and I smiled a lot, even if it wasn't completely genuine. I went on normally on the outside but on the inside I quickly got worse and worse.

I had no idea what to label it, I only knew that it wasn't normal and it was inhibiting me more and more. I never slept in after that. Once my eyes opened in the morning, even if I was still tired, I would not close them again. Then, once I was awake, I found things to be bothered about. I became aware of blinking and that gave me anxiety. I found it hard to watch TV without being bothered because I noticed the actors blinking. Looking back, the thing that bothered me the most was not the actual blinking but that it represented what I feared most—being crazy. Normal people got lost in the movie or TV show. I had a hard time getting past the blinking! I must be going crazy! No one can ever find out, I thought.

I started junior high that fall. It was the sixth grade. I was nervous but still excited for a new beginning. Maybe that would get me out of the funk that I was in. That is what I hoped every new beginning would bring. Unfortunately, every new beginning was entered by the same old me. And every time I was disappointed to see that the old me kept coming along for the ride.

I made the most of my new junior high experience. I was elected to be in the sixth grade student council. I had a genuine caring for others even before my life exploded, but afterwards it increased. It was fueled by my inner pain. Although I was what you might call popular, I knew firsthand the pain of low self-esteem. Thus, I tried to be kind to those who I thought might be needing a lift. I said hi to everyone, especially the unpopular.

My mom taught me to do that; however, I think she had underlying motives in teaching us to be nice to the unpopular. It was her way of controlling the direction of my life. She wanted me to win the school elections and she knew there were many more unpopular kid votes than popular ones. That declaration about my mom's motives may seem really harsh, but it's forgivable. I wasn't completely innocent either. Although, most of my kindness I believe was genuine, some was definitely premeditated to get votes. I, too, wanted to win elections. I wanted to keep up the façade that everything was perfect in my life. We are human and we often find selfish reasons to be good, but sometimes that is the best we can do.

If it was winning the elections my mom was after, she came out a winner because I was in student council for four years in a row. The fact that I was in student council for that long shows that I kept on going—on the outside, at least. I kept pretending everything was perfect, in hopes that someday, if I pretended long enough, that it would be.

My 6th grade homeroom teacher had the worst reputation. Unfortunately, he lived up to his reputation. He wasn't good at teaching but he was really good at giving out homework. That is never a good combination. Add OCD in there and the bad gets worse. Since my OCD had just started the summer before sixth grade, this was the first time that I had to deal with it while in school. It kept getting worse now that I had to sit in classes all day. Writing started to bother me, reading bothered me, my legs bothered me and got antsy, and another big one was my tongue. I was hyper aware of whatever my mind wanted to focus on. If it was my tongue then I wouldn't know how to relax it in my mouth. The best way to explain it is to compare it to Restless Leg Syndrome (RLS), except this would be "Restless Tongue Syndrome." The definition of RLS is "feeling of uneasiness and restlessness in the legs after going to bed (sometimes causing insomnia); may be relieved temporarily by walking or moving the legs" (Restless Legs Syndrome, n.d.). My "Restless Tongue Syndrome" could be defined comparably by stating it this way: "feeling of uneasiness and restlessness of tongue and mouth all the time (causing anxiety and a feeling of craziness); may be relieved temporarily by chewing gum."

That I did. I started chewing on a lot of gum just like someone with RLS wants to move their legs constantly because they can't relax them. I felt so scared, so crazy, so in need to keep this secret. I had never heard of someone as crazy as me. I thought, I must be the worst of all mankind. Unfortunately, no one could see my pain and no one believed me when I tried to tell them and so I kept my shameful secret to myself. Secrets are never good.

It was so hard and at times got even harder. I remember seeing my teacher in front of the classroom teaching and in my mind I would see him naked. He was a nerdy old guy to me and it wasn't sexually gratifying in any sense of the word. In fact, it was horribly obscene to me. I was only 11 years old. I felt like I must be the worst crazy person in the world.

Nothing was off the table. Almost everything in my everyday life could become a weapon of my brain. It seemed as if everything was bothering me. If it wasn't blinking, it was my tongue, if it wasn't that, then it was reading, writing, or my legs feeling antsy. My volcano had indeed exploded, yet I was walking around like everything was perfect in my life. I felt I had no other choice. I didn't think of hurting children like my aunt, but because of what I knew about her obsessive thoughts, being around little kids, as well as seeing or washing knives, made me anxious. Once in awhile my brain would have a flash thought of stabbing someone and that was the most sickening of them all. I was deathly afraid that I might start having similar repeated thoughts like hers. I lived in a scary world and I lived it alone. My brain could make anything and everything my enemy. I felt out of control. I couldn't control when another thing would manifest itself as the supreme annoyance and I would have to hurdle over it or get around it in some creative (or "compulsive") way in order to feel semi safe again. It makes me cry to think of it today. I was so young to have such pain, to fight such battles, and to be so alone.

OCD has its basis in anxiety. The basis of the anxiety is fears. In order to suppress them (your real fears) your mind forces you to focus on something else (for me it was mostly my eyes and tongue). It causes marked distress and is very time consuming. In response to the unwanted obsessive thoughts, there comes a compulsion to do something in order to relieve yourself of the thoughts. The obvious and often most common compulsion is excessive hand washing; however, it can be whatever one's mind creates and it doesn't necessarily have to relate to the obsessive thought. For me, it was excessive gum chewing, putting pressure on my eyelids while I prayed, and later I became compulsive about food. With OCD, it's almost as if a person becomes a slave to a certain behavior in order to relieve their anxiety. They are no longer free and are hardly ever at peace. They feel crazy even as they try with all their might to feel normal.

A typical day for me in sixth grade was an emotional torture chamber. My alarm goes off. "Oh no, I'm awake." I immediately remember that something is wrong with me and my heart goes from peace to gripping fear. I want to go back to sleep and just forget the world but I can't close my eyes. They won't stay closed. "Oh no, now I can feel myself blink. I am so crazy. I must get up. I need to get ready. Oh, and I still have some homework to finish before school." I get out of bed and immediately roll down to my knees. I want to pray but I don't want to close my eyes. I close my eyes anyway. The anxiety in my gut skyrockets. I put pressure on my eyelids with my hands while I pray. "Please, Heavenly Father. Make me forget. Please. Please!" I get up and go to pick out some clothes. My eyes feel dry and teary all at the same time. I squint a bit to try and help. I don't want to know when I am blinking but I do. I try to concentrate on what I am wearing. I get dressed, look in my full length mirror. I wonder, "What is wrong with you? You have so much. Why are you such a mess? No one can know what is in your head. They would laugh at you. Your life would be over." I go in the bathroom to do my hair. My mom tells me that I never wear the cute clothes that she has bought me. She makes me feel guilty for not dressing the way that she wants me to. I do my hair. I get my mom's approval. I go in the kitchen to eat. I remember my homework and so I sit down with my paper and pencil. My legs start feeling antsy. I feel annoyed by writing. It's as if my hand forgot how to write. "Why am I so crazy?" The anxiety builds. My heart pounds uncomfortably. I notice my blinking. "Come on, Misti. You have got to get this homework done." I somehow focus enough to finish.

I don't ride the bus. Mom needs me to need her and so she takes me personally to and from school each day. Mom talks to me about everything superficial on the way to school. I don't hear any of it even though I am responding in all the right ways. I am not a normal child yet I get out in the school parking lot and try to act like one. I smile and say hi to everyone. I go to my class and sit down. I gear up for the almost seven hours of torture as I try to listen to teachers, be normal with friends, and do my work all while I fight my brain. I go to write. My brain says, "You are so weird. Your hand feels weird. It bothers you." Anxiety. "Your legs are so restless. Move them." I resist. Anxiety. "You're blinking now. No one else knows when they are blinking. You are crazy." Anxiety increases. "What did the teacher just say? You don't even know, do you? You are too busy not knowing where to rest your tongue. What a weirdo you are. You are so messed up."

By this time, I have so much anxiety that my heart sinks into its next survival mode—despair. However, I am still smiling on the outside. I don't know what else to do. I am trapped in an annoying body, an uncontrolled mind, and an obsessively controlled life in which I have few choices offered me by my parents.

After school, my mom picks me up. Again we talk of superficial things. She asks how was school because it is the right thing to do, yet I know from my experience a month or so earlier that she doesn't want to know how it really was and so I look at my day as she would and tell her it was good. She brings me a snack and takes me to Grandma's to quickly change into my leotard and drive thirty minutes to my dance class in Logan. There is no rest for me. I can't close my eyes on the way there to sleep. I can't keep them open without feeling them blink. I want to cry but I stuff it down. I try and act normal and talk of normal things to distract myself. It never works for long.

I go into dance class where I see my aunt. My mind tries to suppress thoughts of what her mind obsesses on—stabbing children.

More anxiety. I try and focus on the music. I actually find some relief in dance, but all the while I know that everyone I see at dance has a better life than I do. They aren't crazy.

Afterward, I wait for my mom to get done teaching, and for another 90 minutes I try and do my homework and distract myself. The ride home is the same. I climb into bed at the end of the day after pleading with Heavenly Father to take away my pain. I lie in bed with anxiety about closing my eyes until I finally fall asleep and pray that I don't remember the next morning that I am crazy.

I dealt with this same scenario daily and I dealt with it alone. My parents did not have a loving marriage at the time. I thought they had enough problems and so I didn't want to give them any more. Plus, I didn't feel safe to tell them anymore anyway. I don't know if I actually thought this, but I think somewhere deep down I thought that if I wasn't perfect then their lives might get too overwhelming and they might get a divorce. It seemed that divorce was always a word that accompanied their fights. I remember them yelling and fighting so loudly that I would hide in my room after my attempts to stop them didn't work. I can still see myself crying in my room.

No child should ever have to worry about their parents' love for one another. Children do not emotionally mature properly when they are looking up at their parents with worry. From my experience I've learned that a child's normal growth is then stunted as they change their natural emotional growth and behavior in order to try and alleviate the parent's emotional pain. The child is no longer true to themselves, but becomes a skeleton of what they once were. That skeleton moves and acts only to satisfy their painful worry for their parents. They are then not acting and growing as children should but as an adult would. The scars of this can linger all the child's life unless a divine miracle occurs or through much relearning. Most of the time it takes both. It is ever so important for parents to learn early that it is the their job alone to look down with worry and loving concern for their children and never vice versa.

My parents' volatile marriage, coupled with my huge mental trial that I was enduring alone, made it seem as if my whole world would come crashing down at any moment, and I had no voice to stop any of it. I felt like I was in a bad dream where everything is going wrong and you are about to be destroyed if you don't yell for help, yet that is the one thing you can't do. You can't even speak. I was taught to pretend and I got very good at it; however, I couldn't lie to my spirit, and my spirit kept getting sicker.

One of my happiest memories was while driving in the car with my family. A love song came on and I saw my parents smile at each other and then hold hands. I felt so safe at that moment. That, obviously, wasn't a normal occurrence at my house, however, when it occurred, it was wonderful.

Like I said earlier, my parents did not marry in the temple at first. My dad had a Word of Wisdom problem. He liked his morning coffee at the café, as well as beer and cigarettes. Thankfully I never saw him partake of any of it. He never brought it home. I guess one time he did and my mom threw it all away and that was the end of that.

His Word of Wisdom problem was a big part of my parents' fighting. My mom wanted to coerce him to quit. She wanted a temple marriage, but she wasn't going about it in a Christ-like way. She admits that when she began to give up on changing him, that was when he started to change. I, too, wanted so badly for us to be sealed in the temple. It was torture for me to go to Primary and hear the teachers teach how families can be together forever. I was taught that if you weren't sealed in the temple when someone in your family dies then you wouldn't be together again. Although that is partially true, I didn't understand the whole doctrine yet and so it scared me terribly.

I am told that one night my dad caught me crying in my pillow. When he asked what was wrong, I told him I was crying because I wanted us to be a forever family. I hear that that was what helped my dad decide to quit his habits of smoking, drinking alcohol, and drinking coffee. My mom was asked to talk in Stake Conference on temple marriage before they were sealed. That helped them actually set a date. We were sealed as a family on July 31, 1987, the summer before my eighth grade year. I was so excited and so happy. I thought that surely this would be the end of my parents' marital problems. Unfortunately that wasn't so, but it was the start in the right direction for them.

It was a beautiful experience getting to actually be in the temple. Especially for me it was poignant. Because of my OCD (which at the time I had no idea what to name it or if it even had a name), which was frightful and peace stealing, I yearned to be in the presence of my Heavenly Father. I yearned for any experience that brought the Spirit so strongly to my heart that fear couldn't stay. I loved being in the temple. My sister, my brother, and I stayed in the temple playroom for about three hours while my parents performed their other ordinances. We played games like checkers and we were there with this angel-like woman with white hair and a white dress on who served us banana cream pie and root beer. Who would have thought an angel would be allowed to give you junk food? Needless to say, I could've stayed there forever. I'm sure I was looking for real angels in the temple. That was my faith. I wanted to be in heaven. If heaven meant peace, then I couldn't wait to get there.

Not that I was suicidal, I was taught that suicide would only land you in Hell. I wasn't what you might call the depressed type either, although I know now that depression is often what I would feel when I couldn't take the OCD and anxiety anymore. But, on this temple day, I was oh so happy. The reverence I felt as our angel took us from the playroom up to the top floor to meet our parents in the sealing room was unspeakable. It topped to overflowing when they opened the door and I saw my parents kneeling at the altar waiting for us to enter. That was a sight too precious to ever forget. My mom and dad, dressed like angels, clean from sin, kneeling at the altar of the temple, with smiles that beckoned us to come join them. I hardly noticed, but the room was full of emotional family members. We knelt at the altar with them. The sealer asked us to hold hands. As we did so, he sealed us together forever. One of my greatest desires had come true

Soon after our sealing, I began to believe there is no "happily ever after" in this world. (As a side note, I now know that that's not exactly true. There can be some aspects of our lives that can actually fit into the "happily ever after" category.) After my family was finally sealed, life went on as it had before. I still struggled silently, and my parents still fought. But there was, in my mind, a huge sigh of relief—we were a forever family. My dad went to church with us every week and his testimony seemed to be heading in the right direction. I actually can't remember my dad not coming with us, but my mom told me she often took us to church alone when we were little. I am so grateful that she did that. That would be very hard. Sacrament meeting is hard enough with two parents when you have little kids. Although, I'm not sure how often she even stayed for sacrament meeting when my dad wasn't coming to church. Before we were sealed, we often missed sacrament meeting. After we were sealed, I think we pretty much always stayed.

We were young in the gospel but we were slowly heading in the right direction. Thankfully, that is what the Lord expects. However, I did wish we were like the families I would hear about in Primary. I wished we said family prayer morning and night. I wished that we read scriptures together. And I wished that we had Family Home Evening. We did pray over our meals, and once in a while we knelt around my parents bed for family prayer, but I don't have one memory of reading scriptures together. The only Family Home Evenings we ever had were the couple that I put together as I got older.

It was my pain that propelled me forward spiritually. I thought that if my family could be more righteous, I could be happy and pain free. I thought that if I could somehow change them, then I could change my pain to peace and joy. Looking back I can see that that was a typical co-dependent way of thinking; if you can change someone else THEN you will be happy. I now know that it is impossible to change someone else. However, at the time I didn't know any better. I did understand, however, that if my attempt to change my family failed then at least I would still be doing my best to be righteous and obedient. I had faith that with those two in place, the Lord would finally answer my prayers. Maybe if I were righteous enough He would provide me with a miracle.

And this He did. It wasn't on my timetable by any stretch of the imagination, but through this trial He drew me close to Him. He was like the positive side of the magnet that my negative life could not help but go to. He used this trial to draw me close to Him. Although I was very angry at Him over the years for taking so long to heal me, looking back how could I be mad at Him for drawing me close to Him?

I began reading my scriptures every day around sixth grade. One night when Heather and I were having a sleepover, she brought her Book of Mormon. She read it in front of me. I was so impressed that I decided to start doing the same. From what I remember, I have been reading them pretty much every day since. Amazing, what one great example can do. The scriptures, especially the Book of Mormon, have literally been my lifeline. I hung onto it every step of the way.

CHAPTER 7

Dual Realities

~

M Y JUNIOR HIGH years were two different experiences. There was reality, and what was the prison of my reality. I wrote in a journal regularly, but it was usually just about my life as it would feel without the prison. I was too scared to even write about the prison.

My younger year journals are a great example of Reality #1. It was the reality that others saw me having and that I wished was the total truth. I almost can't explain it. For example, if I went swimming with my friends I would write, *"I went swimming with Heather today. We had so much fun...."* Although that would be true, what was also true was that I hated to "lay out" in the sun. It would cause me great anxiety to close my eyes and just lay there. I would be thinking about how weird I am, how no one can ever find out my secret, and how gut-wrenchingly sad I am that I ever thought of this trial in the first place—I literally thought I made up the whole thing. I had no idea that I had a real condition and that it was a form of OCD. I thought that no one in the whole world was like me and so no one in the whole world could help me.

I do remember being at the State Fair and seeing an exhibit on hypnosis and wondering if someone could hypnotize me into forgetting it all. I felt bound by my own secret into a strong prison. If ever I had a thought that something might help me, all I could do was wonder. I was bound by my own rules of not asking for help. The desire to keep my shame a secret was more powerful than my desire to get help, mostly because I didn't believe anyone could help me. It's not like I could never get away from the body parts that seemed to grab my mind's attention and torture me. I must always blink, I must always have a tongue, I must write, I must read, and so on and so forth. I felt trapped with my worst irritations, with no way to escape. That was my Reality # 2. Both realities were real, but more and more I felt the two realities splitting. I felt like a fake.

I loved it when I would go moments without remembering I was different, weird, or had a problem. Those were golden times. I had many of them. Sometimes it would even be weeks, but then I would remember. I would sink and struggle to forget but I always knew exactly how many days or weeks it had been since I began obsessing again. It's not like I would "forget" on the good weeks. Of course I would remember, but there was a strength somewhere in my brain that allowed me to roll over to the next thought. It was wonderful! Never take for granted a brain that allows you, the user of that brain, to control where you want your focus to be. What a wonderful thing a healthy brain is!

Unfortunately I didn't stay in control of my brain for long enough. It was never long enough. I wanted to be in control all the time! I now realize that I could only keep that control as long as things were going almost perfectly and in an exciting manner on the outside so as to keep my attention. As soon as anything came up that was the slightest bit uncomfortable for me emotionally, my brain would choose an escape from that real life problem. It escaped to OCD. Doesn't it seem a little ironic that the brain escapes brain overload from life's natural difficulties by going into overload? It's like a scratched CD that won't play the song but keeps repeating the same annoying sound.

As I look back, I am amazed that I was able to concentrate enough in class to understand the concepts being taught and thus get the good grades that I somehow managed to receive. I did have coping mechanisms, though. As I said earlier, when my brain would hyper focus on my tongue and it seemed I could find no way for it to relax, I would go for a piece of gum. That seemed to help. When I prayed, I would clasp my hands together and put pressure on my eyelids with my thumbs. The firm pressure on my eyelids made it so I couldn't move my eyes and be bothered by their sporadic movement. It was also easier to keep my eyelids closed, which was a big part of what bothered me to begin with. I later learned that these outside ways to deal with the obsessive and anxious thoughts were the compulsive side of the Obsessive-Compulsive Disorder.

Life seemed to get almost unbearable when I started maturing physically. What? I have to hurt and bleed every month? When I first started my period, I hated it! I threw myself on my mom and dad's bed, looked up at the ceiling and thought about how I hated being a girl. It wasn't fair. Not only because girls have periods, but because I only knew woman with emotional problems and I thought that that too was a girl thing. Boys had it way too easy. If I were a boy, I thought, I would be carefree. What I didn't know was that my brother was struggling emotionally too. Later, much later, I found out that imperfect brains come in all shapes and sizes as well as in both genders.

If hating having a period wasn't enough, I could not figure out the tampon thing. It hurt like crazy to put one in. My mom and older sister would be like, "It's not that hard. Just relax and put it in. It's all in your head." As if I didn't already think that something was wrong with my head, I now knew it. Everyone else, who was "normal," could use a tampon. Figures, that I couldn't. I would be in so much pain after trying to put a tampon in that I would lay on my mom's bed in the fetal position. It wasn't until one terrifying day at the OB-GYN right before I got married that I found out the truth. The doctor tried to examine me. I was in immense pain. He pushed his stool back from the table, helped me sit up and told my mom and I that I needed surgery. The hymen had never receded like it should have. Finally, I could release the shame I was holding onto! It wasn't "in my head" after all. I had felt that not being able to use a tampon was just another indicator that I was defected. Now I knew that I had a real physical issue. What a relief!

I did feel some resentment toward my mom because she didn't take me to the doctor several years earlier. But, resentment toward my mom wasn't anything new to me. I resented her for many reasons. I thought that if on that epic day that I first confided in her about me not being able to close my eyes comfortably, she had just held me in her arms and responded lovingly that I could have released it right then and there. I thought that I never would have had an issue. Maybe I was right. Maybe I never would have struggled with OCD all those long years. However, when I heard the story of Francis Webster I felt akin to his very poignant feelings about his own suffering while traveling in the Martin Handcart Company across the plains to Utah.

Years after Francis' company finally made it to the Salt Lake Valley, he was sitting in a Sunday School class where people were criticizing the Church and its leaders for allowing the handcart companies to trek across the plains so unprepared. He listened to the criticism for long enough when he finally stood up and with emotion said, "I ask you to stop this criticism…. Mistake to send the handcart company out so late in the season? Yes! But I was in that company…We suffered beyond anything you can imagine and many died of exposure and starvation, but did you ever hear a survivor of that company utter a word of criticism? Every one of us came through with the absolute knowledge that God lives for we became acquainted with Him in our extremities!

"I have pulled my handcart when I was so weak and weary from illness and lack of food that I could hardly put one foot ahead of the other. I have looked ahead and seen a patch of sand or a hill slope and I have said, "I can go only that far and there I must give up…I have gone to that sand and when I reached it, the cart began pushing me! I have looked back many times to see who was pushing my cart, but my eyes saw no one. I knew then that the Angels of God were there. Was I sorry that I chose to come by handcart? No! Neither then nor any minute of my life since. The price we paid to become acquainted with God was a privilege to pay and I am thankful that I was privileged to come in the Martin Handcart Company." (Palmer, n.d.)

Just like Francis, I, too, feel that it was a privilege to pay the price I've paid to become acquainted with God. I can hardly believe I am saying it. All those years of hardcore emotional insecurity and suffering often from sun-up to sundown was horribly lonely and difficult, but I wouldn't trade where I am today. I know Heavenly Father. I really know Him. I know He loves me. The things I suffered were the vehicle I needed to get me here.

Also, like Francis, I have looked ahead and said to myself, "I can make it to there and then this trial must be over." When I got there, I would have brief reprieves, answers to prayers, whisperings of the Spirit that I could do this, that God was with me and that I would be healed one day. And on I would go. And on fired the trial. I would not trade all that I am now for never having had the trial in the first place. God did heal me when He could see that the refiner's fire had done its job. But, oh was that fire ever hot! And oh, how it seemed it would never end!

I received my patriarchal blessing on December 18, 1988. I would turn 14 that April. That morning I knew I was supposed to fast but mom told me I didn't need to so I ate a bowl of cereal. Mom hated to see any of us suffer even if it was hunger for a good cause. She just didn't have a testimony of fasting yet, and obviously I didn't either.

I loved the spirit I felt as I walked in Patriarch W. Gerald Simmons' home. He welcomed my parents and me warmly and then took us in a small room. I sat on the chair and he placed his hands on my head and gave me a blessing. He had a tape recorder in there so his wife could type it up later and then send it to the Church office headquarters and then back to me. I remember sitting in the car in the grocery store parking lot afterwards as my parents did a little grocery shopping (I didn't want to go in the store since it was Sunday) and feeling a bit disappointed. He said I had a mission to perform, but I wanted to hear that I was going to change the world in some manner. I really wanted to hear that the Lord needed me to do some really great work for Him. I felt like He did have an important work for me to do, yet it didn't say those exact words in my blessing. What I know now is that we all have a great work to do. In D&C 18:10 we are told to "Remember the worth of souls is great in the sight of God." If we help one of those precious souls, then we have indeed done a great work for the Lord.

Although somewhat disappointed in my blessing, I quickly learned that I found great strength by reading and pondering those words. It was so full of hope and joy and enthusiasm that I often wondered how it could be mine. I talked earlier about my two very real but contradictory realities. In my Reality #1, those words of enthusiasm and joy fit me perfectly, yet in my Reality #2 I felt void of all that was light. Often my friend Heather would ask me how come I was always so happy. The devil on my shoulder said, "You're a fake, Misti." Another girl once told me in high school that she wished she were me, obviously sensing joy in me. I hated that she wished she were me. I felt like a hypocrite and a fake because in my Reality #2, I was an emotional mess that lacked what she was seeing on the outside. I remember thinking that I wished I were her, or anyone else for that matter because they weren't in pain, or so I thought.

I have come to know that the Lord knows me more than I know myself; thus His very positive description of me in my blessing. He knew that one day my Reality #1 would become my only reality. He knew that He had already felt and paid for my pain. He knew the words He spoke in my blessing would give me the strength during hard times to keep hoping and to keep working. He knew that somewhere deep down, sometimes very deep down, that I would believe Him, that I would lean on Him to persevere until I saw "the salvation of the Lord" (D&C 123:17). I knew that it would take just that to ever feel completely healed and safe. Sometimes I hoped that healing would come in forgetting, or in time, or when I was in high school, or college, or married, but as each one of those failed to do the job, I knew more and more that it would indeed take a miracle.

I loved those wonderful church stories where someone was given a priesthood blessing and was healed on the spot. I wanted that to be me. One night, in high school, when I just couldn't close my eyes, relax, and sleep, I couldn't take it anymore. I lay there in my bed. The night felt so dark around me. I was exhausted in every way, yet I couldn't close my eyes to fall asleep. Everyone else was asleep. I felt so alone. My gut was ridden with more anxiety and despair than I thought I could handle. My thoughts felt as if the devil himself were controlling them. He was telling me, "You have nothing to hope for. You will never be able to live life like you want. You are so crazy that you can't even control your own mind! No one can help you. You are wasting all of your youth. Your life will never get better."

All while the devil spoke, my eyes twitched and hurt. I couldn't roll my eyeballs back or forward for comfort. Where are they supposed to rest? Why is this so easy for everyone else? Why am I so weird?

I pushed the pillow over my eyes to help, but even more than the awkwardness of my eyes was what it symbolized—craziness and lack of life. It was the despair that hurt worse than my eyes. It was the resultant fear and anxiety that crippled me more than my obsessive and uncontrollable thoughts. It was my secret that kept increasing Satan's power over me.

Finally around 2:00 a.m. I broke through the black hole around me as well as the secret I had been guarding. I went to get my dad. I had mentioned my problems to him before, but I hoped that maybe this time he would really help me. I woke him up, told him about my eyes and my thoughts haunting me, and asked him to give me a blessing. He gave me the blessing right there in my room. I did fall asleep but I remembered all too clearly my embarrassment in the morning. More astounding than the embarrassment was the despair. It was getting worse. And to make matters worse, my dad acted as if nothing had even happened the night before. Everyone kept hoping that pretending it wasn't real would make it go away. The opposite was true. Pretending only deepened my wounds.

School was also hard. I felt a lot of academic pressure, but it was also hard for other reasons. As I mentioned earlier, my mom and her family sent me the message that I would only be important if I were cute and popular. They didn't mean me any harm; it was just a false belief system that they inherited or acquired. They just thought they would pass on the "good" information to me.

I wasn't a complete sponge, though. I was torn between that belief and what I was learning through church and scripture study. I was learning that what was on the outside didn't matter, but that it was what a person was on the inside that truly counted. Those two beliefs didn't gel well. As a teenager, I started to associate what I thought was worldliness on my mom's side with the pain I was feeling. Thus the wrong conclusion I deduced was that poor people were more righteous and thus happier. When I received a new Easter dress, for example, I wasn't proud to wear it to church. I was worried that people would think that I was worldly and not righteous. I was taught to base too much of my self-esteem on what people thought. Ego goes both ways. It's prideful to want others to think you are better than them because of what you wear, but it's also pride that tries to get people to think you are righteous because of the nice clothes that you aren't wearing. Either way, it is pride. Either way we are worried more about what others think of us than what Heavenly Father thinks of us.

Even amid the internal conflict of what was more important, the inside or the outside, I did like to go shopping to get new clothes. I did like to look pretty. Everything, even within a single person, has two perspectives, two ideas that contradict. It's not until they mesh into the one truth, that a person finds peace. Unfortunately, for me, there were seemingly hundreds of these fights going on within me. From what I learned at home, to what I learned at church. From what I saw my parents do, to what I saw other parents do. The list went on and on. Life became a quest for the one truth in all the many different battles that were going on within me. I had a quest for peace. I am not sure I would've ever been on that quest if it weren't for the pain I was in. Although I hate to admit it, that is another reason why pain can be good. I wish it weren't true, but unfortunately it is.

CHAPTER 8

Abandoned By All

~

DANCING WAS ALWAYS a huge part of my life, but in high school it seemed to be increasing. Not only was I dancing every day but now I was dancing daily at several different times and places. I was on the drill team, which practiced every morning and some evenings. I was also still taking classes, teaching classes, teaching private lessons, as well as competing individually. Even though I don't remember ever choosing to dance for myself, I found a lot of satisfaction from realizing that I was pretty good at it. That is where I received most of my accolades. I could lose myself in dance. While dancing, I had to focus so hard on what I was doing that I could forget my obsessive thoughts and the accompanying pain. I knew I was in a bad place when even at dance I was suffering. There were many times when I was obsessing in my mind while trying to focus on the dance practice. It was very hard.

Again, the two realities hit. On one hand there was despair and the question of "when will this pain go away?" However, on the other hand life was sometimes joyful because of what I was accomplishing in dance, the friends I was making, and the many pats on the back I received. My Reality #1 was looking more and more perfect from the outside in. I won several dance competitions. My mom told my sister and me that if we didn't win and we cried, then we would not compete again. I'm not sure if that taught me to be a great loser or winner or if that was just another lesson in pretending. By that time I was getting pretty good at it anyway.

I enjoyed my sophomore year the most. I became good friends with two girls that were on my drill team with me. They were a lot of fun. We had a great first two-thirds of the year until they both turned on me. At the end of the year, they were constantly leaving me out. Behind my back, they decided to try out for cheerleader. I could have tried out anyway but didn't want to. I felt hurt and betrayed by those that I thought were my friends.

It is amazing how much those teen friendships mean. What did I do wrong? I wasn't certain, but I had a clue while writing in one of their yearbooks at the end of the year. I read what the other girl wrote in her yearbook. It was about me. I guess they had nicknamed me "Bubbles" and mocked me by saying, "It's a good thing Jesus loves everyone." I was what people might have thought as a little too righteous and a little too straight, but that's how I wanted to be—I needed to be. If God was my lifeline, I was going to hold on with all of my might.

When they quit being my friend, I felt alone and again, like life wouldn't turn out like I wanted it to. I began to feel worse emotionally again.

My junior year was really one of the hardest. From the outside in, no one would've ever believed it. My Reality #1 looked perfect. I won homecoming royalty every year, yet I still felt nervous socially. I knew by word of mouth that most definitely my two old friends did not like me. I hated how I felt when I was around them. I had other friends, but I never got in the groove again and had as much fun as I did my sophomore year.

The next year as seniors, one of the two girls, who hated me, became head cheerleader and I was appointed Drill Mistress (head of the drill team). How stupid it all seems now, but at the time she caused me a lot of heartache. It wasn't until the actual day of graduation that she hugged me and told me she was sorry. That was cool of her (you can't write about high school without saying the word, "cool"). I was grateful for her brave recognition of the problem and for her sincere apology. Unfortunately, the damage had already been done. She had made an already difficult high school experience even harder.

As I look back on my school years, I realize how scared I was of being abandoned. I didn't feel capable on my own, yet it seemed that everyone was abandoning me. At first I felt scared that I might be abandoned by my parents getting a divorce, then my mom abandoned me by not helping me when I first came to her for help with what I now know as OCD. As time went on and I tried to get help from my dad, he, too, abandoned me by ignoring my problem. My best friend Heather abandoned me when she moved in seventh grade. And later on my high school friends not only abandoned me but became my enemies. Everyone seemed to be abandoning me, and what was completely terrifying was that I was holding in a secret that if discovered, I feared would leave me utterly alone in the world. I believed no one could've handled it if I would've told them what my brain was doing all the time. There would be no one left to help me get through life.

To top off the pressure of never being discovered, I had a controlling mom. She was so needy for me to always be her little girl that she never wanted me to think that I could handle myself alone in the world. I was bound by false beliefs. I had nowhere to go. I couldn't leave because I thought I was too incompetent to make it on my own. I had to stay but had no agency because I had to abide by the unspoken rules of the family. I did what Mom and Dad wanted and that was it. I felt trapped, although I couldn't have voiced that at the time.

Inside I felt like a complete, embarrassing mess. It felt as if absolutely everyone I knew would run away from me if they knew I was crazy. I felt crazy inside. It is so sad to me to write that and to know of its validity, in my perception at least, and to know that most of what I really needed what a good listening ear, an arm wrapped around me telling me that everything was going to be okay, and my freedom back. Something so simple and seemingly so easy was so impossible to have at that time.

CHAPTER 9

Puzzle Pieces Everywhere

~

M Y JUNIOR YEAR was eventful and difficult even without my friend issues. It began with no drill team advisor. My mom and sister helped us for about a month. After that we had a different advisor almost every month. It was frustrating. Add drill team problems to my friend problems as well as my family issues and I was on more than overload. As I've already explained, whenever overload happened, my brain would think, "I know, I'll take over and give her a distraction from all those hard things." It thought it was doing me a favor, but OCD was never a favor. Yes, my OCD did begin to dominate my thoughts more than my outside problems, but it was just like adding insult to injury. Life was getting heavier to bear than ever before.

I began early that year to practice my routine to try out for Miss Drill and Dance Team Utah. It was held in Salt Lake City and was, at the time, the largest and most prestigious dance competition in Utah. I don't know if I actually decided to try out or if it was just what I knew I would do because that is what my older sister did, my older cousin, and my aunt before her. It is just what we did.

I was very intimidated by the competition. It seemed big and scary. I practiced very hard. My sister and her friend choreographed it. My dad would often drive me to Logan to practice. Mom was busy teaching dance. I remember one time in particular. I was so fed up with my obsessive thoughts. I wanted them to go away! I wanted someone to say something that would help me. I finally told my dad again on the way to practice. I said that blinking bothered me and that holding my tongue comfortably in my mouth was a bother and my brain would keep focusing on it. I'm sure it all seemed absurd to him! He did tell me that when he was a kid it bothered him to close his eyes and see all those colors floating in his darkened vision. That did help a bit. It brought a little normalcy to what I was experiencing.

I asked Dad if he would fast with me. He said he would but the next day I came home from school and he was making bacon and tomato sandwiches quite early. I don't remember when we started our fast but I do remember feeling like he didn't care enough for me to actually go without food for a whole 24 hours. I don't think we even prayed together about it, other than a passing plea while asking a blessing on the food. That really hurt me. No one was going to help me, not even my dad.

Funny thing is that after I got told by my mom in 6th grade to "quit dwelling on it because she didn't have enough money to take me to a psychologist," I never told her anything of this problem again for years. I tried to get through to my dad, but it wasn't working. My dad said it was because I wasn't eating enough. Good one, Dad. I wished it were that easy. I left him alone.

I don't remember what year in high school it was, but my dad and I were once in a class at the church about mental health. I felt so anxious there. The lady said that mental illness was hereditary. During the class I asked my dad if I could have gotten mental illness through Mom's side of the family. I knew that my mom's sister was mentally ill. I am sure I didn't actually use the words "mental illness." Those words were too scary for me to say. But Dad understood what I was saying and I think he was too scared to believe that it might be true because he more than quickly denounced that theory. "You are fine," was all he said, and that meant, "Don't say it ever again."

I often heard at church that what we are here on Earth and how we feel now, is exactly how we will feel and who we will be in the next life. I heard that when we die we can only take what is inside us. That doctrine scared me to death! I did not want to be what I was then for all eternity! I also learned that those who were righteous had peace. I had no peace. It didn't make any sense! Why would I not have peace if I was doing all that I thought I should? I concluded that I wasn't good enough, that I didn't have enough faith. I was taught that if I did, then I would be filled with peace. That is when the gospel became confusing. I am grateful, though, that I did not conclude that the gospel must not be true. From very early on I knew it was true. I just didn't understand it all yet.

Just recently my husband and I got puzzles for Christmas and after putting one together with our little family, I realized that putting puzzles together was a parallel for my testimony. When you first purchase a brand new puzzle box, you have complete confidence that every piece you will need to complete the puzzle is inside the box. That is how I feel about the gospel. I know the gospel comes as a brand new puzzle box would—complete with every piece. As you begin to put it together, some parts about the gospel are like the end pieces of a puzzle, very easy to know where they go. Other parts of the gospel don't make as much sense, but I know that eventually they will and so like a puzzle piece that doesn't seem to fit anywhere, I set it aside until one day it becomes obvious as to where it goes. My job is to study, ponder, and listen to the prophets and then wait for the Spirit to whisper in my ear where an awaiting piece fits into the puzzle. It is kind of funny how when a once frustrating orphan puzzle piece fits in, it seems obvious and we have to ask ourselves why that one piece took so long to figure out. What I do know is that one day all those gospel puzzle pieces will fit perfectly and without a single one missing. It will make a beautiful and complete picture of God's Plan of Happiness. Although I don't know where they all go yet, I have always trusted that all the pieces are found in Christ's gospel.

What an understatement it is to say that knowing I was working with the sure source of truth, The Church of Jesus Christ of Latter-day Saints, was crucial to me. It was an absolutely crucial part of me surviving and overcoming the tremendous challenges of having an emotional and mental disorder. I could have easily concluded that I was putting the wrong puzzle together and then gone outside of the gospel to search for happiness. That, right there, is why a testimony is life saving, as well as eternally life saving. I had a testimony. I am so grateful for my grandparents as well as my church teachers that provided me with the opportunity to be taught by the Spirit that the Church is true. I don't remember many specific lessons, but the Spirit penetrated my heart. Whoever thinks a Primary teacher is a "lesser job" in the Church is wholly confused! That is where a child's foundation is laid and how important is a foundation! I needed my foundation to be strong before the beginning of sixth grade. I didn't get it at home. I got it from my grandparents and from Primary.

The highlight of my junior year was winning the Miss Dance and Drill Utah Competition. I never expected to win, and so when they called my name, I was jumping up and down even in my evening gown and heels. I felt very honored, but even that couldn't compensate for the pain I was living with day to day. In my Reality #1, I was so proud of myself and what I had accomplished, but in Reality #2 I couldn't have cared less about winning a stupid dance competition. I mean, what did it really matter anyway? Did it change the fact that my every waking second was laced with private struggle? Did it change the fact that I felt like I was wasting my high school years feeling either anxiety or despair, all under the guise of Reality #1? The answer is a resounding "no!" I learned that nothing the world could give me would ever compensate for the lack of peace. I learned to focus even more on the only people who could give me that peace. Striving to please Heavenly Father and Jesus Christ became an ever more earnest quest. As much of an honor as winning Miss Drill was, I quickly learned how worldly honor is just empty calories compared to the feast I longed for.

The summer before my senior year, I thought I needed to lose weight. A fellow Drill Team member told me she got a diet supplement at the health food store and so I went and got myself some too. I didn't tell my parents. I became quite obsessed with food. My other OCD symptoms lessened when I was obsessed with food. I tried to eat less than 1000 calories a day. Plus, I was dancing at least 15 hours a week. I started losing weight quite quickly and that fueled my need to continue. I never became ill, thank goodness, but I did quit menstruating. When my mom made a fattening meal, I wouldn't eat it. She started threatening me with never being able to have kids if I didn't start eating more.

Again, all my mom knew how to do was to "fix" the symptom. She did it by using fear and threats. She didn't dare look at the inside of me. I don't believe she ignored the inside of me on purpose. I just don't think that she was capable of doing that at the time.

People began asking Mom if I had an eating disorder, and that increased her coercive pressure. I only lost about 10 to 12 pounds but that can be quite a lot when I wasn't fat in the first place. I got up early every morning and ate a bowl of healthy cereal, went to drill team practice, went to school, and then around 10:00 a.m. or so, I would take my diet pill and then for lunch I would eat a piece of fruit or a salad with no dressing. After school I would eat fruit or a bagel, then teach dance, take dance, and then go to drill practice. I would eat a plain potato when I got home and always tried to go to bed hungry.

My life was misery, at least in Reality #2. There was no peace, not even in eating. My joy was in getting on the scale and seeing the number go down. Even that was fleeting. I was constantly thinking about food and calories or how hungry I was. And if my mind wasn't on that, then it was on my different OCD obsessions. There was no rest for the weary. Thankfully, sleep has almost always come easy for me (meaning, even though my eyes bothered me, I could fall asleep quickly). At times that was truly my only real rest other than when I was feeling the Spirit.

My parents wondered what was wrong with me, not because I flat out told them I felt crazy inside (which I had done), but because I loved to go in my room and shut the door. I felt like they wouldn't feel a brick if it hit them on the head. How could they not know? So, instead of trying to prayerfully help me on the inside, they tried to fix me by controlling me. They tried to guilt me into eating more food. They tried to guilt me into not going in my room so much. By this time, these were the only two things that I could control, and so I kept doing them both.

My room was my temple. I had a picture of the Savior on my wall above my desk. My scriptures and journal were both by my bed. I wasn't your typical teenager with posters all over the walls. My room was simple and pretty. I loved being in there alone to think, read, and write in my journal. That is how I replenished my strength and received the energy to keep going, keep fighting, and to keep hoping for relief.

The fall of my senior year I had a psychology class. I hated that class. I felt like everything that was being taught was about me and my crazy brain.

I remember vividly sitting in that class the day that I learned about OCD. I was sitting in the second row, close to the windows. I was wearing navy blue Levi's, a brown belt, and a light blue shirt. I could hear my teacher's words about obsessive thinking, but I didn't dare look up at her for fear she would read the horror on my face and know that I was OCD in actual form. Instead, I looked down and fidgeted with my bony wrists and arms. I tried to distract myself with how much weight I had lost, but all I could think about was that I was a statistic in a psychology textbook. In fact, I was worse than a statistic. My exact symptoms were so weird that they weren't even in the psychology book. I felt weirder than all the weird in the world. There wasn't even a label for my weirdness. I was crazy and there was no cure was all that I heard the teacher say. I would die crazy was what the devil on my shoulder said, even while I was fighting my mind from firing off words like "tongue," and "blinking." I couldn't get out of that class fast enough. Unfortunately, Satan had more ammo now. The despair was sinking in even while I was smiling and saying hello to my friends in the hall.

As I write this and I look back at myself at that time, I feel like a parent who is watching a small child walk next to a cliff. I just want to take that young teenage girl in my arms and pull her far away from the cliff she was walking by. I want to tell her that everything is going to work out; that her hope is real. That she will get everything she dreams of and more. This is one of the reasons why I am writing this book. I want others who are walking by that same steep cliff to have the strength to walk away from it by knowing they, too, will overcome. I would have given anything to know of just one person who was healed from OCD, anxiety, and depression. I was so ashamed of that part of me that I would have never believed I would one day write about it in a book. But with the healing of my physical body has come the healing of the emotional, and I am now ready to shout it on the housetops: "I am healed! You can be too!"

CHAPTER 10

Beginning Eternity

~

M Y SENIOR YEAR became a pivotal point in my life. Heavenly Father was leading me in the right direction. October 17, 1992, will always be a special day. It is the day I met my eternal friend and companion.

It was a Saturday. My sister had won Miss Utah State University the year before. She was to give up her crown that following Monday. She and I were going to perform a dance together at the pageant. We had a rehearsal time to practice on the stage at Kent Concert Hall on the USU campus at 10:00 that morning. But before we went there, we headed to the mountains in between Tremonton and Logan. Channel 2 News in Utah filmed a segment on my sister up there. It was called "Beauty Queen Hunter."

My sister had her hunting license and often went hunting with my dad. My cousin, Rod Zundel, worked for Channel 2 at the time and he was the one heading up this story. I had to go with my sister and my dad early that morning to the mountain to shoot the story. It was a beautiful, bright fall morning. I remember standing near the top of the mountain that overlooked Cache Valley and feeling very tender. I said to myself, "I wonder who I will marry? Could he be down in the valley at this very moment?"

Little did I know, I would meet him in a matter of hours that very day! I don't think that was a coincidence. I think the Spirit was giving me a heads up.

After the news segment was filmed, we hurried to the concert hall to practice. All of the performers had their own separate rehearsal time so there was hardly anyone in the audience. As we were dancing, I did notice one particular person. He was a handsome young man sitting near the front of the auditorium by himself. He was looking at me. He had on a purple and black Utah Jazz shirt. He had his elbows on his knees and his chin resting on his clasped hands. I thought he was the most handsome boy I had ever seen. I was so aware of him that I felt embarrassed to take off my sweatshirt while we were practicing. It felt immodest to wear a leotard in front of someone that handsome. Eventually I had no choice—I was too hot.

After we were done practicing, I needed to wait for my sister to practice the routine that she was going to perform alone. I wanted to sit in the audience and watch her. By this time, this handsome boy was sitting alone in the middle of an almost empty auditorium. I went and sat several rows ahead of him. After awhile, in order to break the awkward barrier, I turned around and said, "So, where are you from?" I can't remember if he answered me or not, but he did get up and walk to the aisle where his sister, mom, and nephew were sitting. He picked up his 18-month-old nephew and (I later learned) said, "Come on, you are going to help me." He brought his darling nephew and sat one row behind me to talk to me.

Within the first few seconds of talking to him all I heard was, "Hi, I'm Jed, and I'm going on a mission in July." It was the only two things that mattered to me—his name and the disappointing fact that he hadn't already served a mission. I never wanted to wait for a missionary and I already knew I could fall for him fast!

I went home that night and wrote in my journal. *"I met a guy named Jed Stevenson. He's really cute and nice! He goes to USU and leaves in July for his mission. His sister is trying out for Miss USU."*

The Miss USU pageant was two days later. I was nervous and excited to perform with my sister. We were dancing to the song, "Don't Let the Sun Go Down On Me" by Elton John. I also couldn't wait to see Jed again.

I wrote about the experience:

October 19, 1992: *"My sister and I said a prayer before going back-stage. After we said a prayer, our nervousness turned to excitement. We were so excited to perform together. The announcer introduced us. He said we were performing to "Don't Let the Sun Go Down on Me." We walked on, hit our beginning pose, and performed to the huge audience as sisters. It was one of the most fun times I have ever had performing in my life. It was the feeling I had of unity, love of my sister, and a love of dancing that made that performance so…great! I loved it!"*

"The guy I met last Saturday, Jed Stevenson, was there. His sister won second. He is so cute!…He started laughing and told me his older sister had just held up a pen and mouthed the words, 'Do you need this?'"

I was so excited when he asked for my number. I remember asking him if he did need a pen (like his sister had asked) and he said, "No, if it's important, I'll remember it." It must have been important, because he remembered it!

That was a perfect night. I have very good memories from that night. Reality #1 and #2 were meshed into just one very good real-ity. My sister and I had a wonderful experience of dancing so well together and on top of all that, I was so head-over-heels about this new boy. Reality #2 must have been on hold that day because this is what I wrote about an assembly the very next morning:

"This guy that came and talked to us was an awesome speaker, comedian, singer, and piano player. He changed the words to famous songs and made

them so funny! I was laughing so hard once and he got really quiet and my laugh could be heard everywhere. He said, "Has anyone ever told you that you have a funny laugh?" The whole audience laughed! It was so funny. At the end, he played and sang this song about life and how we shouldn't give up. I needed this assembly today. It was a blessing. I know I'm only 17, but lately I have had so much stress. It's not just emotional, but sometimes I can feel it physically. Then I worry about worrying myself unhealthy. It's all so stupid. Sometimes I wish stress could be fixed like a broken arm is casted. Don't get me wrong—I do love life, it's just that some days are better than others."

That journal entry may seem like a fairly positive entry or at the most a pretty common teenager-like day, but I can see through myself. I never allowed myself to get too negative about anything, especially in my journals. And so when I read my journals now and see myself open up just a teeny tiny bit, I know that those words were imperceptibly weighted with heavy hopelessness. "When will these feelings and thoughts go away? Will they ever?" "Will I ever feel normal?" I felt like I was such a naturally happy person, as you can see with my loud laughter at the assembly, but I was trapped in a see-through prison. No one could see the bars around me. All they saw was a happy, beautiful, Misti that laughed very easily. In fact, the previous Saturday, after I met Jed, I went to proof some pictures that were taken of me at a professional photography studio and the lady said sarcastically, "Life must be hard for you." I was flattered and angry at the same time. I wrote in my journal, *"Looks have nothing to do with a happy life."* And I meant it. I did like trying to be beautiful, and sometimes I felt like I succeeded, but I knew from my experience that it didn't bring happiness, at least not the kind I was searching for so diligently.

The following weekend was the Utah State Homecoming Parade. I rode on the back of a car in the parade for winning Miss Dance and

Drill Team Utah. I saw Jed and his family as I passed them in the parade. They waved and took a picture.

That night I went to a girl's choice dance with a boy from my school. I remember laughing really hard at my bald chemistry teacher who had the most real looking wig on. It wasn't a forced laugh. I literally lost all control. After that my date looked at me and said, "Everyone loves being around you. People can't help but smile when they are with you. You must've had a happy childhood."

People said those kinds of things to me quite often, and although I was pleased by what I was hearing, I felt like a big phony. It was so confusing to me. Why did I have to have two realities? He was partly right. On one hand, looking from the outside in, it looked like I had a very happy childhood. On the other, it was as miserable, painful, and lonely as seemingly possible.

The following day Jed called for the first time, and two days later He came to see me. He still jokes to this day that while giving him directions to my house I had to include a dirt road.

On October 27, 1992, I wrote of this momentous occasion. *"Guess who came over? You're right! Jed Stevenson! I was so happy he came to see me. We just sat and talked about everything. We laughed harder than you could ever believe, but that's not all, we were also very serious.... The thing that I loved the most about him is his personality and I just love the way he laughs. Just listening to him makes me happy. Somehow we got on the subject of his principal. He told me his principal won "Principal of the Year." When I asked him how he won that he said, 'Well 40% is based on swimsuit, 15% personality . . .'! I laughed so hard I thought I would die!...He asked me out for Friday. When he left, I shook his hand. It is so weird, but I really think I like him."*

Jed and I still talk about that first handshake. We were standing on the sidewalk in between my front door and his car. We shook hands to say good-bye. We didn't let go right away. We both felt something special. It was literally like electricity flowed between us. He felt familiar and new and exciting all at the same time. That is a special memory for us both.

Life was looking up for me as I met Jed and began dating him. I remember almost every detail of our first date. We both wore Levi button-up shirts. Yes, Levi shirts were the big thing then. He took me to Sizzler to eat. Sizzler was cool then, too. I was too embarrassed to get a salad like I really wanted, so I got what he ordered. We both ate a plate of grilled chicken, rice, and a shrimp kabob. I was impressed that he spent $18 on our meal. That seemed so expensive for just a casual date. We laugh about that now. I thought I was really moving up in the world with a date that would spend a whole $18 on me! We went to the show *Pure Country*. The best part was that we held hands during the movie. Jed and I still get a kick out of how we held pinkies first. Again it felt like electricity going through me. The whole thing surprised me. I was not easy to win over. I couldn't believe how little I knew of him yet how much I liked him. Looking back, it's easy to see it was just meant to be. I think I even knew it back then but was too scared to admit it.

A few days earlier, the morning before Jed was to come to my house for the first time, my friend made a prophetic statement. She said, "Misti, I think you will marry him. I just have this feeling that you will."

I didn't want to admit it because I had just met him, but I, too, had the feeling Jed was "the one."

The day after our first date was Halloween. My friends and I went to Utah State University's Halloween Howl. It was a big dress-up party. I was hoping to see Jed there and I did. He took me and a couple of my friends home because our ride left earlier. He kissed me for the first time that night. I won't mince words—it was wonderful! It was the best kiss and the best feeling I had ever had. It was so different from the two boys I had kissed before. This felt real.

From that kiss on, Jed and I were steadily dating. We were together as often as we could be. He drove over from Logan once or twice a week to be with me.

Neither one of us necessarily liked the situation we were in. He never wanted a girlfriend when he left on a mission and I never wanted to send a boy off on a mission. One dark night after a date, we sat in his car at the bottom of my driveway. We were talking about this very thing. We tried to break it off between us or at least find a way to lessen our attachment to one another. However, I distinctly remember feeling the Spirit tell me that it was right that we keep dating. We needed the experiences that we were both about to have together as well as apart while he was on his mission. As Jed often says of those two years, "They were worth a million bucks that I wouldn't pay a penny to do again." I echo that.

As much as I loved Jed and all the fun we had together, I still battled my Reality #2. I hated it. I often hated myself for it. I thought that if Jed knew about my struggles, he would run away from me as fast as he could. I really believed that and it brought with it an underlying hopelessness. I thought I needed to "forget it" quick or he would never love me. I knew I was lovable from the outside and I didn't worry about him liking me. I was quite confident that I could date anyone I wanted…as long as they didn't know the "real" me. I was even too afraid to write about the "real me" in my journals because I was afraid someone might read it and then I would be abandoned by everyone. I was so deeply afraid of my own hopelessness that I would often pump myself up by saying or writing things like, "I love life," or "keep smiling." I soon found out how incredibly perceptive Jed was and worried that he was seeing through me.

One time as I wrote in my journal, he looked over my shoulder and saw the "I love life" statements written big at the end of almost every entry. He said, "It sounds like you are trying to convince yourself of something." That stuck with me. It scared me. I quit writing those positive comments at the end of my entries. I could not afford to have another person abandon me, especially Jed.

Meanwhile, my OCD and underlying despair was getting to be more than I could handle. I tried very hard to never talk to my parents about it because I usually ended up feeling more abandoned. I did talk to them once my senior year. The problem was that after those "good talks," no one ever said anything to me again about it like, "How are you feeling?" or "Are you doing any better?" I wanted them to show me that they were really concerned, that they were praying for me, that they would do anything to help me. Instead, our talks, which were few, were band-aids for my bleeding soul.

December 20, 1992, *"I'm confused right now in my life. My feelings and emotions are in an uproar and I can't seem to get them into perspective."*

December 24, 1992, *"I had a small fast this morning on behalf of myself in hopes that the Lord would bless me that these feelings of uneasiness would go away. I know that it helped because my burden was lifted and I had a wonderful night. I love the Lord so much. Without His strength and wonderful Spirit I know I would die—inside, at least."*

I was just beginning to be the tiniest bit more honest about my Reality # 2 in my journals. I literally would have died inside had it not been for the Savior. My pain was deep. It was emotional torture. To wake up in the morning and immediately remember what I had to face every second was enough to make me want to curl up and die. Depending on what my mind had fixated on at the time, I would immediately feel my eyes get dry and blink or not blink or I would feel my mouth and tongue tighten and know that all day long it would never feel at rest. There were other things too, but those two were the worst. Those things alone were enough to drive anyone crazy, but worse than the actual misfiring of my brain was what it represented to me. With every anxiety ridden blink or every notice of my tight mouth I considered myself crazy, unlovable, a fraud, weird, stupid, weak-minded, less than the whole human race, and doomed to be caught and abandoned by everyone someday. It carried with it anxiety that made every moment torture, or depression that made every future moment seem hopeless. I was a miserable mess—yet because of the way my parents did not respond to my pleas for help, I was a miserable, pretending-all-is-perfect, smiling mess. I knew of no way out and so I did my best to just survive.

My cross that I carried, seemingly alone, was what propelled me to become closer to Heavenly Father. One of my new favorite hymns comes to mind as I write this. It's "Nearer, My God, to Thee" (Adams, 1985).

> Nearer, my God, to thee, nearer to thee!
> E'en though it be a cross that raiseth me,
> still all my song shall be,
> nearer, my God, to thee;
> nearer, my God, to thee, nearer to thee!
>
> Though like the wanderer, the sun gone down,
> darkness be over me, my rest a stone;
> yet in my dreams I'd be
> nearer, my God, to thee;
> nearer, my God, to thee, nearer to thee!
>
> There let the way appear, steps unto heaven;
> all that thou sendest me, in mercy given;
> angels to beckon me
> nearer, my God, to thee;
> nearer, my God, to thee, nearer to thee!
>
> Then, with my waking thoughts bright with thy praise,
> out of my stony griefs Bethel I'll raise;

> so by my woes to be
> nearer, my God, to thee;
> nearer, my God, to thee, nearer to thee!

This song outlines my emotional and spiritual life. It was, indeed, my "cross that raised me" up and gave me deep reason to seek the assistance of Heaven.

CHAPTER 11

Mental
Tourette's Syndrome

~

A T THIS POINT in my life, when I was a senior in high school, I lived off hope, I fed off hope, and when it was gone I did everything I could to get it back again. I struggled. I really want to be able to explain it, but unless you are going through or have been through it, it is almost impossible to really understand. In Reality #2 every hour, every minute, and at times every second was a struggle to stay on top of my thoughts and my emotions. I would basically say to myself, "No, I'm not going there," or "What else can I put my energy into?" But, mostly I would pray and pray until I received a boost from the Spirit or until I had no choice but to get on with doing whatever was expected of me at the moment. Between drill, school, parents, church obligations, and Jed, I had a lot expected of me.

I added things on myself just to keep me focused on other things. They weren't always healthy. For example, as I said earlier, food became a big mental escape from the OCD and the accompanying despair. I thought about food. What I ate, and how little I ate, how much I exercised verses my intake, and how much I weighed were on my mind almost constantly. It was a war between food and the obsessive thoughts that went through my mind like a Tourette Syndrome victim uncontrollably moves. There was no rest for the weary. I guess

I did have some rest. It came in the form of my handsome prince, Jed. The only problem came when I realized that even a handsome prince couldn't make me well. In fact, I'm sure Satan had a heyday with that one: "Jed can't even change the fact that something is deeply wrong with you, and if he finds out, he will leave you."

How sad it makes me to stand in the place I am now and see the awful pain and aloneness I was in then. Alone, even amid so many people that loved me. The problem was that I believed they only loved the facade that was me, the Reality #1 me, and thus in my mind, they didn't love the real me. The real me was hidden and so flawed, and if I didn't even love that part of me how could anyone else?

I lived the best I could at the time—moment to moment—doing all that I could to be good, to please Heavenly Father, and to wait for one of my favorite scriptures to come to fruition: "Whatsoever thing ye shall ask the Father in my name, which is good, in faith believing that ye shall receive, behold, it shall be done unto you" (Moroni 7:26).

I am so thankful that the Lord didn't tell me that I wouldn't be fully healed until I was married and had five kids! That would've crushed the hope that I was living off of. To a 17-year-old, that was a lifetime away!

I wrote in my journal almost daily, and I rarely, if ever, missed a day of reading in the scriptures. My lifeline was the Holy Ghost. I couldn't risk Him leaving me. Yet through all of this trying, I still felt inadequate and unworthy. Why? Because in my mind if anyone knew that I was almost constantly bothered by my eyes, my tongue, and almost whatever else my mind grabbed ahold of, they would deem me crazy and I felt I would be an outcast. Even when given the kindest of compliments, I would find little joy in them.

I felt like I was going through the motions but everyone else was really living. I felt guilt for having so much to be joyful about, yet not feeling much of it, for I knew the very next moment would remind me that I was still in prison—a very lonely prison.

OCD, to me, is like Tourette's of the mind. A person with Tourette's uncontrollably makes the same bodily movements over and over again (Tourette's Syndrome, n.d.), much to the dismay of the person. People who suffer from OCD have the same thoughts fire over and over again in the brain, much to their dismay.

Most of my life I never even had a name for my problem. I thought that I was the only person in the whole world who was weird enough to be bothered by body parts. Little did I know, that just like the physical misfiring of a Tourette's victim's body, mine was just a misfiring of my brain. I—meaning my spirit—was not flawed. My body was flawed. If I could have understood that one truth very early on, I believe I would've been able to have greater joy amid the struggle. I would've felt more equal to mankind and the "normal" weaknesses I beheld in them. If there is one thing I would wish for those who are led to read this book, it would be this one truth—there is nothing wrong with your spirit, which is who you are. There is just a thorn in your flesh (see 2 Corinthians 12:7). That's it! A thorn to teach you whatever it is you need to learn or experience so that you can then choose to propel yourself towards the only true healer. Jesus Christ is the one who will pull out the thorn and deliver you.

This I know, Heavenly Father allowed me to suffer extremely to try my faith and my patience. He allowed me to have this thorn in my flesh, which was not a flaw of my spirit, but a flaw of my flesh—a flaw that was built up from the generations before me and was brought out by the environment I was raised in. It was mine to wrestle with. He knew I would learn from this thorn things that I could learn in no other way. My thorn was deep and it seemed to be getting deeper.

CHAPTER 12

Life Without Jed

~

BY THE TIME I was a senior in high school, I felt I had learned enough. I had suffered for over six years. Why wouldn't the Lord take it away? I would surely be a much better instrument in His hands without it. I even wondered at times if the Lord *could* take it away. I mean, He most likely wouldn't erase my memory and I thought that forgetting was the only solution. I also knew He wouldn't mess with a person's agency and I thought it was my fault. If I could just quit obsessing then all would be well. In some strange way, I thought I was choosing it. My testimony of the omnipotent power of the Savior was weak. I felt more flawed than the Atonement could handle.

Emotional and mental issues can skew rational thinking. It is a fight to stay rational but I testify that it is a fight worth fighting. It's also important to remember that it is easy and normal to vacillate between hope and faith and doubt and despair. Sometimes I had great faith, but often I felt the despair of feeling out of the Atonement's reach.

The rest of my senior year of high school was bittersweet. Jed and I grew closer and closer, which made the inevitable separation of his upcoming mission more dreaded. I honestly didn't know how I would be able to be happy while he was gone. He, more than anyone else, helped me forget all of my pain. He made me laugh almost constantly, yet he loved serious conversation as much as I did. He complimented me effortlessly. He loved me. I knew he did. On one hand I felt so good about myself when I was around him. On the other hand, I had deep-set fear that what he saw on the outside of me could only go so far and that if I didn't get the inside of me straightened out, he would never want me as his wife. That was a huge fear because I loved him so very much.

Jed got his mission call on April 30, 1993. I sat next to him as he opened the envelope containing his call. As he read out loud where he would be serving, I silently read the same words. He was called to serve in the Chile Antofagasta Mission.

At this point, I fully admitted to myself and to him how much I loved him. I described my love for him as well as my fears that night in my journal. I wrote, *"I cried nonstop all the way home. I was crying so hard that I even had a hard time seeing the road sometimes. I love him more than I have ever loved anyone and I think my biggest trial in my life so far will be learning to live without him. He's my best friend and he treats me so good. I already miss him and he hasn't even left yet."*

From that moment on, we were 100 percent committed to one another. We filled our days and our nights with as much time together as possible. It was filled with lots of laughter. We fasted together, we laughed together, and cried a lot together. Jed's tears were for fear that I would be married by the time he got back and my fear was surviving life while he was gone. My sobbing was a cry of desperation; Jed had become a lifeline of sorts and I feared with him gone that I might sink into the black hole within my mind and never get back out.

Having an emotional and mental sickness made what would have already been a hard time even harder. Taking him away from me felt like all that was good in my life was going with him. Again, I felt like I was being abandoned, left alone. I knew I would act strong and keep my façade up, but inside I felt like I might die.

Jed left for the Missionary Training Center on July 28, 1993. I said good-bye to him the night before he left. I didn't go see him get set apart. Whenever I read that journal entry for our last day together, I still get teary. I sobbed like a baby that day. I told Jed that I felt like a little girl who just got her dolly taken away and in typical Jed fashion, he replied, "Just as long as you don't get a new dolly while I'm gone." He could always make me laugh through the tears. Both of us cried a lot. We really loved one another. As young as we were, we knew it was love. I sobbed all the way home.

Life after he left seemed to drag on and on and on. It was amazing to think of how fast time went by when I wanted it to slow down and how slow it plugged along after he left. The stress of him leaving was very real. It showed up in me physically as well. One day I had some kind of seizure or fainting incident during sacrament meeting. I quit breathing and had to be resuscitated. The ambulance took me to the hospital and after a few hours at the hospital and several tests, they sent me home. Nothing ever showed up. All the tests came back good.

That experience was helpful. It was like the electric shock that is given to someone whose heart has stopped to help shock it into beating again. It helped me realize that I needed to pick myself up and get on with life. Heavenly Father helped me with that by blessing me with two things—busyness and a great new friend named Amie.

The previous spring I tried out and was chosen to be one of the assistant choreographers for the Glen Miller Show up at Utah State University. I was also a dancer in the show. We were called the Sunburst Dancers (I always hated that name—it sounded so cheesy). There were twelve of us, as well as twelve Sunburst Singers.

Three other girls and I helped Irene, our advisor and head choreographer, with all of the choreography for the whole show, including the singers' choreography. The Glen Miller Show was held every year in February and March. It was a dinner theater. People spent good money to come in their fancy clothes, enjoy a live band, dancing, and, of course, the show.

I started doing choreography in Logan at the end of August right after my fainting ordeal. We were there eight hours a day, five days a week for about a month before school started. To be busy is a blessing when you want time to go by.

I was doubly blessed because Amie, a fellow choreographer, and I instantly became best friends. We laughed and laughed constantly. We were always together and always laughing. We had a class together the first trimester of college. It was an anthropology class. We hardly believed a thing they were teaching. The professor taught human evolution. Often Amie would make me laugh in class. One day he was showing a slide show of the supposed evolving primates when Amie whispered in my ear, "That's your grandpa." The way she said it and her perfect timing made me laugh so hard that I am surprised I didn't get in trouble. Like Jed and I, she was the funny one and I was the laugher. We made a good team.

Anthropology was a really hard class. Amie and I often tried to study together. "Tried" is the key word. We didn't ever get very far. One time we went to study in the library and ended up in a private library room, standing and marching around on the tables laughing uncontrollably. I can't remember at what. She was a Godsend. Her friendship really helped me make the adjustment to college as well as life without Jed. She brought a little sweet into a lot of bitter.

I did love college and obviously had great moments at times, but was disappointed that I couldn't just "forget" being bothered with the constant firing of the same thought. Moving away from home was just one more milestone that felt more like a millstone around my neck—a millstone of disappointment. With every new step in life, I hoped that I would forget the OCD. (It is important to note that at this time in my life I had talked myself out of believing I had an actual illness called OCD for two reasons. First, every definition of OCD that I had ever read did not include any of my exact symptoms; and second, admitting I had OCD was too scary for me. It would take me many more years before I would really know and admit I had it. For the sake of this book and to eliminate confusion I call it OCD all along.)

As I read through my old journals, I remember Reality #1 more clearly and I see how absolutely perfect my life seemed. Not just seemed, but in Reality #1, it actually was perfect. I had a wonderful missionary who I loved, plenty of guys asking me out while he was gone, and great friends. I was on the prestigious Sunburst Dancers Team and was one of the few choreographers. I had the lead dancing part in the whole show, and compliments that never seemed to cease.

If it wasn't a compliment about my dancing or how I looked, it was a compliment of some sort relating to the inner self. All of that added together looks like a pretty darn good experience for the first year of college, but I hated what I perceived as my self-made mental weaknesses, and that hate carried to the main core of who I was. Everyone else was seeing the person I wanted to be, but I didn't feel like I was really her. I wanted to be at peace with the person I was portraying. Thus, the compliments made it into my journal entries but not into my heart.

I felt like a bicyclist who when going up a really steep hill fears he can never make it to the top, yet if he quits pedaling for even a moment he will fall clear to the bottom in a heap of metal. I, too, felt like I could never make it to the top of my emotional Mount Everest, yet if I quit pedaling for a second, dropped the façade, and admitted that I needed professional help, everyone would know I was a fake and my Reality #1 would crash at the bottom of the hill in a heap of broken façades never to be repaired. I was absolutely terrified on the inside of anyone discovering the "real me" and just kept thinking and hoping that just around the corner I would suddenly find relief that would last forever, hoping that I could quit killing myself by pedaling up an impossible hill that never seemed to end.

CHAPTER 13

Growing or Withering?

~

THE LAST SIX months before Jed came home seemed to be the hardest for me emotionally. I leaned on the Lord a lot hoping to find relief. At one particular stake conference I received the boost I needed. A General Authority named Elder J Ballard Washburn spoke. He did such a good job that I wanted to tell him, so I went up to him after the meeting. I wrote this about that experience, *"When I came up to him, he shook my hand and smiled. He didn't let go. He just held my hand. I thanked him for speaking and told him he did a good job and he said, 'Did I step on anyone's toes?' and I said, 'No, it was needed.' He thanked me for coming up. As long as I live I will never forget what he said to me as he held my hand and looked at me with this most pleasant face. He said, 'I like the light I see in your eyes.'"*

It is amazing the power for good that another's words can have on us. I felt so honored and so complimented. I actually felt that compliment! It went deep within me. I wanted light. I needed light. I had hope that if I could get closer to Heavenly Father, He would hear my prayers and make Reality #2 disappear.

In Mormon 9:21, Moroni teaches one of the affixed laws decreed from before the foundation of the world. He says, "Behold, I say unto you that whoso believeth in Christ, doubting nothing, whatsoever he shall ask the Father in the name of Christ it shall be granted him; and this promise is unto *all*, even unto the ends of the earth" (emphasis added). In that same chapter he states, "And whosoever shall believe in my name, doubting nothing, unto him will I confirm all my words, even unto the ends of the earth" (Mormon 9:25).

I held fast to those words and all the scriptural verses that say the same message. They were my literal iron rod. I held on to them for dear life. I exercised my faith that if I kept trying and kept repenting that one day "it shall be granted" even unto me that which I most desired.

I desperately wanted a release from my internal hell. That is what it felt like, an almost constant hell, a damning of my progression. It felt like a huge handicap kept me from who I felt was trapped inside me. I was trapped inside the prison of my Reality #2. No one, to my knowledge, even suspected that I was in prison.

When we do seek the Savior, even in faith, there is an interesting balance between asking in faith and being told no. It can get very confusing, especially for those of us who have experienced emotional turbulence. "Why isn't the Lord answering my prayers?" Or, "Why isn't the Lord healing me so that I can serve Him better?" I asked questions like that a million times.

Like I wrote earlier, Nephi sheds some light on the subject of not getting what you ask for, even when you ask in faith. In 2 Nephi 5:1 he writes, "Behold, it came to pass that I, Nephi, did cry much unto the Lord my God, because of the anger of my brethren. But behold, their anger did increase against me, insomuch that they did seek to take away my life." ·

Did Nephi have faith? I am certain he did. Yet, the Lord did not answer him in the way he wanted. In fact, Nephi said their anger not only didn't go away but it increased. It even got to the point where his brothers sought to take away his life again.

Nephi's enemy was the hate and harassment of his brothers. My enemy was the almost constant harassment of my mind. I often asked the Lord to take it away and what a test of faith it was for me when at times it became worse. And like Nephi's brothers seeking his life, I often felt like the OCD/anxiety/depression was seeking mine. Satan must have laughed as the pain became almost relentless to the point where death seemed pleasant (again, I was never suicidal, but death isn't naturally supposed to look good). It is the same for someone who is in almost unbearable physical pain. They too can get to the point where death seems like a pleasant option. Like the person who is in horrible physical pain waits it out and hopes it will pass, that is what I did. I waited the hard times out with a hope that it would soon pass.

My hope wasn't in vain. Even the hardest times gave way to relief. Like Nephi, my pain wasn't taken away, but because of my faith in His care He guided me to respite. Nephi's prayer wasn't answered the way he wanted it to be, but the Lord led him another way. The Lord didn't take away his brother's anger but He did lead Nephi and his people to another place where they were a safe distance from it. This paralleled my experience in almost every way. I wasn't blessed that my enemy be taken from me, but many times the Lord put enough distance between my mental enemy and me that I felt safe and was able to prosper. Those experiences increased my faith so that the next time the OCD/anxiety/depression seemed more terrible than I could bear, I hung onto the knowledge that if the Lord was with me then, He would be with me still and that hope would get me through to the next respite.

And so my life went on, and so did its ups and downs. Often the ups and downs were simultaneously a part of my experience. In the October 2010 General Conference, Elder Richard G. Scott gave a wonderful talk on the transforming power of faith and character. The whole talk is not only a must read, but a must read over and over for me. He said, "As you walk to the boundary of your understanding into the twilight of uncertainty, exercising faith, you will be led to find solutions you would not obtain otherwise. With even your strongest faith, God will not always reward you immediately according to your desires. Rather, God will respond with what in His eternal plan is best for you, when it will yield the greatest advantage. Be thankful that sometimes God lets you struggle for a long time before that answer comes. That causes your faith to increase and your character to grow" (Scott, 2010).

I am thankful now, but during the hard times I wondered if I was growing or withering. I can see now that it was indeed growth. Sometimes we can only see our growth after the growing period is over and we can step away from the pain.

Jed came home from his mission to Chili July 12, 1995. It was almost a perfect day. In my journal entry, I wrote of the perfection in it all. Jed and I embraced when he got off the plane. It was movie-like. As I embraced him, I covered my eyes and cried. I knew we had an audience and was embarrassed by my emotion. Jed's mom, Susan, cut our hug short. She laughed as she said, "Hey you're still a missionary and you can't hug her longer than you hugged your mom."

It was as comfortable after two years as it was the day he left. We had both changed, but because of our good communication to one another (we sent hour-long tapes to each other every week for the entire two years!) and help from the Lord, we stayed connected. Even though he still knew nothing of my emotional trial, we knew much of each other's lives along the way. I felt so blessed that day. We still felt so in love, so comfortable and so meant to be, even after being apart for two years.

Unfortunately, in the back of my mind was the inevitable foe of Reality #2. A big part of me felt unworthy of Jed's love and of his family's acceptance. I knew that on paper I was the perfect wife for

Jed and the perfect daughter-in-law for his parents, but they didn't know of the prison I was in. I didn't even understand it. I felt like I was just weak, like it was my fault. I felt like a stronger person would never have troubling repeated thoughts that bothered them. I especially felt foolish that I was bothered by my own body parts. What if Jed found out? Would he still want to marry me? Would Jed's family still accept me? I felt like the answer was a definite "no."

I had heard them talking about and making fun of a "crazy" relative of theirs who had bipolar disorder. I felt that if they made fun of her and didn't accept her, then that meant that what they loved in me was just my façade and that they would never accept and love me if they knew of my internal chaos.

As wonderful as the day was that Jed came home from his mission, the devil on my shoulder said it would all fall through tomorrow if they knew. It makes me sad now to think of the burden I carried alone. I couldn't even tell my bishop. I felt that somehow saying things out loud would make my Reality #1 perfect world come crashing down. I don't know exactly what would have happened had I told everyone the truth of my hidden pain, but I believe Jed knew me well enough and loved me truly enough that he would have never left me. I'm not sure his family would've done so as easily as he did.

I know now that they meant no harm in making fun of this poor lady. She had caused a lot of havoc in their lives by her unpredictable behavior. Humor was and is the way that they deal with their hardships in life—not necessarily a bad way to cope. They didn't have bipolar themselves and so in blissful ignorance they judged and made light of it in order to deal with the fact that she was mean, even cruel to them at times, even to the point where they had to get a restraining order against her so she couldn't come near them. Mental illness can be scary to those who don't understand it. Considering the way she harassed them when her brain was off kilter, I knew that their judgment of her was understandable but I unfortunately and unjustly grouped myself with her and concluded that they would do the same to me if they knew of my secret.

Secrets are never good to hold on to alone. They eat at you. Satan wants us to put on façades, to keep secrets out of fear, to feel less than others, to feel weak, to feel fear of abandonment. He ultimately wants us to quit growing. If we hold onto secrets then we won't put them out into the light where we can actually see them well enough to do something about them. That is what I did. I kept hiding it.

My Reality #1 was absolute bliss, or at least it should have felt like that. I was so in love with Jed, and he treated me like a queen, but Satan kept telling me I didn't deserve it. "It can all fall apart tomorrow if he finds out about the real you," he would whisper. I tried not to listen but he often won and I would give in to feeling worthless, trapped, and full of tremendous anxiety and despair. I never showed it. I kept it to myself. Reality #1 was still there and very wonderful on the surface. At times I thought the world was at my feet, but the devil on my shoulder never left and often won out. "All you do is think about your eyes, your tongue, and your emotions. What is wrong with you? Everyone else just lives life."

CHAPTER 14

Engaged Puppet

~

J ED ASKED ME to marry him two months after he got home. I
was excited. I knew it was right, but I still struggled off and on
during our engagement. If I could do it again I would do it so differently. I wouldn't have lived at home. That was the biggest mistake.
What I really needed was to be on my own. I didn't understand it
fully at the time, but even though my mom loved me, she had been
emotionally abusing me by controlling me my whole life.

She used underlying pulls of guilt coupled with neediness. If it
wasn't so covert and subliminal, her message to me would've said,
"You can't make it on your own. The world is a scary place and so you
will always need me. Your ideas aren't as good as mine. You will only
be okay if you do everything that I tell you to, look the way I want you
to, and behave exactly like I want you to."

That was her powerful side. She also had another subliminal message from her needy side that if said out loud would have sounded
a bit like this, "If you ever quit being my little girl I will be so sad. I
won't know what to do with myself. If you ever quit needing me, I will
have no identity left. I can't take care of myself without you and so
you must never leave me."

One day during our engagement I had a breakdown. After Jed
had dropped me off at my car that was at my friend Amie's house

(she moved back to Logan with her husband to be in Sunburst again), I waited for him to leave and then I went to a nearby church parking lot and just cried and cried. I prayed so hard. I needed assurance that everything would be okay. This was another milestone of disappointment. I was always looking to this change or that upcoming milestone in my life. I would think to myself, "When I'm there, I won't struggle this way. When I'm there I will feel differently." The hard part was when I got "there" and was still struggling emotionally. That is when real despair would easily settle in. My dreams of ever living the life of peace and accomplishment that I wanted would shatter and it was so painful. I felt like I was failing everyone. I was failing Jed because I was hiding a horrible secret. I was failing God because I felt I couldn't do any good for Him while being such a mess. And I was failing me. All of my expectations for myself were like shards of glass in my heart. The pain was heart wrenching. I felt I was a horrible, failing, inadequate, less than all others, pretending fraud. "You don't deserve anything or anyone", the devil on my shoulder said, "and now you are going to ruin the day you get married, the best moment of your life, because you have no power to feel otherwise. You will never get out of this slump before your wedding date."

I went back to Amie's house and cried to her. I don't know what I said but it wasn't the real truth. She and her husband concluded that it was because I was engaged. They said that it was a hard time for them too. I let them think that but inside I knew the truth. I knew I needed help and I didn't know where to get it. It was a scary and very sad feeling. Here I was engaged and at a time in my life where I always imagined feeling so competent, happy, and hopeful for my new life ahead, and instead I still felt so incompetent, scared, and sad. I was sad that I wasn't enjoying this beautiful time in my life like I wanted to. I knew that it would be over soon and I knew from experience what my real memories would be. The memories that I journaled I knew would all be from Reality #1's perspective. I knew they would seem perfect but I knew that I would always know the truth. I would know that I couldn't really feel them. They would feel like empty calories.

I felt so out of control. I had no control over my schedule. School and Sunburst took almost every minute I had. Instead of planning my wedding with great anticipation, I can't remember picking anything out except my wedding dress. My mom was again taking all the control. I was but a puppet going through the motions, saying and doing all the right things to make others happy, and striving with all my might to make myself at peace again before the actual wedding. I did not want to tarnish my memory of that day.

In my mind I was trying not to obsess over my tongue or over the necessary bodily function of blinking. And when that was more than I could bear, I would fall victim to anxiety, and when that was more than I could bear, despair took over. As soon as I got myself out of feeling despair, I would feel great for a while until the cycle repeated itself again. When life was stressful, which was almost always, I would notice myself or someone else blinking, or I would become hyper-aware of my tongue and mouth. I would immediately grip in fear and anxiety saying, "No, no, no not again," or "This is so stupid. Think of something else." I had dealt with this internal battle for almost ten years at that point, and so the cycle was familiar to me.

I didn't understand at the time that I was not flawed. I had just inherited something that manifested itself because of the controlling environment I grew up in. I had the OCD gene in my genetic makeup; however, I believe it would have lain dormant and never manifest itself had my family life been healthy. You could liken it to someone who had a propensity to get diabetes but never got it because they ate healthy their whole lives.

If I could've known that and separated the OCD from myself just like a person separates the flu from the person it has infected, I would have accepted myself and my circumstance much better. Just like the person with the flu still feels the sickness, it still would've been hard but it would've made it less personal. Maybe I could've freed myself from the fear that Jed was better than me and deserved better than me. Maybe I could've allowed myself to see me, the person underneath the sickness, as the strong capable person that I was. I wasn't the weak, out-of-control person I was taught to believe that I was. My parents didn't mean to teach me this but they did. The OCD didn't mean to teach me that *it* was my identity, but it did. Those false beliefs were thriving in my life and thus I wasn't.

On top of my inherited brain issues, of course, I had mom issues. When she knew that Jed and I were talking about marriage, she made up all sorts of excuses why we couldn't get married for a year. They ranged from she didn't have time to plan a wedding to she didn't have enough money. Yet, she wanted me to do the upcoming pageants for a chance to go to the Miss Utah Pageant, both of which take time and money. My mom, although she didn't mean to intentionally hurt me, hurt me very much through emotional abuse. It wasn't mean, berating, verbal abuse. It was controlling-me-like-a-chess-piece abuse. The abuse I suffered from was less easily defined. It seemed like love, but love is never defined with the word "control" in it. Because it was hard to define, I concluded that it was just me that was flawed.

Again, people can be abusive without even knowing that they are. I don't know exactly why my mom was that way. Was it in her DNA from the generations before her? It seemed that neediness was the heaviest rock in her backpack. She was so needy while raising me that it was emotionally abusive. I didn't feel free to grow and become what I wanted.

Even when I was engaged, I was given direct as well as subliminal messages that I needed to do what she wanted me to do. It was always more about her than about me. I felt guilty getting married and leaving her. I knew she needed me to need her.

Here is a simple example of the complex problems I faced. It was hard to put my finger on at the time, which made it all the more difficult to see:

During my second year of college, I had a washer and dryer in my house at school that I shared with roommates, but Mom would come get my laundry or have me bring it clear home so she could do it for me. I didn't know how to start the washing machine until I was married.

She needed me to need her so that I wouldn't grow up and she could still play the mom role. That is emotional abuse. A parent's job is to encourage, from the time a child is small, autonomy and independence. A child should never be thought of or treated like a parent's appendage or trophy. They were adult spirit children before they came down to earth and that is what they are meant to quickly become here—adults; independent and strong, equal in power to create through choice their own lives that they might fulfill their full potential here on the earth. We don't fill our potential if we remain the puppets of our parents. Why? Because we need our full agency in order to do it!

The best thing for my emotional health at the time of my engagement would have been to be out on my own—all the way. Yet, it was better for my mom's ego to be needed so I played the part. I lived with her at home to "save money." Yes, it is partly my fault. I could've shut her out completely. However, just like someone who has been sexually abused for years doesn't always run the other way and tell on the perpetrator because (even though it was in no way their fault) in some way it feels good to them; I, too, benefited from my mom's need to be needed. I got spoiled with food, laundry, and a multitude of other favors. A small child does not have the ability to say no to the spoiling behavior of their parents, even though it would be best for them. Yes, I was in college—I wasn't physically a child anymore—but I believe I was still a child inside because that is what she wanted me to be.

My mom always said she wished she had more kids. She was in love with the fairy tale of kids running down the stairs on Christmas morning. She loved kids because it filled her need to be needed. I felt an uncanny need to please her and so if she wanted me to be a little kid then that's exactly what I gave her. I played the part. I kept on needing her because that is what she wanted me to do. I wouldn't let myself learn how to do my laundry because I knew deep inside that if I told her I didn't need her in that way anymore, it might hurt her. I didn't stay at college on the weekends. I knew that would hurt her.

She also manipulated me by telling me it would be safer to have Jed send his tapes from his mission to her house instead of my apartment in Logan. I can see now that that was another way in which she kept me from growing up and not needing her anymore. I had to see her every week in order to get what I looked forward to more than anything—Jed's tapes.

Another example of our dysfunctional relationship was that I didn't get a job teaching dance in Logan, where I lived. Instead, I went home every Monday to teach at my mom's studio where her need to "play mom" would be met every week. She got to make dinner for me, give me my clean laundry, and fulfill her pride quota as I, her daughter, taught at her studio. I was good enough that I could've started my own studio in Logan. It would've been far more convenient and lucrative, but the strings to Mom were too great for me to cut. I was trapped living a life that wasn't my own. I did not have the strength or the know-how to break free yet.

It has been hard, at times, to look back as a clear-seeing adult and not get angry. I have learned that anger is never good, even if it seems justified; anger never heals, it only widens the sore. I sometimes needed to forgive her and my dad over and over again. I even needed to forgive myself repeatedly for not getting the heck out of that dysfunction cycle sooner! I have asked myself many times why I didn't get out of that cycle sooner, but I now know that I was just incapable of it at the time. Heavenly Father still had a lot to teach me and He did it the way He usually does it: "For he will give unto the faithful line upon line, precept upon precept; and I will try you and prove you herewith" (D&C 98:12).

It is a truth that children are mostly incapable of stopping abuse in any form, but especially when it feeds them in some way. The abuse that comes from a needy, co-dependent parent is almost intangible. Until we are given help to see it, either by God or by someone else, it seems like life *should* feel perfect, or at least it seems that it should by the way things look on the surface. We exclaim to ourselves constantly, "What is wrong with me? I have everything. Why do I feel this way?"

We need to trust ourselves. When we feel that way, it is because our spirit is trying to tell us something is wrong so that we can fix it. My body was telling me that it was wrong for my spirit, for my growth, for my life, to not grow up and rely on myself. It was telling me, "Mayday, mayday! You have passed the point of needing your parents! You must disembark now!" But, I didn't listen. I don't think I knew how.

I did, however, begin to really watch how other parents acted with their kids. I especially began to notice a difference in how I was raised and how Jed's parents parented. Were they perfect? No. I thought so then, but now that I know them better after many years of marriage to their son, I can see that they have their own set of weaknesses. However, at the time, I was only comparing my family's weaknesses against what were strengths to them.

In a healthy family, the child quickly learns to make his own decisions. He increases in the ability to make good decisions for himself when he also experiences the natural consequences to those choices, whether good or bad. That is how a child grows to adolescence and then to adulthood. It is by learning through one's own experiences. It is abuse when a child has to channel all decisions through the filter of "is Mom going to be happy with this?" The life of the child is no longer his own, it is the needy parent's life.

If this was or is your life, there is nothing wrong with you. The depression and/or anxiety is just a warning system that something in your relationships (with yourself or others) is not right for your progression. I wish I had really understood that then. I knew something wasn't right in my family and my relationship with them, but I didn't know what it was. Thus, I had no idea how to fix it. I resigned myself to watching other families and thinking that my own future family would do it right—whatever "right" was.

I didn't know what "right" was, exactly, but I falsely concluded after watching others that it was living the gospel to the letter of the law. If I read scriptures, prayed with my family every day, had Family Home Evening every week, fulfilled church callings, went to church every week, the temple every month, etc., then my kids would grow up happy. I learned, however, if I just did the letter of the law in order to check it off my list and I didn't let it in my heart to change me then I was no better off. I had a lot to learn about the letter of the law and what the law was meant to do for my heart. This is where suffering was my friend. It was like a bridge that took me from where I was to where I wanted to be.

Suffering taught me. It encouraged me to not just read the scriptures but to search desperately for the knowledge I needed. I often searched until the Spirit entered my heart enough to outweigh the obsessive thoughts, anxiety, or depression. Suffering taught me to rely on the Holy Ghost. Sometimes His power was the only power that could make those dark feelings leave. Suffering taught me how important it was to keep myself worthy of His companionship. Suffering taught me of the power of Priesthood blessings. Suffering taught me much more over the next fourteen years, and in one way or another, it will continue to teach me my whole life. Suffering is God's tutor. It helps us get our hearts ready for our final exam—the one on judgment day.

I went through the Logan, Utah, temple and received my endowment on December 8, 1995. I loved it. I thought it was beautiful. I felt the Spirit so strongly that I cried almost the whole time. In the Celestial room, I cried so hard that it was difficult for me to not make too much noise. It was because that room represented the gift of eternal peace, joy, happiness, and progression. It represented why we toil to overcome and sometimes just endure the trials of life. It represented all that I longed for—peace. I was so grateful that I felt peace there that day. It was never something I could count on. It wasn't perfect peace because I knew it was momentary. I knew I was still different from others and that I might be struggling tomorrow or even the next moment. I think that is why I cried so hard. I was extremely touched by the amount of peace that I felt.

One week later on December 15, 1995, Jed and I were sealed together in the Salt Lake Temple. We had been looking forward to and waiting for this day for over three years. We knew we wanted to be together forever pretty much from the day we met, but a mission and a lot of growing up had taken precedence. And so there we were, finally looking at each other across the altar and it wasn't a daydream anymore!

Elder Lynn A. Mickelsen of the First Quorum of the Seventy married us. Jed got to know him while serving as an assistant to the president on his mission. I was in awe to meet such a servant of the Lord. He taught us all deeply while in the Celestial room. It was a beautiful moment being sealed to Jed. I loved him deeply and I knew that I had made the absolute right decision.

I wrote, "*I can't even describe the feeling I had. The best word I can find to describe the whole moment is glorious. It was so glorious knowing that after waiting my whole life and especially after waiting for two years while Jed was serving a mission, the moment I have been waiting for is now! I can't repeat the words of the actual ceremony because they are so sacred, but I can say that the blessings bestowed upon us if we live right are absolutely beautiful. The tears were just streaming down my face as Elder Mickelsen looked into our eyes and sealed us together for time and all eternity. I was so emotional that I could hardly say the word 'yes'. Then, Jed kissed me over the altar. That whole moment was the neatest moment so far in my life. I love Jed so much that I can't even explain it. I have never been so happy and the great thing is that I know it will continue.*"

I am not sure what I meant by that last statement. I knew I would be happily married but I think I also meant that I hoped this would be one of those milestones in life that had absolute power to close the door on all skeletons and pains from the past. What I know now is that no mortal ceremony, even a celestial one, can do that. Only the Atonement of Jesus Christ can heal us and not only shut, but slam the door closed on past pain. Only He can make that pain stay behind that door forever.

It wasn't long after I got married that I realized that I was fooling myself to even hope for a new emotional life as a married woman. I had a new and wonderful roommate, but I still carried the same fears and the same shameful pain. I didn't dare to even tell Jed. Telling Jed would have meant admitting it to myself. To say it out loud seemed like it would be a life-sentence of "crazy" stamped on my forehead. Instead, my own pride kept me in an invisible prison, even to my husband.

Nonetheless, I still have some great memories together as newly-weds. We had a lot of fun together. One of my favorite things that we did was go rollerblading together. We went rollerblading in church parking lots and on USU's campus. We hung out with Amie and her husband and laughed until our stomachs hurt.

Jed and I read our scriptures together, prayed together, went to the temple every month, and even shared the same calling as Primary workers for the 7- and 8-year-olds. Still to this day we call the scriptures "squishburts" because of a cute little girl in our class that couldn't say it right.

There were lots of good times but still an adjustment period. One morning as we were cuddling in bed I got teary eyed as I told him how sometimes I felt like he doesn't even need me and he admitted that it was his fault. He said, "I get too egotistical sometimes." And then he hugged me.

I wrote (April 17, 1996), *"I just like to feel needed and Jed seems to show his love by trying to make me perfect by criticizing everything I do, at least a little. And that is good to a point, but it starts to eat at your self-esteem after awhile."*

As I look back now, I can see clearer. Being observant, confident, and critical was as ingrained in him as was my being sensitive, unconfident, and low on self-esteem. He was good to me, he was my best friend, and I knew he truly loved me. Those things outweighed his weaknesses. I've never asked him, but I'm assuming my tenderness, laughter, and love for him also outweighed my weaknesses. No doubt about it, weaknesses and all, we loved each other very much.

CHAPTER 15

First Breakthroughs!

~

O N THE NIGHT of my 21st birthday, I stayed up way past when Jed went to bed. I had been praying for an answer on whether or not to try out for the USU Sunburst Dancers again. On that night I undoubtedly received an answer. I wrote, *"I was quite surprised at how directly Heavenly Father answered my prayer. I feel happy and sure that for some reason I don't know, . . . I am not supposed to try out again."*

That was probably the first really important decision I had ever made without my mother's approval. She called one morning to ask if I really wasn't going to try out for Sunburst again. She told me, "You'll be sorry," and then she hung up without even saying good-bye.

I wrote, *"I don't think my mom really believes that God really hears and answers our prayers."*

That decision to quit performing was hard on me, too. I had danced since before I could even remember. I had been on at least one performing dance team all my life. To say no to trying out again was like saying a writer could never print his writings again or a comedian could never again make someone laugh. Performing dance had been my whole life thus far, and to not perform anymore I knew would be a monumental change. However, that didn't change the sweet assurances of the Spirit that I was doing the right thing.

It wasn't easy for my mom to accept that I was doing something beyond her control. I don't blame her. It was a first. I had never blatantly chosen my will over hers. What she didn't understand or believe was that for some reason, it was God's will. I had received a clear answer.

To my mom, it was just one more reminder that I was no longer hers to control. She didn't like losing that. Even after the tryouts she tried to prove that she was right and I had been wrong by saying, "You will be sorry you didn't try out. You just wait, you will be sorry."

Jed was so sweet that night. He took me on a late walk and we just talked. I needed that. I needed his assurance and I got it. We moved a bit further away after that thinking that the extra distance might somehow cure the Mom issues. If only it would've been that easy! I never wanted to hurt her feelings. I just didn't know how to escape it. I didn't even know what "it" was at the time. I didn't know the puppet syndrome would last until I fearlessly faced my parents and cut the apron strings myself.

We moved into a basement apartment. I dreaded moving there. There was no natural light in the kitchen and family room. When we were cleaning and painting it before moving in, Jed's sister came over. She said, "I would be depressed living here." I went in the bathroom and cried. No one knew that that was my biggest fear.

We ended up adjusting quite well there. Jed started a lawn maintenance company and I started my own dance studio. Within months I was teaching almost one hundred students weekly. That included the local high school's drill team, which I taught technique to a couple times a week. I felt quite successful. With my income and Jed's summer income, we lived comfortably. We weren't big spenders but we weren't too tight either. We rented movies, went to dinner with friends, and played lots of UNO. I kept my OCD at bay with the hope that it would soon fade away. Soon, I would say to myself, I will start feeling like a grown-up and it will all be gone.

However, I could only keep it at bay so long. We had been married just a little over a year when I began feeling the effects of OCD, anxiety, and depression so much that I finally broke down and told Jed. I realized I couldn't keep it in any longer. I remember that night very clearly. We were on our way home from attending a session at the Ogden Temple when I finally cracked open the door of my invisible prison.

I wrote in my journal on February 1, 1997, *"I hate to even write about this, but I feel I should. Sometimes I get really down and then I get down about feeling down and so on and so forth until I feel so lonely, and I can stay that way for days. I have never told Jed this because I felt like he would look down on me and I thought that if I never told anyone it would just go away. Well, after Christmas I started feeling this way and it lasted until almost two weeks ago. Jed and I went to the temple and what a blessing that was! I started crying when we got home. I finally opened up to Jed. Even though I know he doesn't understand I felt so much better knowing that he still loves me. He gave me a blessing after that. Immediately after the blessing I felt at peace. Although for days after I still had to work on not letting myself get down."*

That was the first time that I ever wrote anything of substance in my journals about my Reality #2. I had two huge breakthroughs in just one day—I told Jed and I wrote about it in my journal. That was the very beginning of accepting that I had a problem that wasn't just going to go away on it's own. I hoped again that maybe just telling Jed would be one of those milestones that would free me from the past. However, it wasn't.

But I will say that Jed said the very best thing he could've ever said to me. I had just told him a tiny bit about how stupid things like my eyes and tongue bothered me and he said, "I remember being a kid and at night my nose would itch and then my other nostril would itch and then I was hyper-aware and I couldn't sleep cause I would itch." He made me feel less weird. Then he ended with, "Someday I'll tell you all my secrets too." Again, he made me feel like I wasn't so abnormal even though I don't think he really had any more secrets to tell. I will always look back at that moment with love for him. He could have ruined my already tender heart with an insensitive comment. Instead, he gave me strength, as well as perspective.

Jed didn't bring it up again after that night. I'm not sure if I really wanted him to but I still felt quite alone in the bearing of my trial because of it. He unknowingly did exactly what my parents did when I tried to tell them—after "the talk" they ignored it. I was on my own as a child and to my disappointment I was on my own again. I wanted someone to take the bull by the horns and find out how to heal me. I wanted someone else to take care of me—the emotional, messy me. Jed may have taken that role if I had had the courage to ask and the faith that someone out there could really help me.

That was the problem: I didn't think anyone out there could possibly understand me, and even if they did understand, it seemed that no one besides God could have the power to change me. I even wondered at times if God could. I trusted that He must know how, but it seemed that nothing besides erasing my memory could heal me. How could it be anything less than that? It was my own memories of the things that bothered me that obsessed in my mind and created the havoc of anxiety and depression. So basically I felt that it was hopeless unless I could one day wake up and be healed—that no matter what I thought about, nothing would bother me.

My daughter taught me how erroneous that line of thinking was. When I had just had my fifth baby, my 3-year-old daughter, Sadie, was eating up at the bar one day when she asked me this question: "Mom, when will Brinn be my sister?" I tried to explain that she was already her sister. She was quiet for a moment until all of a sudden she got so excited because she thought she had the answer. She stood up on the barstool, threw her arms up in the air and said, "I know, I know. She will wake up one day and look down and say, 'I'm a SISTER!'"

We all got a good laugh out of that one. Unfortunately, I was just about as juvenile about how I thought I would grow from who I was then to the healed person I dreamed of being. I wanted to one-day wake up in the morning, look myself over, and with arms flung in the air declare, "I'm healed!"

I wasted so many years holding onto that silly belief. I know now that that just doesn't happen any more than you can go to bed young and wake up old. Nothing short of a miracle could make me "forget." I believed in miracles. I just wasn't sure that I would ever be the recipient of one.

Telling Jed of my pain didn't change life a whole lot. The best thing was that he knew my secret and he still loved me. I knew that I had only scratched the surface when it came to the amount he really knew of my pain, but it was a start. He left me with the assurance that he wasn't going to be scared of me like I was scared of myself. At least with the amount that he knew. Because Jed felt that all was well, I did what I had always done—I went on pretending. He was still funny and I still had a sensitive funny bone. He liked to tease, and if he caught me in the right mood, I would laugh until I had no strength to hold myself up.

On March 29, 1997, I wrote of a funny excursion we had at the grocery store. *"Jed and I were in really funny moods. When Jed wasn't looking I put this huge ugly platter of Easter looking things in the basket. When Jed turned around and gave his famous 'What!?!', we both broke out laughing so hard.... He got me back. He grabbed my wrist and pulled me away from the candy aisle as he loudly said, 'You have already had three Kit Kats today. You don't need any more chocolate. We need to get you to a rehab!' I was laughing so hard that I had no strength to pull my hand away."*

I was all right as long as everything was going smoothly and everyone was happy with me, especially Jed. But to be real, how long are things in anyone's life ever really smooth? So in order to keep calm around and in myself, I was a pleaser. I did everything in my power to please Jed. I needed his approval because if he approved of me then I was still an okay person. When he didn't approve of me, it was like he was confirming all my worst fears—that I was not normal and thus not worth loving.

It just so happened that the Lord led me to marry the most observant and highly-vocal-about-his-observations person in the world. To be fair, he is not critical to be mean, he is just so observant and his brain so computer-like that he would point out anything that wasn't perfect, which I decoded to mean, "You didn't do it well enough, Misti." Sometimes he may have meant to say that, but most of the time I just added those words in my mind.

For example, in the past he might have opened the fridge, noticed that it was dirty, then without condemnation, said, "This fridge is dirty." I would automatically think, "I'm a horrible wife because I can't even keep the fridge clean." I then would be hurt and act like he was such a mean person for saying that to me. I placed my insecurities and self-loathing on him, when he was just stating a fact.

Now, today, when he says something observant like, "This fridge is dirty," I just say, "Yeah it is. You better clean it." He loves this change in me. He gets to be free to be his observant self and there are no hurt feelings or contention over it. I get to keep my self-worth by throwing the responsibility to fix whatever he is noticing back on him. We usually both smile at each other when this happens. Through unspoken communication we are saying that we accept one another and ourselves.

I love to give this as an example of how observant Jed is because I will never forget it. One day while living near Salt Lake City, Utah, Jed left for work. He came home a short time later and said, "Where did you go?" I asked, "Why?" He said, "Because when I left the tires on your car were facing this way and when I came home they were facing the other."

Seriously, I don't know if there is another person alive who is more observant than he. I think Heavenly Father must have thought that it would be really funny to put us two together—me unobservant, and him hyper-observant. I was mostly unobservant, not as a genuine characteristic, but because I had to be hyper-observant about what was going on inside of me in order to keep my head above water. Thus, when it came to things on the outside, I had less mental capacity to be observant. The tangible world didn't matter as much to me as it did to Jed. I was trying too hard to avoid my emotional pitfalls or get out of them if already in there.

I wanted to be more like Jed but the fear of my pain kept me bound in my internal world. It was such a scary moment—the moment I would feel myself slipping back into those emotional pit-falls. Many things could trigger it, but the triggers didn't work unless I was stressed about something, even if it was stress that "life is too good for me, and what if I get prideful if it goes on this way too long?"

Some of the main triggers were commercials that had anything to do with eyes, noticing someone blinking, someone talking about their eyes or their tongues, hearing a commercial on depression or anxiety medication, and noticing my own eyes while trying to close them to sleep or pray.

After any one of these triggers, I would have a full-fledged battle in my head. I hated it. I felt so weird, so flawed, and so embarrassed of my own self. It was a battle between my spirit and the powerful firing of the neurons in my brain. Stop! I would say. Stop it! But the more I tried to get it to stop, the more I had to focus on what the problem was, and the more I did that, the worse it got. It felt like a no win situation. It was always there. Everywhere I went and whatever I did, it was like there was a connection between the obsessive misfiring in my brain and every uncomfortable emotion that you can think of. I couldn't have one without the other.

I have heard others use the "elephant in the room" metaphor and that was an exact likening of me. After I experienced a trigger, it was like a big neon pink elephant just appeared in my line of vision. The elephant was like a floater in one's eye; no matter where I turned, it was still in the center of my vision. I couldn't see anything else very clearly at all. Only peripherally was there anything else in my life.

I tried everything to not see the elephant, in other words, to not notice myself or others blinking, or my tongue in my mouth, but no matter what I did or where I turned, there it was. It caused tremendous anxiety. In order to survive and not sink into what I thought would be craziness, I had to pretend the elephant wasn't there even though it was very much there. The neurons in my brain kept firing and firing, repeating and repeating the same message to me until the only relief available to me came. Unfortunately, as I said before, it came in the form of another torture, equal if not worse than the first, and that was depression.

For some reason, depression didn't make the elephant disappear but it made it shrink some because depression hurt so badly that my focus then changed to doing everything I could to get rid of it. I had always prayed, read my scriptures, and read my patriarchal blessing, but I increased the intensity of my study during the hardest of times. When I felt the Spirit, I found temporary relief, or at least increased in hope.

My patriarchal blessing was a huge hope builder for me. Although sometimes it seemed impossible that it was meant for me, I hung onto the hope, joy, and peace promised me. Sometimes it was only by my fingernails. Nevertheless, the important part was that I was holding on.

Again, the hardest part of these difficulties was feeling shamefully alone. I was ashamed of myself for having brain issues. I thought that if I were a stronger person, I would have "real" problems. I was embarrassed to lean on Jed too much, especially at first. I feared he would regret marrying me. I not only put on a show for Jed, but I felt I had to put on a show for everyone else. I didn't put on a show for others as much as I did it for me. I needed them to think I was great or I feared I might fall in a black hole and never get out. Holding onto Reality #1 with all my heart felt like my only choice.

On May 29, 1997, I began to open up about my struggle again. I wrote, *"Today my life is going to change. Lately I have had a hard time and have begun to make myself depressed and then I would get more depressed from feeling guilty about being depressed. It feels awful! I have just not been myself lately. I talked to Jed about it and he has been so good to try and help me, but he just doesn't understand. He suggested I talk to Bishop and so I did."*

I remember that visit very clearly. It was the first time I tried to get help for my emotions by actually telling my bishop. I didn't say anything about the embarrassing OCD. Bishop only helped me a little. Part of it was my fault—I didn't disclose any of the hard OCD details. He did help me a great deal by telling me a lot of other people in the ward experienced feelings of depression too. It was nice to hear that I wasn't completely alone, but it wasn't the depression that was so shameful and lonely, it was the stupid reoccurring thoughts. It was the Tourette's of my brain.

I felt lonelier than ever after someone tried to help me and then it didn't work. It felt hopeless. If my bishop couldn't help me then who could? The tender mercies of relief came in different ways. Sometimes it was only a sentence or two from the scriptures or the prophets and then some good old-fashioned determination that could get me out of the slumps. I would finally gather up enough energy and anger to break free. I would say, "If this is my life, I am not going to be down about it," and then after forcing myself to do a lot on my to-do list, I would have more energy to ignore the elephant in the room until it disappeared.   ·

It was wonderful, yet I knew I was still walking on the edge of the cliff and just one trigger at the wrong time could send me falling off. It was still a hard place to be, but I would take that scenario any day because that was the best place I could be at the time. I didn't know how to ever be a safe distance from the edge. I was always feeling fear in the back of my mind, and worse than the fear was the feeling that I was just getting by in life; that I wasn't really living it the way I would if I didn't have the elephant waiting offstage hoping for the next chance to be center stage. I felt I was watching others live while I was just pretending. That, in and of itself, was extreme torture.

CHAPTER 16

Shamefully Admitting the Truth: I Didn't Like My Mother

~

WATCHING OTHERS AND how they seemed to obtain peace became really important to me. If I wasn't happy and others were then I wanted to know what they were doing that I wasn't. I went through all the gyrations. I evaluated everyone's family versus my own. My family confused me. I couldn't figure out why I felt uneasy at the thought of being with them. I enjoyed them on the surface. I had fun with them. But something was missing. Why did I feel such underlying pain while being with them or even just talking on the phone? What was it? I didn't really know and so I began guessing. Were they not living the gospel? They always went to church, they held callings, and later Dad was the clerk in the bishopric. They didn't do everything perfect, but neither did anyone else. My parents didn't have a perfect relationship but neither did most other people. What I concluded for the time was my family lacked confidence in themselves and thus lacked in true joy. My family had never learned that it was healthy and okay to debate, discuss, and even disagree with one another without being offended. We had never learned to take interest in anything besides other people's problems and the superficial things of life.

My mom did everything she could possibly do to make her home, her physical appearance, and her life look perfect. Jed used to tease her by putting a tissue in the bathroom garbage can and then see how long it took for her to take it out and throw it away in the kitchen. I'm not sure why she had garbage cans in the bathrooms because we weren't allowed to use them. She loved Jed's teasing. She would laugh right along with him. She was good at planning fun activities. But maybe that was it—maybe there was just too much planning for how things should look and what memories needed to be made and when. It was more the talking about the fun things we did with others than, in my mind, actually enjoying them. In my family growing up there was less loving of one's self, of leaving the kitchen a mess for a while if that was what was best for the family. There was less service, less genuine laughter. There was more of living through others' experiences than through your own. There was always someone else's drama or tragedy that was easier to feel than dealing with the drama and tragedy on our own backs.

My mom loved to talk on the phone, partly because it was her job. Along with the necessary calling came, what seemed to me, gossip. Gossip has to be one of the most tempting of sins when living in a small town! I hated hearing her gossip when I was young because of the yucky feeling it caused. Unfortunately, leaving home and getting married didn't cut that out of my life. I began dreading her phone calls to me. She didn't call to see how I was or what she could do for me. As soon as I said "Hello" I just listened to her to-do list (because that made her feel like she was projecting her life in a good light), and then I heard all the latest in town. Most of it was tragic stories, which left me feeling drained and dragged down from all the trials of others.

I had always been the dutiful daughter but now I was getting angry—anger that I felt I could never express because I feared my family hating me if I ever told them I didn't like something. That is the complete opposite of a healthy family. In a healthy family people are free to express what they like or don't like. The other person is then free to accept it or disagree with you. Either way, just expressing it is freeing to both parties. Love and acceptance is able to thrive in that environment.

Freedom of opinion and speech in a family is huge! I greatly feared ever telling my mom that I disagreed with her or that I didn't want to do whatever it was that she wanted. It would crush her ego too much. I felt very torn. I wanted my mother. I wanted to be with her, but I dreaded it at the same time. I saw emptiness in her. I saw a lack of confidence. I saw an insatiable hunger for fulfillment and love that she tried to fill with worldly things and through me. Although I knew material possessions would never satisfy my needs, she was like a mirror of everything I didn't like in myself. As a true co-dependent, I tried to change her so that I could then feel better about myself. If I changed her I could do what I had always wanted to do: love to be with her.

I wanted to love her. I really did. However, I found it harder and harder as I grew older. I realized, much to my own dismay, that I didn't admire her. I felt guilty even thinking that, but more than that, I felt cheated. I wished that she had known how to mother me better. Silently I asked God, "Didn't you know that I needed a mom who could be there for me emotionally?" What I know now is that I got exactly the mother that I needed. There are no coincidences with the Lord. God loves her and knew her weaknesses and tendencies as well as my own. He knew what we could learn from each other. Growing up under her false beliefs was very hard for me. What I am writing in this book will probably be very hard for her. I guess that God knew we both needed the hard things that the other one could give. We could only learn what we needed to through each other.

When I was newly married I didn't know or understand these truths. In spite of my feelings about her and our relationship, I didn't know what else to do so, again, I pretended all was well.

Pretending makes you sick. It is not good for the soul. Pretending a relationship is perfect when it isn't is like pretending a sliver isn't in your foot when it really is. At first it is annoying but not too hard to ignore. After awhile it can get infected and so painful that you know you must do something about it. You can no longer pretend that it is not there. By that time the infection is so much harder to get rid of than if you had just removed the sliver when you first noticed it was there.

Families who remove their slivers quickly are much happier, and if done lovingly, their wounds are never there long enough to get infected. Even within families there are some who do this and some that don't. Some lack the confidence to go right to the source to work out troubles, yet others have no problem with it.

I noticed this with Jed's family. Jed is a tell-the-person or get-over-it type of person. I have known other people that go back and forth. They generally tell the other person what they really think, but over time I have noticed their wounds become more and more infected because they often tell the wrong person what they are really thinking. If you tell everyone except the person you really need to talk to, nothing changes except the size of the wound. I wish I had known and really understood this principle many years ago. Today I try and go directly to the source when I find a sliver. There are still those that I find it harder to do this with; namely my parents. I am getting better and better at it, but only because I am consciously working at it. When I do it lovingly, they are getting better and better at accepting that I am speaking out of love for our relationship. I love them for that!

My study of other families became even more heightened when I was expecting our first baby. Without a doubt, the one thing I wanted more than anything was to raise my child to be a happy, independent person—happier and more independent than I was. Was that possible? I had already noticed that my original family was lacking in those areas. With heightened anxiety, I noticed almost all of my mom's siblings and children lacking in those things as well. I didn't know my dad's siblings well enough to decide what category they fit.

Was I doomed to raise my family in the same dysfunctional way? That really scared me! I wrote several comments in my journal about the fear I had about not being a good enough parent. What I really meant to say was I feared I would raise my own child to feel as insecure and emotionally weak as I did. We learn from our parents by emulating their mannerisms as well as their behaviors. Doesn't the son often walk like the father and the daughter often laugh like the mother?

When we are little, our parents are all we know and so we learn everything from them. No one is born into a perfect family and so we all must take inventory when we are old enough to do so. What behaviors and family traditions do I want to emulate? What worked? What didn't? These are hard questions and it takes time, study, and a lot of prayer to really understand.

The Book of Mormon talks a lot about the "traditions of their fathers, which were not correct" (Mosiah 1:5). It isn't easy to change any tradition in a family. For some reason, families, especially parents, take offense easily if another family member wants to change a "tradition" or false belief in a family. Parents think they are being abandoned or unjustly judged by their children. What their children are really trying to do is abandon all of the junk. The junk represents the lies or false traditions that through the generations we are unknowingly taught to believe.

The truth is that if parents will let down their guard and go through the process of evaluating false traditions with their children, they can actually become closer as a family. They can all learn to strip themselves from those untrue traditions or the things that if believed and emulated, without ever being questioned, actually take us away from love instead of toward it.

Though it can be very difficult, a child who recognizes their false traditions and works with the Savior to try and change it within themselves can actually change the course of history for their children after them. They lovingly strip the false traditions away from their future generations that otherwise would've been blindly passed down.

I love this quote from a short story called "He Who Travels the Road Best." "He who travels the road best is he who makes the road smoother for those who follow" (Clark, 1997).

That is what we can do for the generations who follow us. We can make their road smoother when we do the work first. No matter the false traditions that we are taught as children, we always have the choice to change. Otherwise, where is the test that we came here to take? We all get different test problems. We all have a choice as to whether or not we will swim upstream.

The Savior has helped me see the false traditions that I learned as a child. When I asked for it, He gave me knowledge on how to escape it—line upon line, precept upon precept (see D&C 98:12). As He helped me pull away, He simultaneously helped me to forgive and love those who, without ill intent, taught me the untrue traditions in the first place.

That process of loving your family yet separating from their traditions is hard. They can make you feel like you are a bad person for doing so. It can take time, study, prayer, a lot of effort, and at times some pretty tough skin. However, through the Atonement I have found it is more than possible—it is wonderful!

It is important to note that the "wonderful" can come almost immediately. Other times, like in my case, it can take years of progress, setbacks, and ultimately accomplishment before the "wonderful" is set and enjoyed. Freedom from the bondage of false traditions is very much worth the effort. After a lot of work, and a lot of prayer and tears, I am now free from my family's control abuse and false traditions, however I still don't have their blessing in doing so. At times it is still hard for me to not feel like a "bad child" when I act in accordance to my own conscience and not theirs.

In Zechariah 1:2–4, the Lord commands us to be different from our fathers if they are not hearkening to all of His commandments. "The Lord hath been sore displeased with your fathers. Therefore say thou unto them, Thus saith the Lord of hosts; Turn ye unto me, saith the Lord of hosts, and I will turn unto you, saith the Lord of hosts. Be ye not as your fathers, unto whom the former prophets have cried, saying, Thus saith the Lord of hosts; Turn ye now from your evil ways, and from your evil doings: but they did not hear, nor hearken unto me, saith the Lord."

If there is a contest between following your parents and following the Lord, there is no question that the commandment to honor parents will be fulfilled if we choose the Lord in all things. It may seem counterintuitive, but we honor our parents by following the Lord even if it means saying no to their way of living. Of course, we will only qualify for His Spirit if we try and do this in a Christlike manner.

This is what Christ said on this subject: "He that loveth father or mother more than me is not worthy of me: and he that loveth son or daughter more than me is not worthy of me. And he that taketh not his cross, and followeth after me, is not worthy of me. He that findeth his life shall lose it: and he that loseth his life for my sake shall find it" (Matthew 10:37–39).

My battle between father and mother, God, and self was yet to be waged. I had no idea how to pull away from their demands and cut the strings of my puppeteered life. How to escape the OCD caused by such a life was a saga yet to be enacted.

CHAPTER 17

Healing in Stages: Stage One

~

WHEN I HAD my first baby, our son, Jeren, I was amazed! How could anyone not believe in God and yet see the miracle of a baby? The whole pregnancy I was enamored by each new stage of growth. When I saw his tiny fingers on the ultrasound, I couldn't wait to hold them. It was a spiritual experience to participate in that process of creating a beautiful little person.

After he was born, the second night in the hospital, I had a special experience with Jeren. I was nursing him in the semi-dark. I told I loved him so much and to my surprise, he quit nursing, looked up at me, and sighed as he gave me the biggest smile you have ever seen a baby give. Then he went back to nursing. I wrote in my journal, *"He melted my heart and engraved his name on it."*

Being in the hospital wasn't all rosy. My mom was waiting in the hall while I was in labor and left the hospital to go teach dance, and while doing so she missed him being born.

I wrote, *"This was the thing that I was saddest about. I cried pretty hard because I felt Mom was putting her work before me. She could have stayed with me. Last year she got so mad at me and Jed because we missed one of my brother's games, yet she missed being out in the hall waiting to hear her grandchild cry for the first time and being right there to come in and see her daughter after she had her first baby. She didn't how bad that hurt me. I never said anything to her because I didn't want... any fighting at the happiest moment of my life."*

In her defense, I dilated quicker than the nurses anticipated and so she didn't think she would miss it, but she still took the chance. It was more than her not actually being there; I wanted a storybook-like mom. I wanted a strong, solid mom to be there to give me strength and hope in my own ability to mother. I'm sure my mom wanted to be that for me too, but she didn't know how. I understand now that most of us really do the best we know how. That is why knowledge is power. If you couple a habit of obtaining divine knowledge with that of humility to apply the truths learned, there is no end to what you can become. Increasing your knowledge increases your ability for good. My mom never read anything but the sensational parts of the newspaper. She had a false belief that she was not smart and thus couldn't learn from the scriptures. With that crippling habit of omission, she never had a chance to learn how to be better.

Somewhere deep down I knew that I had to separate myself from her and become someone new, someone unlike the chain of dysfunction that was in the generations before me. I prayed to know how. Little did I know how much work it would be to do so and how much pain it would cause the ones that I chose to set firm boundaries with.

A couple weeks before Jeren was born, my brother left on a mission to Nicaragua. He was in the MTC for six weeks where he experienced a mental breakdown and needed to come home. It was so sad. He didn't want to come home. He wanted to serve a mission. He had just served the previous summer as captain of the Sons of Helaman camp (this was a camp that the Church put on to prepare young men spiritually) and was a spiritual giant. He couldn't understand why the Lord would do this to him and why He wouldn't just heal him so that he could serve him. Wouldn't that be a good trade? To our finite minds, that is what would make sense, but Heavenly Father says, "For my thoughts are not your thoughts, neither are your ways my ways, saith the Lord" (Isaiah 55:8).

As I think back to this time, my heart hurts. I was more scared than I had ever been in my life. My own mentally ill brother, a counselor saying it's genetic, remembering my mentally sick aunt, and having it all close in on me like a black hole. As it was all sinking down on me, it was like I was hearing in my mind, "All your worst fears are confirmed. You and your whole family have a prison sentence of craziness. You are crazy. You tried to fight it off but now you know. You will never escape it. Your aunt still struggles even with medicine. Medicine doesn't work. Now your husband will mock your family and you. You don't deserve him. His family isn't crazy. They don't have any mental illness. You won't be a good mom if you have mental issues. If it is genetic, you could have given it to your son. Life will never be good for you. You can't escape your own genetics."

It's hard to explain how dark that hole was. I felt like all my hopes and dreams of escaping my own prison had just turned black and I could hear someone double-lock my prison door. On top of this huge burden was the burden I was already carrying of trying to figure out how to be a good mom. On top of that burden was the fear of my own OCD thoughts, anxiety, and depression. And on top of that was the ultimate burden of pretending it all didn't exist. After a few weeks, I couldn't handle it anymore and I made the best and hardest decision I had made thus far in my life. I went to see a counselor.

I was so nervous that Jed gave me a blessing the night before my appointment. I went to see a wonderful older man named Woody. He looked so much like my dad's dad, who I loved. He used to be a minister for another church before he was baptized at age 52. Since then he had served as a bishop. Immediately I felt comfortable with him. For the first time, I opened up and told him things that I had never told anyone before. He heard me. He understood me. Then he taught me.

He taught me about prayer, real prayer. I learned that I had been praying with a list of give-me's, instead of having a real conversation with Heavenly Father. He also taught me about listening. He showed me a little notebook that he kept in his pocket. He said, "It's amazing what kind of personal revelation you will realize you have received and would have brushed off if you hadn't taken the time to listen."

He asked me about my parents and our relationship. As I told him, he seemed to instantly get it. He said, "It sounds like your anxiety is a result of your mom not loving you the way you thought she should have. There is no doubt that your mom loves you, but it seems it's conditional on what you look like, and other insignificant things instead of what you are inside and how you feel." He also said, "It's sad, but I don't think your mom knows true happiness because she hasn't made the connection with Heavenly Father. She isn't a hypocrite, it just sounds like she hasn't learned to pray. She is looking for happiness in getting attention from her kids' awards, her house, job, etcetera." He said that this life is my test from the Lord and not my test from my mom, dad, Jed or anyone else. I only need to answer to God.

After talking with him, it was as if my body and spirit heaved a collective sigh of relief! He got it and he helped me get it. Overall, he fed my hungry soul. I told someone the whole truth about all of my symptoms. By responding with understanding and love, he helped lift the shame that was weighing me down. He helped me understand a hugely important thing that I could never quite put my finger on. I knew something in my original family was wrong, but I was trained to look from the outside in and from out there everything looked perfect. House perfectly clean, perfect honorable kids (except when my brother came home early from his mission, which put a huge flaw in my parent's resume), fun family, lots of laughter, successful kids that won popularity awards as well as prestigious dance and beauty pageants, and kids that graduated from college and married in the temple (at the time my brother wasn't yet married). The family resume was pretty much flawless, so I couldn't understand it until Woody rescued me.

I only had a few sessions with him, but each time I left there I felt a little less crazy and a lot more hope. In some weird way, I felt too much hope. He assured me that I did not have a chemical imbalance. I took that to mean that I didn't have OCD. I jumped the gun a little bit. I came out of there with the false hope that nothing was wrong with me physically when, as I would learn later, I did have a physical issue. I had OCD, and that was coupled with scars from emotional abuse and feelings of abandonment.

I still had a lot yet to learn and a lot yet to heal. However, this was the beginning of my journey toward complete healing. It was a small step, but still important. Sometimes we are delivered all at once, and other times He shows us the way little by little. We learn in the New Testament that the Savior has power to heal in stages. I learned this by reading the book *Jesus the Christ* by James E. Talmage, "A blind man was brought, and Jesus was asked to touch him. He took the sightless one by the hand, led him outside the town, applied saliva to his eyes, laid hands upon him in a ministration, and asked him if he could see. The man answered that he saw dimly, but was unable to distinguish men from trees. Applying His hands to the man's eyes, Jesus told him to look up; the man did so and saw clearly.... The Lord sent him away rejoicing. This miracle presents the unique feature of Jesus healing a person by stages; the result of the first ministration was but a partial recovery" (Talmage, 360). The scriptural account is found in Mark 8:22–25.

I, too, was healed in stages. I suspect that I will continue to heal in stages throughout my entire life. All the different facets of my mortal self will need to take their turn to be healed by the Atonement. If we follow God's plan, the Atonement is never done with us in this life. The Savior keeps lifting us inch by inch closer to Him.

After those few sessions with Woody, I began to look at my relationship with my parents, mainly my mom, through different lenses. Even though my healing journey had just begun, it was like I had just had blinders removed and I could suddenly see more clearly the dysfunction in my mom and our relationship. Before, I had felt sinful even thinking about what I didn't like about my mom. We were taught to never—I mean never—hurt mom's feelings, so even recognizing this fault in her almost made me want to shun it the very second I recognized it. There was a false tradition in me at work. It did not want me to believe the truth.

I was torn. I felt angry, yet didn't know how to voice it. I became angrier when I noticed it in real life situations. Here is an example: When Jeren was a couple months old, we took him to church in my hometown for a missionary farewell or baby blessing. When we got there and sat by my parents, my mom looked displeased at what I had dressed Jeren in and said, "And he has so many cute clothes." She didn't like what I had dressed him in.

I was hurt and angry. I was less hurt about the actual comment and more hurt when I realized even further that Woody was right. Her love was conditional. That is a terrible realization. I had convinced myself for so many years that my family wasn't the problem. It was me that was flawed inside. It almost felt worse to know that my problems stemmed from somewhere less in my control than the little control I felt in myself. Inside I turned to my mom in anger and thought, "You did this to me! You ruined my adolescence and the wreckage continues to destroy my peace! You loved me conditionally and still do! If I don't perform to your liking, then I am punished by less love and snide comments."

As I thought these things, the guilt mounted because, again, I was taught to never think ill of her. That false belief wouldn't even allow me to evaluate the situation. I turned these feelings inward for the most part because I feared standing up for myself. I was afraid of being abandoned by my family. I was afraid of doing something wrong. I was afraid that I wouldn't be honoring my parents.

Turning my feelings inward kept me from healing. I heard once that depression is just anger turned inward. I turned my anger away from them and took it out on myself. I let myself feel anxious and depressed, or I let the OCD take over to distract me from my realization. It was easier that way. I didn't have to face them. It was too scary to do that.

However, soon after that incident at the farewell, my mom and I actually fought. That hardly ever happened because I was always the dutiful puppet and did whatever I was told. When I tried to stand up for myself, my mom told me that I had changed since I had gotten married and "even her sister noticed it." What she meant was that I had become less of a trophy and more of a person with opinions and she didn't like it when they differed from hers. A prime example was when I cut my hair to my shoulders soon after having Jeren. She doesn't like short hair and would never let me cut my hair very much when I was under her thumb, so when I cut it to my shoulders without her permission, she never said a word about it. She didn't even acknowledge that I cut it. Again, I wasn't performing to her liking.

Another example happened when I was first married. I had gained a few pounds from the birth control pills I was on. She told me, "You better watch it or Jed will look elsewhere." I wasn't as skinny as she liked me to be and so she used my one security blanket, Jed, to threaten me. Basically she said that he would leave me for someone skinnier if I didn't lose weight. I didn't think Jed would leave me but I couldn't stand her disapproval of me. Without Jed knowing, I went with her and my dad to a doctor to get the diet pill Fen-Phen.

Things progressively got more confusing for me. I was always the good girl, the pleaser, the peacemaker. I began to realize that in order to be good to myself, I might have to stop the abuse and thus the abuser would consequently hurt. I didn't know how to be good to myself and still maintain that kind part of me, the part that never hurt anyone's feelings. I tried to find the "me" that I wanted to be—the "me" that I knew was inside me somewhere. However, I didn't have the courage or the knowledge to stick up for myself. I fell victim yet again. I pretended that I wasn't angry with my parents. I found myself continuing to give in to old habits of pleasing everyone else first and then just going to prayer to find relief from the anxiety and disconnectedness I felt inside.

I never learned as a child that I was competent. Mom needed to feel needed and I needed to have stuff done for me since I learned and believed that I couldn't do anything myself. We were a good dysfunctional team. But it carried over to when I got married. I felt incompetent and Jed, being very competent, took over that role of my mom. I had to literally teach myself to be a "big girl." I had never made my own haircut appointments until I got married. I rarely ever went shopping by myself because Mom always had a need to be there with me. Even up to the time I was healed, if I went shopping without my mom, I'd feel guilty and I'd have to remind myself that I am not a mean person for doing it. (Sometimes false beliefs need to be confronted and challenged even way after the time that you know they are absurd beliefs.) Bills, money, decisions of all kinds, and even decorating were other areas that I had no confidence in. I found myself calling my mom out of obligation and feeling good for making her feel needed. When I tried to pull away, there were definite subtle comments and even unsaid messages sent to me. She was warning me to shape up and get back in my position. She desperately needed to feel like the mother no matter how old I got.

Over time I tried to inch away, yet my position only altered a bit. As I adjusted, she put new layers of cement around me just to make sure I didn't try to get any further away. I can't blame her. She also had a false belief at work. She thought that she needed me in order to be happy. Underneath her need for me to perform to her liking, I had to believe there was some unconditional love there, however buried it might have been. She didn't know it was buried. She believed her love was unconditional, but conditional it was. She was blind and didn't even know it.

Chapter 18

San Diego Freedom

~

I WAS JUGGLING EVERYTHING: my relationship with my mom, my husband, my baby, my brain, and my dance company. I started the studio to help our financial situation while both Jed and I were in school. When I became pregnant, I realized that I couldn't do all three, and so with a semester or two away from graduating, I quit school. Most people get an "ouch" feeling when I tell them that, but I have no regrets. I have my Associate's degree framed and I can confidently declare that with four and a half years of schooling, I received an education.

I wouldn't have quit school with such little time left if I had felt passionate about my field of study. When I did the math (which I learned in school), I realized that I would be making as much money, if not more, teaching dance twelve hours a week than I would working forty hours in my line of study. It just made sense, especially with a baby on the way. It was a good decision. Between that and Jed's lawn maintenance company, we made good money for newlyweds and Jed could just focus on school in the winter. Financially, we also benefited when we left the state for law school because I was able to sell my business and so was he. We were definitely blessed.

Jeren was 1 year old when Jed graduated from Weber State. He decided that he wanted to go to law school. He applied to several universities but because of a few careless grades before his mission (he claims that it was because he was dating me), he wasn't accepted to any of the law schools that we preferred. We visited one school that he was accepted to. It was in a different state. We were turned off by the school and area; it just didn't feel right. Thinking it was our only option, we began wondering if he should just bag law school and begin helping his dad at his nursery. However, the Lord had different plans for us.

Soon after we returned from visiting the law school, I was calling my dance students one day when our course changed drastically. My student's mom, Nell, answered the phone. She sweetly asked about Jed and me and how we were doing. I told her that Jed was looking to go to law school. She said, "You remind me of myself. My husband went to law school and I was a dance teacher." I asked her where he went to law school. She said, "Cal Western—California Western School of Law—in downtown San Diego." I had never heard of that school before. That night I told Jed about the school. He looked into it and within two weeks he had not only been accepted but had a full scholarship for the first year!

We were so excited about the opportunity to move away for a little while and establish our own little family. Jeren was twenty months old and I was six months pregnant when we moved to San Diego.

It was the strangest thing to send Jed off to law school that first day. It was January 3, 2000. We were both nervous but especially him. I wrote in my journal, *"I made him smile for a few pictures before he headed off for the trolley. After waving good-bye, I shut myself in our new but strange apartment not knowing exactly how to handle this new situation. This is the first time in my life that I have no other work besides that of being a wife and a mother. I think this is the scariest job I've ever had.... Today was kind of hard especially because I kept watching the clock wondering when Jed would come home. I kept thinking, 'This is going to be a long three years.'"*

A few days later on January 8, 2000, I wrote, *"Well, this week has been one of the longest in my life. Part of me wants to bawl it has been so hard, yet part of me wants to thank Heavenly Father it has been this smooth and easy."*

My biggest fear about moving away was my own mind. I feared getting stuck in the cycle and having horrible memories there. I prayed and prayed very hard for peace while there. I asked Jed to give me a blessing before we moved there that I might be granted that desire. I was thus blessed.

The whole time that we lived there was absolutely wonderful except for one tiny emotional bump and the last three months. I didn't have to worry about taking care of anyone but my little family. I felt especially free from taking care of my mom. I had a great excuse—I was in another state. I felt like I could define myself as a grown woman for the first time. I went where I wanted to go. I went shopping by myself. I decorated my apartment by myself and added my own touches when holidays came around. I made every meal and every Sunday meal. I decided when, where, and how I would spend all of my time. I used my extra time (the time that I had previously spent worrying about mom) having fun and performing service. I no longer felt forced into a role of pretended love. I was choosing to love. It felt wonderful!

I soon met my most cherished friend. From my point of view we were best friends. Her name was Annie. She was from Australia. She had the cutest accent. She was my visiting teacher, although she only visited me at my house once or twice. We decided to go walking together in the mornings instead. Oh what a godsend that was! She taught me so much. I wrote, *"She makes me want to be a better person."*

Annie was a good listener. She gave me permission to have dreams other than motherhood. She didn't feel guilty about those dreams and so I followed suit. She loved homes and wanted to be a realtor when her kids grew older, so every week she had one day that she set aside to walk through open houses. She felt capable and I gleaned from her all that I could. I began to feel capable, too. It was an amazing feeling and an amazing time. I loved our daily walks. Our conversations were uplifting, inspiring, and therapeutic. I learned a lot about how to be the mother that I wanted to be by watching her. She had the instinct to love unconditionally. She helped me deal with Jeren's newfound strong personality with love. Although Annie didn't know of my specific emotional trials, I talked a lot about the things that bothered me about my upbringing and she helped me by really listening, understanding, and sometimes offering clarity. She was also very healthy, budget conscious, and organized. I didn't have it in me to be too budget conscious or on a certain daily schedule, like going to the store every Tuesday with coupons and such, so I let that go. I did, however, adopt a cleaning schedule. I cleaned the whole house and did all the laundry every Monday. It was amazing at how accomplished I felt by doing those mundane tasks every week like clockwork.

Annie really did inspire me. She loved me and sincerely complimented me. She saw people's hearts instead of what they looked like on the outside. Even though she was a friend, in many ways she became a mother figure. She was an answer to the many prayers I said before moving to San Diego. I am so thankful that she was assigned as my visiting teacher. I have no doubt that it was an inspired calling. The Lord knew that we could bless one another's lives. She fed my soul daily with unconditional love and optimism.

CHAPTER 19

Discovering the Joy of Service

~

O UR SECOND CHILD, Hannah, was born just three months after we moved to San Diego. We call her our California girl. Holding her and Jeren together on my lap for the first time was surreal. We weren't just a young couple with one child anymore. It felt in that moment that we became a real family. The next year was almost magical for me. I had never before gone a whole year without getting stuck emotionally (although I did have one bump for a week around Thanksgiving). I began to see the realities of life better and even get frustrated by them, which was quite new for me. Before that, I just wanted emotional peace and after that was given me, I began to realize that "real life" was hard too. I started to write about my frustrations in my journal. I wrote on August 5, 2000, *"If I sound really negative it doesn't mean I think my life is the pits, it just means I am expressing the realities of life more."*

My next-door neighbor was Noelle. I also don't think it was a coincidence that we were neighbors. She needed me and I especially needed her. Because of several brain hemorrhages she had experienced, she found herself without the use of the left side of her body and slower speech. Because of a mistake during one of her surgeries in which her right eye's optical nerve was cut, she only had the use of her left eye. She was in a wheelchair for the most part. She couldn't work and her husband went to school in the day, worked at night, and had a drinking problem. She was lonely and I needed someone to serve. We became a great team.

I wrote, *"I have always wanted a chance to serve and Noelle has given that to me. She will never know how much joy she has given me by happily letting me serve her. Jeren has felt that same happiness. Whenever I am taking food to her apartment, Jeren has to be the one to give it to her because he loves it when she takes it from him and says, 'Thank you.'"* I can still hear in my mind the exact way she deliberately and meaningfully told him thanks.

We often went for walks with her. She had an electric wheelchair so we were quite the parade. I walked next to her pushing my double stroller. The San Diego River was right behind our apartments with the most beautiful river walk running next to it for a few miles. It was surrounded by natural vegetation. It had wild-growing trees, bushes, and flowers. They grew so thick and tall that you could almost forget that you were in the city.

We loved our walks. We always stopped by the river where Jeren would get excited about the ducks and then equally excited when the red trolley would zoom over our heads. We would then walk up the hill to the pet store. Seeing Jeren (and later Hannah, too) in there with tons of excitement for animals was enough to make both my day as well as Noelle's. From there we sometimes went to a store or out for some cheap pizza. We did this field trip often.

She came from a family of preachers for a Christian church. She and her husband were going into the ministry at one time, but after her worst brain hemorrhage left her incapacitated, she was angry at God. She also couldn't have babies. She said that all she had ever wanted was to be a mother. I felt her pain. I understood her disappointment and her anger. She was still in the mode of not praying anymore when I first met her. Our trials were different but both were very difficult to bear at times.

I love this poem called "Gethsemane" by Ella Wheeler Wilcox (1910).

In Golden—youth when seems the Earth
A summer-land of singing mirth
When souls are glad and hearts are light,
And not a shadow lurks in sight,
We do not know it, but there lies
Somewhere veiled 'neath evening skies
A garden which we all must see—
The Garden of Gethsemane…

Down shadowy lanes, across strange streams
Bridged over by our broken dreams;
Behind the misty cap of years,
Beyond the great salt fount of tears,
The garden lies. Strive as you may,
You cannot miss it in your way,
All paths that have been or shall be
Pass somewhere through Gethsemane.

Noelle's Gethsemane was her physical handicap and her disappointment that she had no children. My Gethsemane was my emotional and mental handicap, which often meant I couldn't fully enjoy my children. Although one was more obvious, both of us, at times, suffered more than we thought we could bear.

While in San Diego my thirst for knowledge increased like never before. I read Elder John Groberg's book, *In the Eye of the Storm*. I was so impressed by all of his spiritual experiences. My faith in personal revelation increased. I began listening more and realizing more and more that the Lord was answering my prayers as well.

I asked Heavenly Father for help in sharing the gospel with Noelle. I wanted to take her to Old Town to the Mormon Battalion visitor's center but didn't know how to ask her. She called me one day saying that she wanted to get out of the apartments while they were testing the fire alarm system. It was perfect timing. She agreed to go with me to the visitor's center. I felt the Spirit so strongly there. I was disappointed when she declined the missionary's offer to come teach her. I hoped a tiny seed of faith had been planted.

A few weeks later when I was having the sister missionaries over for dinner and Jed couldn't make it, I asked Noelle to come. I felt that her misconceptions of Mormons were being straightened out. I was so excited. Not long after that, Jed and I had her and her husband over for dinner with the sister missionaries. They listened to the first discussion. It didn't go very well. I was disappointed but was happy that at least by the time we moved, Noelle was again praying. Her emails ever since have been full of faith and uplifting stories. Although disappointed that she never gained a testimony and was baptized a member of The Church of Jesus Christ of Latter-day Saints, I was happy for her that she was again turning toward God. I knew that she would find joy again in her life by allowing Heavenly Father in.

Around October 2000, I started taking control of my schedule and that brought a lot of blessings. I wrote, *"I am so excited that I have finally implemented into my life four things that I have unsuccessfully tried to do many times—1) going to bed early; 2) waking up early; 3) studying scriptures in the morning; 4) and exercising five mornings a week."*

For the first time, I began to truly feast on the scriptures. I woke up extra early before my morning walk with Annie to study the Doctrine and Covenants. I used the institute manual as my study guide. I felt my testimony of the closeness of the Savior growing. I felt power flow into my life like I had never before felt. I loved reading what the prophets had to say about each D&C section in the student manual. I began to feel and experience personal revelation more than I ever had before. I was intrigued by the prophesies of the last days. I look back at that time with fondness because that was when my relationship with Heavenly Father and Jesus Christ really grew. My faith grew and thus so did the miracles in my life.

Unfortunately, my past still haunted me and frightened me. My mom's frequent calls about the upcoming holidays threw me for my first emotional spin since moving to San Diego. On November 21, 2000, I wrote, *"Jed's parents and Amy and Sam (Jed's sister and new husband) came today to spend Thanksgiving with us. They went to take their stuff to their hotel while I stayed here with Hannah. Two days ago I started feeling a little anxious. It got really bad for parts of the day yesterday.....Jed gave me a blessing. It was a beautiful blessing. I can't express in words how grateful I am for Jed and to my Heavenly Father for giving Jed the priesthood. It seems like every year I get an anxious episode about this time when the holidays start kicking in. I don't quite understand it—I'm trying to.*

"My mom has been driving me crazy lately. She gets so in to Christmas. She calls me three or four times a day sometimes as she is shopping. It is so hard for me to talk on the phone with Mom because either she is rock bottom or she is bouncing off the walls. She loves the holidays. I feel like it is so superficial and stressful. She acts like everything is perfect in her world yet when she is in her other mood, everything is wrong in her world.

"When the holidays come around and she works until she's frazzled to make everything perfect and she's saying things like 'My house looks so happy' and 'It will be so fun'—I just see through her how she is so high strung and I get angry. Angry that she never changes—angry that as many times as she cries to me and I strongly suggest she read her scriptures,

she doesn't; or that she go to the temple once a month, she doesn't. She never changes—and it's hard on me because I love her and I see her searching for happiness in materialism.

"I see her anxiety and it reminds me of how I used to feel. I know I'm wrong in trying to heal myself by trying to change my mom. I'm just trying to figure out how I can have a peaceful, Spirit-filled Christmas with my family in Utah while still being intertwined with my mom's high-strung, buy-too-many-gifts Christmas.

"It's not that I don't love being at my parents' house and love getting all the wonderful gifts that she worked so hard for and loves giving. It's more the underlying feeling I get when I'm around her and talking to her. When she calls me she acts like I'm her to-do list. She tells me everything she's done and has to do and then says, 'Well, I better go' without ever sincerely asking specific questions about how my family and I are doing.

"I love my mother. She does the best she knows how, but there are so many ways in which I want to be different towards my family. It's like I don't know how to be around her and be nice without condoning her bad spending habits. When I'm around her I revert to a child and I don't like that because I like who I am now, most of the time. I didn't like who I was then. I was trying to figure my feelings out the other day and I had the most beautiful wave of peace come over me and the thought came into my mind that I need not dig too deep. I just need faith in the Savior and things will work out."

As I read that journal entry I almost laugh as I hear myself say that I don't know why I get so anxious around the holidays and then I go on and on about my mom and the things she did that drove me crazy around the holidays. Could I not see it? Or was I just too afraid to admit it was my mom. I think it was more the latter. However, no matter the cause, anxiety hurts and I plead that it might leave me. In Heavenly Father's mercy, He blessed me at this time with a beautiful and quick reprieve. I knew it was a gift from Him. It had never been that quick before.

I wrote on December 1, 2000, *"I am so full of gratitude right now. My children are sleeping, Jed's at school studying, and I'm in bed. I thought I should take a few moments to write in this. When Jed's parents and Amy and Sam were here, we went to the temple. The Lord poured out his Spirit upon me and has healed my troubled heart."*

While I was at the temple that day, the Spirit told me I was loved and poured strength into me. I literally walked out of there feeling healed. I know the faith I had developed by feasting on the scriptures allowed for that experience to happen.

That time of my life was a special time. I was experiencing my own little family like I never could have back home. Because I was away from the domineering influence of my parents, I felt free to explore and be the person I always wanted to be. This time was incredibly special because I began to feel Heavenly Father close to me like I never had before. My faith increased because of my consistent early morning study of the Doctrine and Covenants. I read of the Savior's deep and intimate role in both the restoration of His church and in the individual lives of the Saints. I began to believe that He must also be that aware of me.

I began to notice the quiet peace that would come in my heart when praying for different answers. My trust in Him increased and so did my spiritual experiences.

December 7, 2000, *"I just got back from walking with Annie. Jed was up with both kids. Jeren (two and a half at the time) was up before I left and so I just gave him some milk and turned the TV on. Anyways, Jed handed me Hannah when I returned and said that Jeren tried to leave the house at 7:00 and the house alarm went off. I couldn't believe it. I never turned the house alarm back on when I left. I don't even know how. I knew right then that Heavenly Father had answered my prayers this morning. See, last week when I walked in our courtyard one morning after walking, Jeren was out there in his pajamas by himself and Jed was in the house sound asleep. This morning as I left Jeren in front of the TV I felt uneasy and as I walked I said a distinct prayer in my mind to our Father and asked him that if Jeren leaves the house that Jed will know about it. The feeling that I have in my heart right now tells me that I'm not making something out of nothing. The Lord caused our house alarm to go off so that Jed would wake up and get our little Jeren. I knelt and thanked Him, but not near enough."*

I was feeling more and more in control of my life and I loved every minute of it! On our fifth wedding anniversary, December 15, 2000, I wrote, *"We took the kids to Balboa Park on the 6th. It was a gorgeous day! I wanted to cry as I cradled Hannah in my arms while she giggled and put her hands in my mouth, and then in looking up I could see Jed going down the slides and playing on the jungle gym with Jeren. I thought how I never would have dreamed five years ago that I would be who and where I am right now—in San Diego, happily married, and deeply in love with both my husband and two beautiful children. I feel like step by step the Lord is maturing me and I am grateful."*

We went home to Utah for Christmas. It was fun showing off our cute little kids and seeing them interact with their grandparents and cousins. However, after being away and experiencing much autonomy and growth, I didn't like what I saw. There was some contention over whose house we were at more, there were way too many presents, and our schedules were way too tight. We all had colds by the time the trip was over.

In Utah, it seemed our families' schedules were so packed that there was no time to improve, grow, or enjoy. It seemed that much like the ancient Pharisees, everyone had so many expectations placed on themselves and one another to perform traditions with exactness that there was literally no time to live, grow, or even breathe without worrying about missing the next thing that must be done or the next thing that someone expected of you. It was a wonderful present to finally be back home in San Diego. I felt so free and so wide open with possibilities while there.

January 15, 2001, *"I have found so much joy with our little family alone here in San Diego that I wonder—we wonder—if we should move home to Utah."*

I enjoyed that winter immensely. Jed was doing really well in school and was able to spend a lot of time with us. We took the kids swimming and for walks several times a week. We enjoyed the warm winter weather. We loved our ward and our friends. We especially loved the time that we had to just get to know and enjoy our almost-3-year-old Jeren and almost-1-year-old Hannah. We went to the San Diego Zoo and Sea World. Jeren was fascinated with animals and so we went quite a bit. One of our favorite things was taking the kids swimming. Jed often came home from studying in the day so that we could all go swimming. Jeren and Hannah loved it! We walked to the pool via the beautiful river walk that lined our way between our apartment and the pool. Jeren would take off running ahead of us and Hannah followed suit as soon as she was able. We took a lot of video of us just sitting around playing with our kids. I felt like a grown up. I felt closer to Heavenly Father and the Savior than ever. I felt like a good mom. We felt like a real family.

It wasn't until spring that I began to get uneasy, knowing that within the next year, we would probably be moving back to Utah. I wanted to move back because I wanted to raise my kids in Utah, yet there was no denying that I had been more emotionally healthy while in San Diego than I had ever been in my life. It scared me that going back home would revert my progress. I think deep down I knew it would. I was able to push back those fears until about May, when I knew for sure that we would be going home in August.

It was a high-stress time. Jed was stressed about being a first year associate at a law firm, I was three months pregnant at the time and very sick (this pregnancy was a surprise, but a welcome one), and my best friend, Annie, moved twenty minutes away and we could no longer walk in the mornings. I missed her and really needed her at that time. All of that coupled with the anticipation of moving back to Utah was more than I could handle.

While doing aerobics one morning in late May, I noticed my eyes and the fear of OCD came rushing upon me. I wrote on May 27, 2001, *"I have had a hard couple of days. While doing aerobics on Friday morning I was reminded of the confusing feelings I used to have growing up and wasn't able to shake them off easily.* (Important to note that I couldn't even write that it was my eyes that I was reminded of.) *They stayed with me the last two days.... This morning my answer came when I came out into the quiet living room to pray. Before I knelt down I saw a little figurine that Jed's grandparents gave us of Jesus holding a child and lifting another to safety, and under him are the words—His words— 'Be not Afraid.' My fear left me and the Spirit entered. I knew the Lord was telling me that He is here for me and everything will always be all right. Oh how I truly love Him and need Him. Then, after my prayer of thanks... I went to make our bed and the words to this song came in my mind: 'Be thou humble and the Lord thy God shall lead thee, shall lead thee by the hand and give thee answer to thy prayers.' I cried silently as I realized that this too was from above because I have no idea why I started thinking about that song."*

The Lord was comforting me, His child. As I look back at it now, I can see that He was warning me that the battle was far from over, but that if I am humble, like the hymn says, He would lead me by the hand until He saw me through it. That is exactly what has happened. He led me by the hand through my own personal Gethsemane. Even though He had my hand, it was still gut-wrenching and lonely. However, had He not been holding my hand, I would've never been led out. I wouldn't have known the way. Only He knows the way out of our Gethsemanes because only He has already been through them. He alone knows the way. He alone leads us out. At that time, I still had a long way to be led.

CHAPTER 20

Personal Mount Everest

~

JUNE 1, 2001, *"My heart is full so full of emotion. My depressed feelings have worn on me off and on for a week. I felt just fine yesterday and half of today and then fear sets in. Fear that I might waste more time feeling this way. The Spirit has driven me this week, which filled my heart with peace even while my head ached—literally. I have been walking outside by myself and I have loved it. I meditate and think and talk with my Father in Heaven. I think of Jed and the kids and the new baby and the Spirit whispers, 'fight.' I decided to fight this tendency within my mortal body no matter what because it is when I start giving up or losing hope to fight that I really feel horrible.... This life can be so confusing for me at times yet so clear at others. I hope that through it all I can be a better wife and mother—that our kids might grow up understanding themselves, their emotions, their fears, and most especially who they are."*

That was a huge fear for me. I knew that I was battling within me a horrible cycle that came from my parents and with all of my heart and all of the parental love I had in me, I desired that my own children might be free from this same bondage. I knew that I would do anything to break the cycle in me for their sakes as well as my own. Feeling the Spirit comfort me here and there gave me glimmers of hope that this was possible.

On June 3, 2001, we went to our regional conference where Elder Neal A. Maxwell spoke. We watched and listened to him on a huge screen set up in our chapel, but it was a live broadcast. At the beginning of his talk he said something like, "Everyone of you in these nineteen stakes is known by our Father in Heaven. He knows you individually and all of what you are going through. He knew you each long before you were born. He knows your trials." And then he added, "I felt impressed to tell this congregation that this day," and then he went on with the rest of his talk that had nothing to do with that bit of revelation. I almost felt as if Heavenly Father inspired him to say that just for me because it immediately filled up my whole soul and gave me an immense amount of additional hope. The Spirit gave me no room to doubt that what he said was true.

Elder Maxwell taught about the Savior and what He said of His own suffering, "...and would that I might not drink the bitter cup, and shrink—Nevertheless, glory be to the Father, and I partook and finished my preparations unto the children of men" (D&C 19: 18–19). Elder Maxwell then asked, "Can we partake of our small (in comparison) bitter cups without becoming bitter? Without becoming edgy and irritable, etc...?"

I wrote, *"I won't become bitter. I will one day overcome myself just as Christ overcame the world."*

When I was in my struggle modes, it was so hard to get lost in life. ("Lost," in this instance, was actually what I wanted. It meant that I was "in" life and not constantly ruminating in my mind about how I was feeling.) I searched everywhere I could for answers. I prayed a ton. I cried when I felt I couldn't take one more moment and my thirsty soul praised God when I received drops of inspiration from heaven prodding me along.

June 18, 2001, I wrote in huge letters across two pages of my journal, *"This is my life and my pain....Now what? If I resist my life and my emotions I will be on my deathbed resisting it. Surrendering to the experiences God has given me will fulfill His purpose of bringing me closer to Him and bring peace."*

It has been over a decade since I wrote that down and I can look at those words now as pure revelation. I didn't know exactly what "surrendering" to it would entail but now I know what it meant. It meant to admit that I had a problem and to prayerfully seek for those persons who could help me.

I needed a path, and equally important I needed to get to work. I love this quote by Gordon B. Hinckley. "Work without vision is drudgery. Vision without work is daydreaming. Work plus vision— this is destiny" (Hinckley, n.d.). I needed both. I knew how to work, but I didn't have a vision. From my point of view it was as if I was about to be the first person ever to climb Mount Everest and all I had was prayer to show me the way to go.

I learned that Abraham may have felt a lot like me. Like Abraham, I had been promised of the Lord in my Patriarchal blessing the very thing that I wanted more than anything—peace. Yet, also like Abraham, it seemed impossible for it to actually happen. He was promised "that he should be the heir of the world. . . ." (Romans 4:13). I was promised in my patriarchal blessing that I would have a zest for living and be at peace with myself. At the time of Abraham's promise, he had no children. At the time of my patriarchal blessing I had no peace.

The very thing that Abraham wanted more than anything was to be a father, and he was promised just that. Yet, being old and way past the childbearing age, when most of us would've lost faith, he didn't. Romans 4:18–22 says, "Who against hope believed in hope, that he might become the father of many nations, according to that which was spoken, So shall thy seed be. And being not weak in faith, he considered not his own body now dead, when he was about an hundred years old, neither yet the deadness of Sara's womb: He staggered not at the promise of God through unbelief; but was strong in faith, giving glory to God; And being fully persuaded that, what he had promised, he was able also to perform. And therefore it was imputed to him for righteousness."

Abraham's faith in God's promise was the key ingredient to his miracle.

I love how it says, "who against hope believed in hope." It seemed impossible according to what he knew in the flesh. He and his wife were past the natural age of having children, yet he had true hope anyway. His hope was accepted by the Lord as an offering of righteousness. He was telling the Lord, "I know we are too old to have children, yet I believe you and know that you are able to fulfill all of your promises." The Lord did fulfill His promise. They did have a baby in their old age. He is the "heir of the world."

Sometimes we are tempted to think, "Well, that was Abraham. I am just regular old me." We must remember that God does not, even *cannot* lie. He has said that "all are alike unto God" (2 Nephi 26:33) and that He never changes, even from Abraham's time until now and unto forever (see Mormon 9:19).

Abraham had faith even when it did not make sense. I tried to have faith even when it seemed there was no hope for me. I had seen no one cured of my malady. Mine didn't even seem to have a name. Don't most things have a name before a cure is ever found? My faith was strong at times, but was most definitely tested to the extreme at others. I know what the sting of despair feels like. I know what it feels like to believe there is no hope. I hated that feeling and thus I spent a lot of time on my knees.

Right around this same time of intense struggle (the last few months of being in San Diego) I was praying one day when I had a very spiritual experience. I was in my kids' room kneeling by little Jeren's bed. I started to say, "If there is nothing wrong with my brain..."

when I felt the Spirit so overwhelmingly. It was the most glorious feeling. It was the exact opposite of the pain I had been feeling. I wanted to stay in that moment forever. Heavenly Father was assuring me that everything was going to be all right. Because I wanted to be free of pain so badly, I prematurely assumed He meant that there was nothing wrong with me and everything was going to be just fine right then. When those heavenly feelings left and I was still struggling, I felt that for sure I was going crazy. The devil on my shoulder said, "Those feelings weren't from Heaven, they were in your head."

I felt lower than ever. I felt that I couldn't trust any of my emotions. I decided I wasn't going to wait around any longer and just hope it would all go away. My pride was gone. I was completely humbled. I needed help.

I looked to the only other person on earth besides Jed that I could go to: my bishop. Even that felt hopeless because I had been to one of my bishops before and the result was of no sustainable relief. However, I felt like I had nowhere else to turn and so I went. Jed came with me.

While at his home I, surprisingly, found out that he suffered from depression from time to time. What? A perfectly normal person can also suffer emotionally? Even a bishop? He said he was taking an antidepressant and that it helped him. He and Jed gave me a blessing and then he gave me a referral to go see someone at LDS Family Services. I was quite nervous to go there.

The first counselor I saw helped me understand some of the reasons I experienced so much emotional confusion, but she didn't even touch the subject of what I now know as OCD. She told me that my fears, anxieties, and sadness were validated. She said I was mourning the loss of my childhood. She said that I didn't know how to be an adult because in a very real sense I had to be one emotionally when I was a child. She encouraged me to define myself, to go new places, and to decide things for myself, like my own tastes in furniture and what I want my future house to look like, etc. This, I tried. I took my very pregnant self, 3-year-old Jeren, and 1-year-old Hannah everywhere that next week from Seaport Village to the children's museum. Even though I was still an emotional mess, it did give me a sense of accomplishment, which was better than sitting at home despairing. However, it was of no lasting consequence. I needed more help.

Within those couple of weeks I went to two different counselors. They completely confused me. The first one said I didn't have clinical depression. The next one said that I did because it ran in my family. She basically said to get used to it because it would be lifelong. That was uplifting. Obviously, I didn't like the "get used to it" pep talk and so I never went back to see that therapist again.

Next, I opened up to my friend, Annie. She told me of a counselor that helped her once, so I went to him next. He said he had the gift for discernment and that I had nothing wrong with me. He told me to put an elastic band around my wrist and just flip it every time I had a negative thought. So, a rubber band was going to solve all my problems?

No one understood how messed up I was inside. Maybe the second counselor did, but she offered no hope. I felt alone and at the bottom of my Mount Everest. Was there anyone out there who could help me? I felt like I was in a prison inside my head. I felt I had to be constantly redirecting my thoughts. I felt so low and so scared to go back home to Utah, yet that was where we were going and I knew I had to face it. Jed had gotten a coveted internship with a prestigious law firm in downtown Salt Lake City. Our course was set. There was no turning back.

During our last few weeks in San Diego, we went on our millionth walk by the river with our little family. I remember telling Jed that I just wished the millennium would come. Jed shocked me by saying, "That sounds like a wish for righteous suicide." That scared me. The word "suicide" scared me—probably because in some ways I understood why people did it. I did wish that I no longer had to fight this very hard battle. At that moment it did seem that the only way out of my pain was for the Savior to come again. I had been to three counselors, which in and of itself made me feel crazy, and not one of them seemed to know a way to help me. I felt crazy even to the crazy-helpers, which is what I felt counselors were at the time.

I didn't feel I could go any lower. I felt weak, embarrassed, unlovable, unworthy to be my children's mother, unworthy of Jed's love, and without much hope for what our future in Utah might bring. Worst of all, I felt below the reaches of the Atonement. The Atonement was for sinners and for crazy people with a name for their craziness. My craziness had no name. I was beyond the reaches of the Atonement, or so I began to feel. It was a desperately low time, which wasn't helped by the fact that we were moving, getting a new job, and six months pregnant with our third child under the age of three. I lived from moment to moment with my head in the despair of the past, the despair of the present, and the fear of never-ending despair in the future.

CHAPTER 21

Back Home . . .
Back to Pain

~

MOVING BACK HOME to Utah was a really hard thing to do, but deep down Jed and I felt that Utah was where the Lord wanted us to be. However, again, my spirit and my body were turning on the sirens. It was as if my insides were yelling, "Don't move back! Mayday, mayday! You are going back into enemy territory!"

My insides were smarter than I was. My spirit knew that I was putting myself back under the cloud of dysfunction. I wasn't listening and so my insides tried yelling louder. My symptoms got worse. My mind kept firing the same thoughts over and over in my head. I hated it! Because of the OCD, I was full of both anxiety and depression. They were bullies that took turns attacking me almost every day at almost every moment.

To make matters worse, to save money on rent, the kids and I went home two weeks before Jed was done with finals. Jed's parents drove the moving truck, and along with both of our families helping, I moved us all into our new Bountiful apartment before Jed had finished finals and come home.

I struggled to find the peace that I had felt for so long while living away. I tried to do the same things I did there. I got up early, read scriptures, and found a neat friend to walk with in the mornings, but to no avail. I tried emailing the counselor in San Diego that said nothing was wrong with me. I hoped he would say something that I could get a finger hold on so that I might be able to pull myself out of the hole I was in, but again it was to no avail. I felt stuck. All I could do was to keep pressing forward. I decided I would "fake it 'til I made it." I quit writing about any emotional issues in my journal for several months. I felt like Eeyore in Winnie the Pooh—I always had a black cloud raining over me. But unlike Eeyore, I didn't show it. I laughed, I took the kids to the park, I went on dates with Jed, I served in church, etc., but I was not living in full color.

I delivered our third baby, Kate, on November 5, 2001. She was beautiful. Three-and-a-half-year-old Jeren adored her and 19-month-old Hannah adjusted out of baby position and into big sister position almost without a hitch.

I was busy, sleep-deprived, a bit overwhelmed with motherhood and housework, and, along with Jed, I was stressed over his passing the bar and getting a job. He was an intern at a prestigious law firm in downtown Salt Lake City. He felt very under-qualified to be there, and according to several people he had talked to, it wasn't very likely that he would end up getting a job there. Most of the people that worked there had attended more prestigious law schools than he did. However, Jed doesn't disappoint very often and this was no different. He passed the bar and got the job. We celebrated and were very grateful, but it didn't last long. Although not a huge surprise, it didn't take long before Jed admitted to himself how much he detested sitting in front of a computer all day. And the billable hours were enough to drive him crazy. Like a bird, Jed was never meant to be caged up in an office all day. His personality needed variety, different scenery, and control of his own schedule. Everything seemed so unsure in our lives. What do we do about Jed's great job that he hates?

Meanwhile, from my perspective, my inside turmoil was far outweighing our outer problems. My brain was not letting up. I felt so lonely and I just couldn't handle it anymore. I knew there was joy just bursting at the seams inside of me somewhere. It wanted to come out and be expressed and enjoyed, yet I was still in my emotional prison—a prison that I chose to pretend wasn't there, at least outwardly. I finally broke down and began writing in my journal again about my trial. Pretending it wasn't there, even to myself, was not working! I needed an outlet.

I wrote in my journal in April 2002, *"Last week my anxiety got so bad that I cried and cried. I just sobbed in Jed's arms because I was so sick of it."*

I kept having the thought to call my old bishop's wife from East Layton. As I wrote earlier, her husband was my bishop who I talked to once when Jed and I were first married. I had remembered him telling me that his daughter had OCD. When my brother came home from his mission also with OCD, my bishop's wife had come over to talk to me about it. That was about four years earlier. But the Spirit reminded me of this and told me to call her.

Against my inclinations to keep quiet, I did as the Spirit directed. She was just what I needed. She was so sweet and motherly to me. She gave me the phone number of a lady in Salt Lake that specialized in anxiety and OCD. I called her late one night and she returned the phone call early the next morning. I went to see her for the first time on April 19, 2002.

The biggest thing I learned from her was that I wasn't as weird or as unusual as I thought. When I first got to her office she had me fill out a paper. It had a list of OCD symptoms and I was to check each box that applied to me. I remember being so amazed and relieved when one of the boxes had "blinking" in it. What? Someone else had been down my same road that I felt so completely alone in? I was actually normal in some realm? I had an average symptom of some well-known disorder? Just understanding that was worth every penny that I paid that therapist. All those years of complete and utter shame at what caused me so much anxiety and sadness, she put into perspective in one worksheet.

It's funny how happy I was to finally have a name for my mental disability. Although I had wondered ever since my high school Psychology class if I had OCD, I never knew for sure because my exact symptoms were never written in the books or given as an example of typical OCD. What I experienced had seemed beyond the reach of anything normal, so that is what I believed—that I was more abnormal than the abnormal people. Not a fun rock to have in your backpack for many years.

The OCD specialist told me that I could go back through the learning cycle and unlearn. She said that I needed to accept that anxiety was part of my make-up. In doing so, she said, it could actually lessen my anxiety. She also taught me about nutrition. She told me of four different kinds of B vitamins that naturally lesson anxiety. I immediately went to buy them. I was excited because I thought I had finally found the answers I needed. I was, in no doubt, led by the Spirit to finally understand that I had OCD. There was also no doubt that it was an important step in my healing. However, in wanting peace so urgently, I again prematurely thought that these answers were *all* that I needed.

I felt great for a couple weeks or so, but unfortunately the yo-yo effect of being human was just around the corner. Just when I thought I might have it made, I crashed again. The OCD began to again take over my life. The success and hope I had previously only made the disappointment that much harder to take.

May 30, 2002, *"This last week has been hard. I started feeling the effects of some OCD and I got really down thinking that I had failed. I have just felt so much relief that when I hit a bump I fell right to the ground. It is so hard. I just cried and cried tonight. I feel so bad for Jed that he has to deal with me."*

That weekend on Memorial Day I happened to be driving alone in the car with both of my parents. I don't know what possessed me to do it, but I took the plunge yet again and told my parents of my OCD. I felt like a vulnerable child again.

I wrote, *"I was very disappointed in their reaction. Dad said, 'really?' like he was surprised. However, they knew right what I was talking about when I asked if they remember how closing my eyes bothered me. Within two minutes of telling my dad, he was on the phone and then he quickly drove home and didn't say a word about it again (I was there for another day, too). How could something that has plagued me my whole life just elude him so easily? Mom made me feel better about telling her when the next day at church she asked me about it while I was nursing Kate in the mother's room. However, it wasn't substantial and she never talked about it again."*

I struggled after that even more. How could my parents be so ignorant? Why did I even say anything to them? *I am so hopeless. Nothing will help me,* I thought. However, the Lord, in His mercy taught me clearly one day while reading the Book of Mormon.

June 12, 2002, I wrote, *"I have felt so wonderfully me lately and I am so grateful. I feel the Lord blessed me with my own personal revelation last week while reading the Book of Mormon.…I was reading Alma 32:28–43 when I realized I was receiving an answer from the Book of Mormon to me about my OCD—a thing in which I never thought could happen!*

"Alma 32 talks about faith and how it starts by planting a seed in your heart (meaning Christ and His word). It says if you nourish it, then it will sprout and fill you and eventually be 'delicious' to you. Through the Spirit, I was taught to plant the seed of hope for myself and my life and nourish it

with good healthy thoughts (even if at times I'm forcing it) until it sprouts, takes root, and begins to 'be delicious' for me."

My testimony of God's nearness began to grow stronger again. I was grateful for every spiritual experience that added drops of strength in my bucket.

Another drop was added on June 28, 2002. Jed and I went to our stake center to watch the Nauvoo Temple dedication. We almost didn't make it. I was sick, we had no tickets, and no babysitter.

I wrote, *"This will always be one of my most sacred experiences. The first song that the Tabernacle Choir sang was 'Come Come ye Saints,' and as they started they sang very softly which brought the Spirit in so strongly that chills covered me. The prophet spoke with more emotion than I had ever heard or seen from him before. He wept when he said that he could feel the presence of the Father and the Son. I knew at that moment without any doubt that I was in the right church. I heard a man sobbing behind me. I had tears most of the time. The prophet talked of a large unseen audience including the prophet Joseph Smith and the Saints.... I will draw upon the feelings of those two hours forever."*

Another drop in my bucket came when I witnessed the healing of our son Jeren. He had always stuttered a bit but it had gotten increasingly worse. I had taken him to a speech therapist. She taught me to play games with him in which I learned to model speaking really slowly. He would mimic me and talk slowly back. She said that the quick stuttering such as "mom, mom, mom..." could be overcome if he would learn to slow down, but his other stuttering that he was exemplifying could not be outgrown. At its worst, it was taking Jeren anywhere from 20 to 30 seconds to even get one word out. He would try to say, "Mom," but all he would get out was, "Mmmm...." He would close his eyes and strain really hard to finish the word. It was heartbreaking to watch him struggle so hard to speak when we knew he had, and always would have, so much to say. That's just how he was—a talker.

We talked to a friend of Jed's mom's who had a son with the same terribly hard stuttering problem. He was in high school. He was very smart but it was a struggle socially. We felt scared, so when other options told us there was no help available, we took our faith and our pleadings to the Lord.

On August 18, 2002, we fasted with Jed's grandma and grandpa and then ended the fast with a healing blessing for the sick. I had never witnessed a healing before but after the blessing with tears in his eyes, Jed pointed out that Jeren's fluency was already showing improvement as he directed a game of Simon Says with his great grandpa. He wasn't stuttering at all while playing the game. Ever since that blessing Jeren has only done the regular quick stuttering when he tries to talk too fast. There was no room for doubt. The Lord had healed him through His priesthood. I hoped maybe one day He would heal me too. It added several drops in my bucket and increased my ability to persevere my own trial.

That was a summer of much anticipation as to where life might lead us. Jed was miserable. In fact, I had never even seen Jed miserable before. So it was quite a surprise to see him so down while doing the exact job he had dreamed of having and had worked so hard in law school to get! To make matters worse, he was at one of the most prestigious law firms in Utah. How could he just walk away from that?

He felt trapped and I felt worried. We prayed for a solution to this problem. Jed was so unhappy practicing law that he was willing to quit his most coveted job that paid more than we could have hoped for as a first year lawyer and go to work for his dad for much less. To top things off we were in the middle of building a beautiful home on the hill near Salt Lake City. This made Jed feel even more trapped;

however, he knew where I stood on that issue. I would rather be dirt poor and have a happy husband than money and a miserable one.

As we were going through all this, I remembered Nell. She was the lady who told us about California Western Law School in San Diego. That is where her husband went to school. I remembered that he also didn't like being a lawyer and yet was very wealthy and successful. I thought about calling her for a week. When I finally did, she said her husband also received his MBA (Masters in Business Administration). That was disappointing because Jed only had a law degree. However, she was so nice and said that she would "put a bug in Bob's ear."

About three weeks later Bob called Jed and wanted to go to lunch with him regarding a job in bringing charter schools to Utah. Bob had met with a group in Florida that were successful charter school managers there and wanted a young lawyer to help them bring their model to the west. I don't think it was a coincidence that the Spirit reminded me of Nell at this exact time that her husband was told to find a young lawyer out here to help them.

We were ecstatic about the possibilities! The job explanation was everything Jed had ever dreamed of—politics, real estate, property development, and selling the good idea of charter schools. Jed got the job and humbly acknowledged that everything we had done since being married was because the Lord had led us there.

November 13, 2002, *"Happiness can get no greater than today—simple today. I went walking, then the kids had gymnastics and dance class today along with all of our regular daily chores, but as the day was coming to a close Jed and I spoke of how it just doesn't get better than this. Jed said that he loves his work and he loved coming home and walking upstairs to see all three of his kids watching the computer as Jeren played 'Preschool.' He loved their smiles when they saw him. And then he said he got to come downstairs to see me and a good meal. After that we put Jeren and Kate to bed. Hannah stayed up for a while with us (she had a nap) and snuggled and loved us while we were watching* Count of Monte Cristo. *We then stayed up until midnight cleaning the laundry/storage room, but even that was fun. Jed is so great. I am so glad that he is mine and I am his. We just felt so blessed today that I felt like I needed to write it down."*

I wanted to add this journal entry because it is indicative of the joy that was still present in my life at times because of the tender mercies of our Heavenly Father. Those times never went unnoticed by me. Oh how I valued the joy of everyday activities when the emotional obsessiveness was gone and I could actually be present in my own life. They were always golden moments. I dreamed, I hoped, and I earnestly prayed that one day I could trust in those "real" moments to occur daily. By "real" I mean that I wanted to trust that I could always be in the moment, feeling the feeling that coincided with the moment. Whether it was a good or bad moment didn't matter to me as much as actually being present in the moment.

What I experienced more often than not with my sickness was going through the motions of each day the best I knew how while my mind was preoccupied with doing all that it could to keep emotional equilibrium. The pain that troubled me the most was seeing my kids growing up, knowing that I was living in a dull reality seemingly most of the time. When compared to the day that I just wrote about, I knew I wasn't enjoying them like I otherwise would have had I not been sick. That was a painful thought that I had to constantly push aside, knowing I was doing the best I could.

The other huge worry in my life that troubled me just as much, was the worry that my kids wouldn't grow up happy because I wasn't fully happy. Because of that fact, I worried that I wasn't being a good enough mother. How would I be able to make sure that my own children never felt the pain that I was going through? How would I know how to help them, when I didn't know how to escape my own pain? Oh how I loved my children! Oh how I prayed that the chains of dysfunction would end with me!

I watched other mothers that I thought had it all together. I tried to emulate them for the benefit of my own children, but that was sometimes counter-productive.

November 22, 2002, I wrote, *"I was just thinking about how easy it is to compare yourself to others and feel inferior. It is easy for me to feel like other mothers are so much better in the home than I am. That they are so much more confident, more motherly, better decision makers, more compassionate and easy to talk to than I am. I was also just thinking that every woman that I have ever truly looked up to had a great mother and a great relationship with her as an adult. Sometimes I am scared that because I didn't have the ideal parenting parents that I won't know how to be that for our children. Oh how I would want nothing more than for one day my children and posterity to call me blessed. Not that I want the praise, I just sincerely want to do them justice. I love them so much. They bring me so much happiness. I want to give that back to them so that they can carry that happiness with them for all their lives and thus forever. I have repenting to do. I lose my cool more than I should and I don't always show the best example. Thank goodness for our Savior who truly makes change not only possible, but achievable."*

As I watched other people and studied their relationships I did notice a scary pattern. Those that were good mothers seemed to have good mothers or the kind of mother that I wished my mother was. It was easy to let that discovery make me feel trapped and like all hope was lost. A person can't change how their parents parented. How could I ever change the course that I was set on for the betterment of my posterity after me? Everyone seemed to follow the course their parents set for them. That seemed so unfair. I wanted the course to change for my children. But how? That was the big question.

CHAPTER 22

Lessons in Carrying On

~

I CONTINUED TO STRUGGLE for emotional balance in my life as well as struggle through the normal stresses of life. At this time I had a few big worries. Although Jed loved his new job, it was still a stress as he worked very hard to make it successful. We also had the huge task of building our first house. Picking out house stuff while hauling around three young children was no easy task!

Through it all, I continued to do as had been prescribed by the prophets. I read scriptures by myself and with our little family. We held Family Home Evening and went to the temple almost every month. I knew that I had a lot to lose if I didn't stay close to the Spirit. The Spirit was literally my lifeline. I needed the Spirit to teach me how to be the "me" I knew the Lord had in mind. I felt I was still in the wilderness and needed His guidance constantly. If I turned one degree in the wrong direction I knew I wouldn't make it to the promised land I so desired. I yearned for the peace with myself that was promised me in my patriarchal blessing.

At times I felt like I was treading water in the dark just to keep my head above water, but there were those sacred times that I felt the Lord turn on the light to show me He was still there. It is important to note that I was still treading water even though at times He turned the light on. This was one of those times.

April 16, 2003, *"This morning around 6:00 I got up to go walking. I knelt down to say my morning prayers. Before any words came out I felt and knew, like I don't know if I have ever known before, that Heavenly Father could see me and that He knew me. And not just knew me but knew everything about me and that He was glad I was going to talk to Him. I felt the Spirit so strong that I didn't want to move or talk because I was afraid that sweet spirit might leave. When I did open my mouth to pray out loud that spirit stayed. I am so thankful for that precious strengthener of testimony that was gifted to me this morning."*

That summer I struggled with my emotions. I was adjusting to living in a new place, as well as adjusting to being a mother of not just toddlers and babies but to defiant and discipline-needing children. I questioned my every act and constantly searched for good parents to model. I, of course, still feared my brain and hated to see the signs that I might be going into another funk where I knew I would be tempted to be preoccupied with my emotions at all times. I knew that all-too-familiar dark hole and feared falling into it. I could never come out of it without a huge muster of self-will coupled with the mercy of an all-loving Father in Heaven.

Around August I remember feeling so out of hope. Why was I still not who I wanted to be? I came up with a new motto to help me. I wrote it in my journal, *"Buck up...Do...Focus. I am going to work on forgetting myself by bucking up, doing as much as I can get done, and focusing on my surroundings and others."*

A couple of days later my idea was validated as I read this talk from the *Ensign*: "Our Father in Heaven does not wish us to cower. He does not want us to wallow in our misery. He expects us to square our shoulders, roll up our sleeves, and overcome our challenges. That kind of spirit—that blend of faith and hard work—is the spirit we should emulate as we seek to reach a safe harbor in our lives.... Use your ingenuity, your strength, your might to resolve your challenges.

Do all you can do and then leave the rest to the Lord" (Wirthlin, 2000). I also read in *Mormon Doctrine* under "Healings" that God *wants* us to be whole and healthy so that we can better move the kingdom forward.

Heavenly Father had led me to learn that being in tribulation doesn't make us righteous, but that positively and diligently trying to overcome our trials is what forges us into saints. It was something I hadn't heard before, but the Spirit testified to me that it was true— Heavenly Father wants healthy, strong saints because they can serve Him best.

After hearing that, one might ask, "Well then why doesn't He just heal us all and make us all strong so we can serve Him better?" I think we all know that answer deep down. If we were all instantly healed and made whole the minute we experienced any discomfort, we wouldn't be of much worth to our fellowman and thus to our Savior. We need the education of trial and experience, and then when we are healed of whatever distress or infirmity we had, we are that much more like the Savior. He went below all things that He might know how to succor his people. In going through our trials, however small in comparison our sufferings may be, we are better equipped to succor God's children in that thing we have experienced. In that small way, we get to be a little more like the Savior through this process we call life.

Elder Groberg in his book *In the Eye of the Storm* said, "Sometimes the Lord calms the storm and sometimes he lets the storm rage and He calms the child." When I read that quote it jumped out of the pages and into my heart ringing, "Truth, truth, truth!"

The Lord doesn't leave us alone while we are trying to overcome our challenges. I know this to be true. He calmed me many times amid my storm that lasted almost twenty-five years. Each time He calmed me it increased my faith. It was like a water break for a marathon runner—running was still terribly hard but the water was just enough relief to keep going.

On August 15, 2003, I had several more drops of faith added to my bucket. I had been experiencing gall bladder attacks on and off for several weeks. Late at night on the 15th I ate three small tomatoes. I thought that gall bladder attacks were from eating fatty foods so I thought that tomatoes would be okay. I forgot that the acid from foods can be just as bad and had the worst attack yet. I was throwing up what felt like hot acid. I was shaking uncontrollably. Jed was in bed and already asleep. I didn't want to wake him because his new job was wearing him out. After so long I couldn't take it anymore so I woke him. It was late and we had no other priesthood holder in the house but I felt like I needed a healing blessing with oil or an emergency room. He was a little hesitant to give me a healing blessing without another Priesthood holder but he could see how much pain I was in. I had been on my knees shaking and rocking back and forth on our bathroom floor. I was in so much pain that I felt unable to get up so that is where he gave me the blessing.

Our master bathroom was open to our bedroom with a big arch. After the blessing I was still shaking and in so much pain that I couldn't get off the floor. My tired husband, not knowing what else to do, got back in bed. He wanted me to get in bed with him, but all I could do was lay on the ground. Even though I was putting pressure on my belly, I couldn't quit shaking especially in my hips and legs. I had been lying there a couple of minutes when all of a sudden, like someone had turned off a switch, I quit shaking. It felt like an unseen hand had been placed on my back, which instantly calmed me. The relief was so quick that it surprised me. I was still in some pain but I knew it was going away so I climbed in bed and quickly fell asleep.

The next day Jed said, "I have got to tell you what happened last night. After I gave you the blessing I was so tired that I got back in bed but I didn't want to go to sleep and leave you in such pain. I laid there and in my head asked myself the question, 'Do I have the faith that that blessing can help her?' I answered myself with a 'Yes, I do have faith that it will help her.'" He said that he then saw light with his eyes closed and then almost immediately heard me stop shaking and moaning.

This experience became a rock of security to me. When things got so hard after that and when I felt completely alone, I could find comfort in remembering that I experienced the reality of an all-loving God, that He healed my body, and that maybe one day He would do the same for my mind.

On August 22, 2003, I wrote, *"I have felt the influence of the Spirit this week whisper to me that Heavenly Father is not 'trying to teach me' anything. He wants me to be healthy and whole and to try every day to make this weakness a strength.* (I meant that the Spirit taught me that although I was in the midst of the pain, God wanted me to do all I could to get out of it. That to wallow and feel hopeless wasn't teaching me anything like I thought it was. But to fight with hope would eventually get me where both God and I wanted me to be, which was healed and strong). *He has promised us he would and will do this. I have decided that everyday I will WORK on this and pray until one day it becomes easier and even a strength. I read in the New Testament manual that Satan will try and discourage you in your attempt to overcome weakness and sin. I am prepared that this will be difficult but it is much more comfortable working than wallowing. D&C 90:24 says, 'Search diligently, pray always, and be believing, and all things shall work together for your good.'"*

As I read this now, I remember that I was really struggling at the time but the Lord was giving me knowledge here a little, there a little. The Spirit testified to me that what I was learning was in fact true. It was time to really understand that the Lord wanted me healthy and it was my job to do all I could do and then He would do the rest. Knowing what to do was now my biggest problem. And so, since I was too prideful and a lot scared, I didn't go to my bishop. I, instead, tried it my way.

My way, at the time, was to pray hard and then "fake it 'til I make it." I tried to do more things on my "to do" list and to stay active with my kids throughout the day. I took them on all kinds of errands, to the park often, and to the dinosaur museum as well. I loved to cook new things and so I continued doing that. I learned how to make blackberry pies, which quickly became my favorite. I wrote the good things that happened in my journal as well as the kids' individual journals to help me count my blessings.

This was one such journal entry: *After school we passed the field where Jeren played T-ball. He said, 'Look that's where I played T-ball. That was so much fun. My life is all good, isn't it, Mom?'* My kid's innocent child-like joy consoled me in that maybe I wasn't doing too bad of a job after all. Maybe my kids would indeed turn out happy in spite of my unhappiness.

As I did these outward things that I wanted to do I felt empowered. I was living my life in spite of the OCD. I was proving to myself that I could accomplish my life goals even now. I didn't have to wait until I was emotionally perfect to start becoming who I wanted to be. In doing this, I still had obsessive thoughts that would repeat themselves like a Tourette's victim uncontrollably moves, yet the despairing thoughts that I was wasting my life had less of a hold on me. I felt I was winning…at least for as long as I could hold up that fast pace.

CHAPTER 23

Pride Meets a Brick Wall

~

O N SEPTEMBER 10, 2003, I found out I was pregnant with number four! We were both so happy. We felt it was time. Little did I know that this pregnancy, along with three other little children would be exactly what I didn't need at the time, yet ultimately needed. Even before I found out that I was pregnant I was still struggling to stay on top of my emotions. Yet because I was keeping up with my to-do list I felt like I was doing okay.

One day while Jed was reading the *Ensign*, he pointed out to me something that I had already noticed as well. Sister Kathleen Hughes of the General Relief Society Presidency had given a talk in the most recent conference where she stated that she knew of the debilitating effects of depression. I had never heard that from the pulpit before.

After Jed brought it to my attention too, I thought more on it and decided to do something I had never done before—I wrote a Church leader a letter hoping for some insight. Three weeks later she called me at home. We set up a time for me to come meet her.

On October 22, 2003, I drove to Salt Lake to meet with her in her office at the Relief Society building. I wrote, *"I was very nervous and wondered beforehand why I was doing what I was doing. But, I went ahead anyways—I guess on blind faith.*

"She was very sweet. She greeted me with a warm hug and offered a seat with her at a round table in her office. Her initial question was for me to tell her about myself. That broke the ice and got us started.

"She got tears in her eyes many times and said, 'Looking at you I see myself all over again.' She was 28 when she first experienced emotional upheaval. It was after she had a baby. She had some distressing obsessive thoughts along with her depression. She went to her bishop and got help from there. It took her a year to get better, but an important fact she gave me was that she still battles it sometimes but that she now has the right tools so that it doesn't become debilitating. She said her mother as well as her daughter both have the same trial. I guess her daughter one day said, 'Mom, I bet great-grandmother never had to deal with this' and Sister Hughes said a very impactful comment back to her, 'I bet she did and unlike us she would have no where to go for help or understanding, or even to know the name of the thing that was wrong."

I could feel her charity as we talked. She assured me of God's love and the all-encompassing power of the Atonement. She said, "Christ felt our pains as well as our sins." She told me she would pray for me. That meant so much to me. She wanted me to call her about once a month. She hugged me when I left and told me that she has found a new daughter in me. I left feeling mothered. Of all the things she said and scriptures she quoted, the thing that kept coming back to me was that she told me to go see my bishop and that he could help me and possibly direct me to a therapist at LDS Family Services.

From my past experience I didn't think telling my bishop would help me enough to make it worth breaking the façade that everything was perfect in my life. It was super scary to open myself up like that. History taught me that the second I told someone I was not in full control of my brain that they would distance themselves from me, or worse, they completely ignored the subject. Most people didn't know how to handle it, and on top of that whenever I was around the person that I told, I could no longer go to my happy place of pretending I didn't have a problem. Every time I looked at them I was reminded of what I was trying so hard to ignore. I would ask myself, "Are they wondering if I'm really okay? They know I have brain issues and now I'm acting like nothing is wrong in front of them."

It would make me feel like a hypocrite. Even thinking of taking the chance of telling my new bishop of my shameful nemesis was deeply scary. What if I scared him like I scared myself? What if he made me feel as low as I already felt by affirming what I already believed at the time, neither he nor anyone had any way of helping me? Then I would be worse off than before! I would still have no way out, and now my perfect façade would have no power to protect me. All would come crashing down. I would be reminded every time I went to church that everyone else had normal problems that the bishop could help with except for me. I would feel more outside the box than ever before. Despair would have a greater hold on me. Those were my fears. I was wrong.

Even after telling Sister Hughes, a woman that I would likely never see again, I felt an increase of real anxiety afterwards. Just the telling of this to someone, although a release for the moment, made me feel hopeless. Life felt so unfair. I could handle anything, I thought, if only I could be in the moment of life instead of treading the unstable waters in my head. Every other "outside" problem seemed trite and easy to either solve or just get over but inside my head was a constant war for control. It got tiring treading waters in my invisible prison, all while pretending it wasn't so.

An example of how easy this "war" could catch me off guard and start defeating me again was this:

October 25, 2003, *"Woke up, everything was beautiful and wonderful until I saw a little tidbit on TV news about a depressed woman artist who committed suicide (her art is now displayed in some San Francisco*

Museum). It is interesting how that news saddened me and started making me feel down."

For some time I had been trying to overcome my pride and write truthfully about my intensely private mental struggles, but I had a hard time being too specific. When I wrote, "I'm feeling down again," that meant a whole lot more. It meant that I was almost constantly bothered by hyperawareness of blinking, my eyes were either dry or watery. It was either that or hyperawareness of my mouth and tongue and I would hold my tongue in such a way that it felt awkward and without a restful position. My whole jaw would sometimes hurt. It meant that as I was constantly berated by these thoughts, I had anxiety that plagued me for fear they might never go away. Anxiety was laced with despair as I went about trying to do my daily duties. Emotionally battling, pregnant and carrying three small children around made the sometimes already difficult daily duties seem to be the edge of what I could bear. There was shopping to do, errands to run, laundry to do, meals to prepare, a house to clean, church lessons to prepare, the discipline and worry for each child, and so on and so forth. And all the while, my brain hurt with despair, my eyes and tongue demanded obsessive attention, and my stomach was tight with anxiety. Nevertheless, I did all I could to behave in the way I thought a righteous woman should.

It was deep, it was hard, it was real, and it was lonely. Only once in a while would I feel enough deep pain that I would venture to talk to Jed about it in hopes that he might say some words that would bring relief.

November 22, 2003, was one of those days, *"This week has been noteworthy. I started feeling down again and then I get frustrated that I feel that way again and it just makes it worse. Tuesday night as I drove to and from an errand, I prayed and pleaded with Heavenly Father to give me the next step that I should do that I might be even one step closer to full emotional health. I told Him that I trust in Him. I know if I pray for my family to be watched over and protected that they will be, even down to the little prayers that the kids might feel His peace and comfort and go back to sleep. I know He hears and answers my prayers and has answered many prayers before concerning my emotions, but I pleaded for more information."*

The next day Jed came home unexpectedly around 10:00 a.m. I told him that I was still struggling. We ended up having a very powerful talk for the next two hours. I was grateful the kids stayed downstairs.

I wrote, "*He really understands my pain and he accepts it as his or 'our' trial. He put into words how I feel and then said that I need to have some constants no matter if I am feeling bad or good. He named three things that are to be my constants. As he said these he said, 'The Spirit is bearing witness to me right now that this is truth.' The Spirit also bore that witness to me. These are my three constants.*

This is a physical trial not a result of a weak spirit.

At some future point I will look back on this trial and be grateful for it.

When the pain keeps coming back it does not mean failure, it is just more training to desensitize negative brain stimuli.

"*I am so in love with Jed. I feel so blessed to have him. He is everything that I am not and somehow through osmosis he makes me whole. I am reluctant to write this but I feel that the Lord is pleased with us right now and that we will be together forever. I can think of nothing greater than to be with my funny, wonderful husband and our children forever. Amid this truly soul wrenching trial I see my blessings, too, and have much hope for the future.*"

When I pleaded to the Lord that morning for more information, He used my husband to be part of that answer. The beginning of the rest of His divine answer would come a few weeks later, although not in the way that I would've prescribed for myself.

This was the Lord's prescription:

December 16, 2003. *"This morning Hannah came and laid by me and then fell asleep and I loved it. She is so sweet and so beautiful. I love her so much....As the morning wore on I started feeling worse and worse. Right after Jed left for work, I let it all out and cried again to Heavenly Father for relief. Jed happened to forget something and he came back home and saw my red face. I buried myself in his arms and cried some more. We decided I should call my Bishop and tell him. I had wanted to avoid doing that, but I guess even my pride has been broken down. I did call.*

"The rest of the day I cleaned, took care of the kids, wrapped presents, and hosted the Christmas party for the drill team I coach.

"After the girls left, I cleaned up and put the kids to bed and then waited. Jed came home and then the bishop came over. I have never been so grateful for the office of the bishop in my entire life. Jed explained my situation to the bishop. Then Bishop said that when he saw us Sunday he knew there was something wrong with me but he 'couldn't put a finger on it.' He said that he was glad when I called. Ironically, I had the thought today that Bishop already knew.

"He recalled us telling him last March that we weren't planning on moving here. We just came upon this piece of land. Bishop said, 'I don't believe there are many coincidences in this life.'

"He laid out a plan of action. He is going to pray and he and Jed will fast. He is going to look for a doctor for me and possibly a counselor from the Church's social services.

"He told me he could see much hope and hoped I could as well. He said that everything we hope for is all centered on our hope in Christ.

"He asked me what my patriarchal blessing says. I told him that sometimes I wonder if it's talking about me. I told him how a lot of it is about joy, having a zest for life, showing my love for my Father in Heaven, and love for life, etc. He said, 'That's interesting because I have heard people use those adjectives when describing you.'

"Bishop asked if he could say a prayer. We all knelt down and he prayed and I know Heavenly Father heard and was near. His prayer was a real conversation with someone I could tell he knew. He told the Lord that this was not a usual prayer. He prayed for ministering angels to be with me. He prayed that the Lord would direct our efforts and that by his Spirit we might know if our paths are leading us right.... The bishop afterwards gave me a big hug. He has charity. I hardly know him and I could feel my Savior's love from him. He told me to not hesitate to call but that he would call back in a couple of days. I am so grateful."

For the next couple of weeks I, indeed, felt the administering angels that Bishop had prayed to me. I had the best Christmas that I had had in years. I wrote it was the best that I had had since I was probably in elementary school. I was blessed with a calm assurance that I had done the right thing in talking to Bishop. I felt a certain hope that he would lead me in the right direction to get the healing I desired.

He called me after several days. He said he had an answer. There was a woman named Marilyn that he trusted. He felt that she was the one that the Lord wanted me to go see. I was a bit disappointed. I didn't trust women and hoped it was a man. But I did trust Bishop. She didn't work for LDS Family Services anymore so I would have to drive to Ogden to see her. If she was the one the Lord wanted me to see, then I didn't care how far I drove. I was willing to do anything at this point. It was a good thing too because the following years were full of a lot of work and a lot of driving.

CHAPTER 24

Finally on the Right Ladder

~

OR THE NEXT several years I went once or sometimes twice a week to see Marilyn. I quickly overcame my fear that a woman couldn't help me. She was like no woman I knew. She was strong in her opinions and in her confidence. She was happy. She wasn't afraid to tell it like it is. She wasn't afraid to keep our conversations on track. She didn't let me wallow. I knew she was inspired. I knew that I was on the right track. I likened it to climbing a ladder. I knew that I was finally on the right ladder—a ladder that if I kept climbing would lead me to the peace that I longed for. I also knew that I was at the bottom of the ladder with a lot of work to do. The effort it would take to get to the top didn't scare me at all. Knowing there was something I could actually do to get to the top was actually very energizing.

I felt to praise Heavenly Father for leading me to the right ladder. Just knowing I had a trusted mentor to lead me gave me so much hope. It wasn't a coincidence that the Lord inspired Bishop to send me to a woman. In so many ways she re-mothered me in the way that I needed. In doing so, she indirectly taught me how to mother my own children in a way that combined all that was good in my own mother with all that was good in her. I thought I just needed help in overcoming OCD patterns, but instead I realized that I needed to relearn life. I needed coaching in almost every facet of my life. Just like it took years and countless hours of practice in order to train my body to dance well, it took just as much time and effort, if not more, to train and retrain my brain.

Because I was sick from such a young age, I had a lot of false belief systems that were not serving me well in my adult life. I didn't feel sure of anything, most especially my ability to mother my children into confident adults. Step by step Marilyn walked me through my many daily scenarios. From dealing with my own mother and father, to feeling equal with Jed, to being a righteous and assertive parent, she taught me truths. I did everything that she told me to. I felt like she was my only way so, like a child, I obeyed. I wasn't about to give up.

It wasn't easy though. I did a lot of writing. I mean a lot. But, that worked for me. I was always better at writing than at talking so my notebooks and I were a perfect pair. I filled volumes. Marilyn taught me how to counteract negative thinking. I learned about irrational thoughts and how crucial it was to quickly correct them.

This is what I would do: Whenever I recognized that I had an irrational or negative thought, I quickly grabbed my little notebook (that was either in my pocket or dangling from yarn around my neck), and wrote down the negative thought. I could usually see right away how irrational it was when I saw it written on paper. I would then write an "answer," which was a rational response. I was learning to take charge of my life by not taking my wrongly programmed brain as truth. I was in a sense reprogramming my brain in the way that I wanted it to work subconsciously on its own.

It was hard and sometimes very discouraging, especially when the thought I wrote down seemed to be true. For example, *"This will never go away. I will always have OCD,"* I didn't know how to correct the irrational response because the irrational one seemed true. I would try to counter it by writing, "It will go away. The Lord has promised me it would." But I had to really believe the response in order for it to correct my negative one and make me feel better. (Yes, I sometimes doubted in the Lord's promises.) Sometimes I had to write that response or similar ones several times a day, pray a ton, and just wait for the relief to come.

The brain isn't stupid. It can't be lied to. My responses had to be believable. At times I felt I was just trying to fool myself, but mostly I knew I was reprogramming my brain and that it was an important rung on the ladder I was trying to climb. I wrote in my therapy journal on April 19, 2005, *"Don't avoid irrational thoughts, capture them and practice interrupting the cycle."*

I was five months pregnant when I first went to see Marilyn. She helped me realize (from what I told her of my life) that most of my pain was from the dysfunctional relationship I had with my parents. During those first few months Marilyn kept saying that it would be nice to have the whole family come to therapy. At first I thought, no way! I had put up a brick wall so thick between me and my parents on this subject that there was no way I dared bring it down. It made me feel too vulnerable again, like that little 11-year-old child that was rejected when trying to plead for help. But, as the weeks of therapy went by, I realized that Marilyn was right. I could move a lot faster in my recovery if the whole family got therapy and worked on our relationships together instead of me trying to shift the whole family single-handedly and without anyone knowing I was doing it. I felt she was right, so I took the plunge. I asked my mom and dad if they would come with me.

They came twice. Once they came alone and then once with my brother (my sister lived in Arizona). It was not productive. My mom just cried the whole time. Instead of being strong and willing to see what she could do in order to help her daughter, she took on the victim role. I don't know why I expected any different. They wouldn't come anymore after that.

I couldn't understand why, when faced with an opportunity to help their daughter, as well as the whole family, they didn't. Why? What good could they possibly see coming from ignoring their daughter's pain, as well as her plea for change? Yet that is precisely what they did. All hope for family change was lost. For some reason, they just couldn't do it. Yes, I was very sad and felt extremely abandoned once again; however, my conscience was clear and I needn't wonder anymore—I was, in fact, truly on my own.

Like always, they chose to pretend that everything was fine. They were purposefully silent on the subject of my obvious pain yet they kept calling me and expecting me to play the same role with them that I had always played. And I, in my weakness, continued to play that role. I was no stronger than they. I was their perfect daughter on the outside, yet inside I was dying.

It was a horrible realization that I now had to take matters into my own hands. It became clear that if I chose to pick up the side of the stick that had "healing" written on it, I would also be lifting the other side of the stick that would say, "parents will hurt." I had to break the dysfunctional family rules in order to heal. In doing so I knew it would confuse and hurt my parents (but would, hopefully, one day help them heal too). I had to allow them to hurt in order to heal me. I was always taught that others come first. I felt terribly guilty. At first I tried to do it in small ways, yet it felt like I was just cutting their arms off slowly. They knew what I was doing: I was pulling away.

The first example of this was when I delivered Sadie just a few weeks after trying to get them to come to counseling with me. I was struggling big time. My OCD, namely the obsessive thoughts on my eyes, was way out of control. It was relentless torture of mind. I knew it would make it worse if my parents were there at the hospital all day with me, so for the first time ever, I chose myself over them. I asked them to wait to come see our baby until the day after she was born.

We told Jed's family the same thing in an attempt to not ruffle too many feathers.

In the end, it was worth every bit of selfishness that I felt for making good boundaries. I wrote this about the day our Sadie was born in May:

"We decided to make it a day for just our little family. It was hard to tell extended family that we would call them when they could come visit, but it was worth it.

"By the time I was all hooked up it was about 1:00 p.m. The nurse had a hard time getting my IV in. Jeren stood by my bed watching and supporting me by holding my hand. In fact, for the next five-and-a-half hours the kids took turns holding my hands and feeding me ice chips. I loved it! Kate even took a nap by me in my bed. I especially loved that time with her. The kids were all so sweet. We felt like a truly unified little family all anticipating the arrival of a new member. When I hit 10 centimeters, Jed had taken the girls for a walk so I called him and then I told Jeren he had to go out and sit on a chair. 'Why?' he asked. 'Because having a baby is kind of private,' I told him. 'But, as soon as you hear the baby cry you can come in.'

"As soon as she was born, all I could say was, 'Oh she is so cute.' She looked so little.... She had a lot of brown hair and a little face that we first associated most with Hannah's. As soon as she let out her first cry, I could hear Jeren's voice at the door, 'Can I come in?' He had to wait a little longer, but he was the first one we let in. I got emotional as I watched him so eagerly and lovingly come in to meet his sister. He is such a loving child. Hannah and Kate were so cute as well. Kate kept saying, 'Is the baby out of your belly?'

"Needless to say, as hard as it was to tell extended family they couldn't be with us until day two, it was so worth it! I experienced my own little family in a very sacred way. We were there at that hospital together waiting to meet our little Sadie. It was so special. It taught me a great lesson. Creating boundaries is not a selfish act. It is actually very unselfish. It is hard to do

on my part but very beneficial for our little family. It will help my kids feel closer to us as a family and they will benefit from me healing. A healthy mom is always better for kids than an unhealthy one."

I should've posted that last sentence on my mirror in my bathroom so that I could see it every day. I knew it was true but it was so very hard to create and maintain boundaries with someone that I had never done that with before and with someone who seemed very dependent on me for her happiness. My mom loves kids and, to make matters worse, I was her only child with kids that lived within driving distance from her. I felt as if I were her only source for happiness. If I didn't play the part she wanted me to play, I would destroy her. I would be mean and cruel. That was a heavy load to carry, especially when my health was at stake.

It soon became increasingly clear that I needed to do something different. Working so hard going to counseling each week and then going and playing the same part with my mom was just pulling me backwards again. It wasn't working. Marilyn, as practical as she was, could see that I had two choices if I wanted to get better: move away again (and enjoy a reprieve like I had while living away in San Diego) or go tell my parents that I needed to separate myself from them for a while. That was not a fun situation to be in. I prayed and prayed for divine guidance.

One day I was praying in my closet on the matter when the word "Abraham" came to my mind. I remembered that Abraham was commanded to leave his family. I knew this was my answer even before I reread the account of Abraham.

I read Abraham chapters 1 and 2. In Abraham 1:1, 2, 5 and parts of 6, Abraham says, "I, Abraham, saw that it was needful for me to obtain another place of residence; and finding there was greater happiness and peace and rest for me, I sought for the blessings of the fathers,...My fathers, having turned from their righteousness, and from the holy commandments which the Lord their God had given unto them unto the worshipping of the gods of the heathen, utterly refused to hearken to my voice; for their hearts were set to do evil, and were wholly turned to…[their gods]."

As I read this, my heart was pounding with the Spirit. I too, saw that it was needful for me to "leave" my family of origin. They weren't good for me. When I tried to convince them that our family needed help, "they utterly refused to hearken to my voice." They wouldn't listen and come to therapy with me. They refused to see that the gods or traditions that they thought were right, were actually terribly wrong and tearing our family apart.

And in chapter 1 verse 7, Abraham again says that they wouldn't listen to him. They "hearkened not unto my voice, but endeavored to take away my life."

In my situation, my family wasn't trying to take away my physical life but they were taking away my "life." They wouldn't come with me to counseling to get the help that our relationships needed, and if I stayed in that same unhealthy situation, I, like Abraham, could have died, spiritually at least, and never unfolded to meet my full potential.

I can't imagine how hard that must have been for Abraham. The priests bound Abraham and tried to offer him up as a sacrifice to their idols, when an angel came and loosed his bands. He heard a voice say, "Abraham, Abraham, behold my name is Jehovah, and I have heard thee, and have come down to deliver thee, and to take thee away from thy father's house, and from all thy kinsfolk, into a strange land which thou knowest not of; and this because they turned their hearts away from me. . . ." (Abraham 1:16).

Then in verse 18 the Lord comforts him and tells him, "I will lead thee by the hand, and I will take thee, to put upon thee my name…." I imagine that greatly comforted Abraham. Even though he would be without his earthly father, his Lord would be his father by putting the His name on him.

Abraham 2:3 was the verse that rang in my ears as an answer to my fervent prayers. Was it God's will or not that I "leave" my parents for a time in order to heal? Verse 2, "Now the Lord had said unto me: Abraham, get thee out of thy country, and from they kindred, and from thy father's house, unto a land that I will show thee." The Spirit whispered, yet did so loudly, "Misti, this is your answer." I didn't hear any words with my ears, but my spirit did.

I felt like Abraham might have felt as he wrote in chapter 2 verses 12 and 13, "Thy servant has sought thee earnestly; now I have found thee.... I will do well to hearken unto they voice."

The message was clear. I knew I had received an answer from Heavenly Father. He not only approved of me "leaving" my family for a time, He was telling me to do so. How could I not hearken unto that voice?

As I look back, I thank Heavenly Father for His divine message to me. If it hadn't have been for that, I don't think that I could've ever followed through. I would have been overcome with feelings of guilt. I would've felt that I wasn't honoring my father and my mother. However, God showed me that He commanded Abraham to do the same thing. Abraham was obedient to Heavenly Father and in so doing was "delivered...out of all his afflictions" (Acts 7:10).

Who would have thought that the history of Abraham in the scriptures would help guide me through one of the biggest problems I had had in my life thus far—setting boundaries with my parents? As I studied chapter 1 and 2 even more, I was taught even more on how to handle the situation. Abraham loved his father and after he repented and changed he took him back. They all left Ur of the Chaldees together and came to a place they named Haran. Unfortunately, his father returned to his idolatry and therefore stayed in Haran. Abraham left his father behind when he was commanded of the Lord to leave and go to a new land. He not only loved his father but all of his relatives too. After he had traveled far, he built an altar and prayed that his father's house might be blessed to have the famine turned away from them.

It taught me that Abraham wasn't a selfish or self-righteous person. He kept loving his father and all his father's house even when they were far away from him and even when they didn't repent. I could keep learning from Abraham. I had struggled for so long believing that if I were to keep the commandment to honor my mother and father, I had to do everything that they wanted. Yet Abraham showed me how to truly honor my parents. Follow the will of the Lord, and then no matter what happens, never quit loving them and praying for them. I ventured to do just that.

I knew that Heaven had sent this personal revelation to me. I knew it was right and that was the only thing that could've given me the courage to do it. I now had an even stronger conviction that I was on the right ladder. Thankfully I couldn't see the top from where I was.

I had no idea how much further I had yet to climb.

CHAPTER 25

Following Abraham

~

M Y NEXT HURDLE was to convince Jed that I needed time away from my parents. He did not understand why I couldn't heal without causing such pain to my parents. Thankfully, he trusted me and was by my side as we drove up to my parents to do the hardest thing I had ever done before (besides living through the trial itself.)

I remember well the feeling of dread that I felt as Jed and I drove up there. That hour seemed like an eternal walk to the guillotine. My heart ached for the pain that I knew my mother would be in. I knew of the anger that would follow, both in my mother and my father. I knew that my sister that I loved, but lived far away, would get an earful every day and that she would also be angry with me. I also knew that like my sister, my brother would only hear my parent's side. I would be labeled the abuser now that I was finally determined to pull out of the victim role I had been playing. I didn't have the energy to try and explain my situation to them. It wasn't easy for me to talk about. I hoped that one day they would understand.

My parents were waiting for us. My mom, sensing that something dreadful was coming, was already crying. Jed did most of the talking at first. I surprised myself. I, too, was able to talk to them without shedding one tear. I tried to explain that I wouldn't be "away" forever, that I loved them, and would come back in their lives the second that I felt strong enough to do so. My mom didn't quit crying. The Lord blessed me with a calm assurance that as hard as that was, it was His will and that it was for the best.

We knew the hardest thing for them would be not seeing their grandkids and so we told them that if they wanted to see them, they could arrange it through Jed but that it was best for me if they didn't even call me on the phone for now. We hugged them both good-bye. My mom was still sobbing. We left saddened, yet at the very same time the Lord gave me a feeling of empowerment. I was doing what He wanted and I had great hope that it would lead to healing.

There were many ups and downs. Just days after talking to my parents I surprised Jed for his 30th birthday. A neighbor of ours let us use their condo up in Park City. Jed and I went up there with just our 10-week-old Sadie for the first two days, and then I had invited Jed's friend, Brandon Fairbanks, his wife Heather, and their 1-year-old baby to come join us.

As hard as daily life was for me, vacations were even harder. And what made it even harder was dealing with the guilt of "leaving" my parents. I knew I had done the will of the Lord in separating from them for a while yet I had been enmeshed with my mother for so long that I felt her pain. I felt hopeless while in Park City those first couple of days. I cried and cried. I felt that my trial was almost more than I could bear. Here I was, already a mother of four, and I was still struggling! I was wasting my life! Not only that but I felt I had ruined my parents lives and now I was ruining Jed's life as well. And who knew how terrible my kids would turn out with such a sick mother! Those were just a few of my terrible and irrational thoughts that I was having.

I also punished myself with "shoulds." I "should" be enjoying it up here. That wasn't a helpful thought. Yet, there was some truth to that. I was looking from the inside out as if I were looking at my own life through a window. It looked beautiful out there looking in but inside was hell. I felt that I really "should" be happy. I couldn't feel all the joy that I could see. I felt sick and tired of pretending. I felt sorry for Jed. Here I had planned what I had hoped would be a wonderful celebration of Jed's 30th birthday and now I was ruining it with my own stupid emotions. I felt weak. I felt less than Jed. I felt less than the whole human race. How stupid does a person have to be to have as much as I have and still be so miserable?

I was in a dark hole. I can only imagine that Satan and his minions were surrounding me. I can picture them laughing as they whispered those horrible things to me. They could see that I was buying it. That I was sinking further into a dark hole. I'm sure they could see I was beginning to believe I would never be able to get out. If they could really convince me of that then they would win. I would lose and so would my posterity after me.

I asked Jed to give me a blessing. I called Marilyn from the condo. She helped me gain a finger hold on a rung of my ladder. I determined to hold onto that rung, to put a smile on my face and keep trying. Our friends were coming and I wanted them to have a good time as well as Jed. I think it turned out okay, at least for them.

The thing I will never forget was the first time that I went to see Marilyn after returning from that trip. I was just about to leave the session. Marilyn opened the door to let me out. She had the most hopeless face that I had ever seen her have. It shocked me. She said something to the effect of, "Maybe this is too hard for you. Maybe you should quit." Without a second's hesitation, I boldly declared that there was no way I would ever give up. I was willing to do whatever it took.

That declaration was so strong and came out of me with such fervor that it surprised even me. I realized the depth of my determination at that moment and it sustained me in the years ahead. I would never quit. I knew that with certainty.

One day, not long after our Park City trip, as I was going about my daily chores, suffering yet still doing, the doorbell rang. My bishop had come to check on me. He asked me how I was doing. I wished at that moment that I had better news to give him. He offered to give me a blessing. I only remember one sentence from that blessing but it is one that I held on to as the greatest gift of hope that God had given me thus far. He said, "You will be healed in the not-too-distant future." The Spirit testified of its truthfulness. I didn't know exactly what "healed" meant or how it could possibly be fulfilled, but I was so excited to find out! What exactly did the "not-too-distant future" mean? Three months maybe? This was in the summer of 2004. In God's infinite wisdom, he didn't tell me that it would be in several more years. Yet, in His loving kindness He assured me that what I wanted more than anything would one day become a reality.

Whenever I read the account of King Limhi and his people, I thought of Bishop's blessing. They were in bondage to the Lamanites and did not know how they would escape. When Ammon, who came from Zarahemla to check on them, finally found them, they were ecstatic because Ammon could show them the way back to Zarahemla if they ever did escape. King Limhi told his people what Bishop told me: that their deliverance was "not far distant." They weren't delivered yet, but they had reason to hope that they would be soon (Mosiah 7:18–19, 23, and 33).

Limhi gathered his people together and said, "O ye, my people, lift up your heads and be comforted; for behold, the time is at hand, or is not far distant, when we shall no longer be in subjection to our enemies, notwithstanding our many strugglings, which have been in vain; yet I trust there remaineth an effectual struggle to be made" (Mosiah 7:18).

I, too, had felt like my "many strugglings" had been in vain thus far in my life, at least I did before I knew I was working on the right ladder by going to see my bishop and my counselor, Marilyn. After receiving the blessing that I would be healed in the "not-too-distant future," I, too, felt to rejoice like King Limhi. He knew that they would be delivered and rejoiced in that knowledge, yet he knew there would remain an "effectual struggle" before they would be delivered. He trusted that God would lead them, but he also knew that they would have to work, use their own ingenuity, and possibly sacrifice much.

In verse 22, Limhi talks of their bondage, and in verse 23, my burdened heart sang with his, "And now, is not this grievous to be borne? And is not this, our affliction, great? Now behold, how great reason we have to mourn."

I felt that I had great reason to mourn. I felt like I was wasting my life in my own personal bondage. Of course, now I know that it wasn't a waste. It was actually refining me and giving me experience (see D&C 122:7). Yet at the time, that was one of the most hurtful of my irrational thoughts. My kids were growing up without me being able to fully enjoy them. That seemed to be the greatest reason to mourn.

Limhi then goes on to explain that the reason they were in bondage was because of the iniquities of their fathers. In verse 30, "If my people shall sow filthiness they shall reap the chaff thereof in the whirlwind; and the effect thereof is poison."

I find it interesting that it was their fathers that sowed filthiness yet they were the ones left with the poison. They were the ones left in bondage. Verse 32 states, "And now, behold, the promise of the Lord is fulfilled, and ye are smitten and afflicted." Jesus said in John 4:37, "And herein is that saying true, one soweth, and another reapeth."

I, too, received the poison from those who came before me. And though they didn't "sow filthiness" and do all kinds of wickedness like the people of Noah did, they did stray from the light. It wasn't my fault that they did ("they" meaning, those who were before me), yet I was the one left in bondage.

I received strength from this next verse. After Limhi had described all of the reasons they were in their dire situation, he then ended with this sure hope: "But if ye will turn to the Lord with full purpose of heart, and put your trust in him, and serve him with all diligence of mind, if ye do this, he will, according to his own will and pleasure, deliver you out of bondage (Mosiah 7:33)."

I trusted that I, too, would be delivered out of bondage according to God's will and pleasure. However, I asked myself a million times, "How could I ever be completely free?" It seemed impossible, yet I took comfort in what Limhi reminded his people of. He reminded them that their God was also the God who delivered the people of Israel in a way that they didn't think could happen either (see Mosiah 7:19). God split the sea for them! He sent them fresh bread daily from heaven! How hard must it have been for the people of Israel to trust that God could deliver them from the powerful Pharaoh? Did they wonder how they would survive in the wilderness without much food? Limhi reminded his people of those miracles for a reason. He wanted them to remember those facts in the times when they were tempted to fear and to doubt as to whether or not God could deliver them from their own uniquely impossible situation.

Limhi told them, and he told me, too, that God's promises are sure. He always finds a way. If He can split a sea, send food from heaven, and make water flow out of a rock, then surely He must be able to help me find an escape from my afflictions, too. Remembering God's past demonstration of power and knowing that He never changes gives us real hope, and real hope gives us energy to move forward.

It is important to remember that even after the people of Limhi had this real hope, they still had much more affliction to go through. However, with their renewed hope and energy, they used their ingenuity to devise a plan to escape their pain.

In Mosiah 22:1, Ammon and Limhi consulted with the people for ideas on how to be delivered from bondage. They were guided by Gideon, who was a man of God, to administer wine to the Lamanite guards. When the guards were drunk and asleep, they left in the night with their families and flocks. They had escaped. The God of Abraham, Isaac, and Jacob who had provided miracles to the Israelites, provided them with a miracle too!

Through this scriptural account, the Holy Ghost taught me. He gave me hope that the Lord would provide a way for me, too. He has and will teach millions of other people exactly what they need to do in their own unique situations with this very same account. What an endless miracle the scriptures are! And I sure needed these miracles because of the growing pains yet to come that even affected my most cherished relationship—my marriage.

CHAPTER 26

My Marriage Too?

~

I CAN'T REMEMBER EXACTLY when I invited my parents back into my life, but looking back I can see that it was way too soon. My boundaries weren't yet strong enough to limit the time I spent with them. I felt too horribly guilty to say no. I wish now that I would have stayed away much longer because while I was away they didn't change anything and I hadn't changed enough. Like an alcoholic to alcohol, I needed to feel like a good daughter and so I went back. I thought that I could do it slowly but I couldn't. Once the floodgates were open, they were open.

Mom and I fell right back in the same routine. She called me, gave me her list of to-do's, a list of all the horrible things that were happening to people she knew, asked me to go here or there with her, and then hung up. I listened begrudgingly. I tried to implement the tools that Marilyn taught me but I found it so hard to do anything that might hurt my mom. It was easier to let myself be hurt. I almost always hung up the phone with anxiety left to deal with. I was stuck again. Either do and say everything that she wanted me to and I hurt, or don't behave like she wants and she is hurt. That rule of "don't hurt mom" still had a strong hold on me.

Marilyn and I spent hours and hours of therapy time discussing what it meant to be a good daughter. For example, Marilyn would help clarify it for me by making statements as if she were in my shoes. It is called role-playing. I wrote this one down. She said to me, *"Mom, what kind of boundaries do you have when my decisions make or break your life? I know that's an over-exaggeration, but that is how it feels and that's not fair. It's too much responsibility for me. I feel that your happiness rests on my actions."*

I began to see the absurdity in the dysfunctional part of my relationship with my mom. That gave me greater power to change. Marilyn helped me feel better each time that I met with her. I always talked with Heavenly Father in prayer as I drove to her office each week. When she worked in Ogden it took me almost thirty minutes to get there. It was a good time for me to pray and think about what I wanted to talk about and work on that week. I always prayed for the Spirit to be there with us. I also invited the Savior to be there and asked that He might guide our conversations. I always left there with a lighter heart than when I went in. I often sang the same song as I drove home. I sang, "A Child's Prayer," except that I changed the words a bit. I sang, "Heavenly Father, thou art really there and thou hears and answers every child's prayer." Those words came from my heart. Each time I left Marilyn's office I knew that He had been there guiding us. I knew that He was healing my life. He was using other people as His tools, yet ultimately it was Heavenly Father and the Savior who were causing all my healing, and I was so grateful.

Since my bishop had assured me through the Spirit that I would indeed be healed some day, I had within my heart this new hope. However, my days were still spent, for the most part, fighting all of my negative thought patterns. I wrote in notebook after notebook. I recognized all that I was doing to sabotage my happiness. I had a habit of being outwardly positive yet inwardly degrading to myself. For example, one day I asked a friend to watch my kids while I ran to the mall. I wanted something to wear when I went to my mom's dance studio's review. I wrote this irrational thought in my thought journal:

"Getting ready to take kid's to my friend's and go shopping at mall. I will feel terrible. I'm just trying to look good to show off at the dance review tonight. I'm not good. I'm taking advantage of my friend. Sadie will be too hard. I'm not getting better. This warm weather reminds me of hot and depressed."

My answer: *"No wonder I'm not feeling good. I sabotage myself so I don't have to feel something unfamiliar. My homeostasis is not feeling good. I can remember my relaxation where I pictured my Savior and He said Men are that they might have joy… look upon the blessed and happy state of those who keep my commandments…the devil wants you to be miserable like unto himself…choose endless happiness or misery and woe. I am not being vain when I buy clothes. I am being vain when I love them more than God and I know I love God. That sounds way understated. As a parent I find joy when my kids are happy, when they feel good about themselves. God is teaching me something."*

A negative thought intruded my positive one, *"You're just using that as an excuse to be vain."*

Answer: *"No, I'm not. I won't give up. I will persist. I can work on vanity later if that is the case."*

I wrote this after shopping, *"Had a wonderfully 'normal' and happy time shopping. Sadie was great. I didn't feel that sinful spending money. Felt good about myself physically. I had a good time at the dance review. I felt happy I wasn't there anymore, but also happy that I experienced what I did (in general)."*

That day, journaling was my day-saver. I ended up having a great day because I caught and corrected myself. Combating my negative thoughts and journaling them really helped me. It helped me see how horribly unmerciful I was to myself. I could see how wrong it was to treat myself that way. However, like a cancer, it had infiltrated my whole way of thinking and was not easy to get rid of.

Like I said, I have journals full of irrational thoughts that I then corrected with the rational. Sometimes it brought relief faster than others. Marilyn taught me that Satan had had a hold on me with depression and she warned me that he will work harder as I work harder. I knew that was true and sometimes I was able to use that to my advantage. I knew that he only had my misery in mind and so that fueled my energy to fight and keep fighting. "I won't let him win," I would tell myself. Satan tried to make me believe that feeling good about myself was vain and that if I kept it up I would never make it to the Celestial Kingdom. Even though I wanted to be happy with all my heart, I let him make me believe that I couldn't be happy and confident and still make it into heaven. I had to be "lowly in heart" right?

Of course the real answer is yes; however, I had the wrong definition of "lowly." That was a main core false belief of mine that I worked really hard to overcome. It helped when Marilyn said, "Be honest with yourself. Not conceited. Not unfair. It's a form of dishonesty when you tell yourself wrong things."

That statement helped me because if there was one thing I never wanted to be, it was dishonest. If it was being dishonest to tell myself irrational, wrong, and mean things then I wanted to stop that behavior quickly. Of course, it wasn't quick but it helped to thwart Satan's attacks on me. I was doing the right thing by being kind, confident, and happy with myself. Satan kept trying to get me on that one but I kept fighting back with the truth. That is what journaling rational thoughts can do. When I wrote the truth down so that I could plainly see it, then Satan had no more power to convince me otherwise.

I had other issues that came along with trying to change besides just my internal chaos, false beliefs, and negative thought patterns. My relationships also needed adjusting. Marilyn taught me that when a person changes, all others in that person's life have to adjust, too. She likened a family to a mobile. She said that each person was one of the arms of the mobile. Together everyone balances it, even if it is out of dysfunction. Just like in nature, everything tries to find equilibrium. That is how you get co-dependent people. One person in the family becomes an alcoholic, it throws the family mobile off balance and so another family member tries to make up for it by covering or compensating for that behavior. They find equilibrium that way, even though not in a healthy way.

On the other hand when one person begins to change or move in a healthy direction, it too throws the rest of the family off balance. No one likes being thrown off balance, even if for a good reason. The best thing would be for the rest of the family members to adjust themselves in a healthy direction too. The mobile would find equilibrium again, but this time everyone would be healthy. However, they often try to force the one who threw everything off to go back to their old ways, to get back to a place where no one else has to adjust. Most everyone wants to take the path of least resistance. It is easier to try to make someone else get back in place than to look at themselves and instigate change.

I had begun to change and it began to throw our family mobile off balance.

Jed and I had a relationship built upon his being the strong one. His job had always been to help me because I was the weak one. That wasn't his fault. I gave him that job. Our deepest and most intimate conversations often came because of my heartache. It was the glue that had bonded us in the past. Our mobile was balanced that way. Jed felt needed and I felt cared for. Now that I had Marilyn each week to listen to me and to teach me, we lost a bit of the glue in our relationship.

During the first couple of times that I went to see her, she had me bring Jed. She warned him that as I healed I would change. She said that that can sometimes be strenuous on a relationship. She asked him if he was willing to let me change and support me in that. She warned him that sometimes people get divorced when the sick person in a relationship finally heals. Jed truly loved me and wanted me to heal. He didn't think that it would change anything. He just thought that I needed help with OCD, anxiety, and depression. He didn't realize that the way I thought about everything needed changing and would indeed change.

It did put a stress on our marriage. Whereas he used to be the authority that I looked to for advice, now I was looking to Marilyn more (and eventually to myself). He didn't like it when I did something in our family because Marilyn suggested it. I think he felt a bit removed from his old standing. I quickly learned to just do it and not tell him that Marilyn had taught me this or that. He also didn't think that I needed to discuss "everything" with her. He would often say, "I don't understand. You went to her for one thing and now you are working on all these other things." He thought the other things were not pertinent. It put some stress on our marriage when I wanted to integrate a new concept in our parenting, for example, and he knew that it came from a discussion I had with Marilyn.

The funny thing is that when we talk today about this adjustment that we had to make back then he doesn't even remember it. He has always been the type to just voice his frustration at the exact second of the frustration and then just let it go. I, on the other hand, remember the time all too well because I was the one trying to instigate the change. When he would voice a frustration, I had to go against my old habits of succumbing and move forward anyway. That was hard for me but as I practiced assertive behavior even against pressure, my inner muscles grew in strength.

As I grew in strength, I began to feel an even deeper void with Jed. I had always fed our relationship with talk of my neediness. Now that I was going to a therapist each week, I didn't need Jed in that way as much anymore. Marilyn and I decided that it was best that I talk about my emotional issues mostly with her so that Jed and I might find healthier ways to bond. It was hard, yet it was the right thing to do. Plus, I knew that Jed was getting sick of always being my emotional helper. I also knew it would be best for Jed and I to find other things to bond us together, otherwise I would most likely stay stuck emotionally. I had to get rid of every reward that being sick gave me.

If there is one thing that I have learned, it is this: doing the right thing is usually coupled with words like "hard" and "lonely." This was no different. We both felt a bit of a void for a while. The void that used to be filled with my neediness now needed something else to fill it with.

One thing we did that was a lot of fun was dance. It was a real miracle that Jed conceded to do it with me. Our stake was putting on a program showing all the different kinds of dances that we did through different eras in the church. One sister asked me if Jed and I would learn the waltz with a few other couples and then perform. At first Jed said no way, but then, to his sweet credit, he said, "If you really want me to, I'll do it."

We had more fun than we had had in years every Saturday morning at practices. We got a babysitter and had a morning date every week. As I have said many times before, Jed is really funny, and although he is not a natural dancer (although much better than he thinks), he made me laugh through it all. Making jokes about his perceived lack of coordination made him feel better and entertained the rest of us. We would then leave practice, get a drink at the gas station, and drive around looking for house lots to build on. We wanted to build one more house to settle in forever. We wanted to build on a flat piece of property. As we drove, we would pick out the things that we liked in the different houses we passed. It was wonderful to bond in a different way, other than my trial. We did other things, too, but that was a really fun one for me. Nonetheless, we needed more than just dancing; we needed to relearn each other in a healthy way.

Marilyn and I felt like it would be helpful if Jed and I had a few sessions together. We needed a "small but big" shift in our relationship—"small" because most things were right in our relationship but "big" because it is hard to change any dynamic in a couple. She wanted to teach us how to fight fair. We hardly ever fought but when we did I was usually the peacemaker even to my own detriment. I had never learned that what I felt and thought was as important as what Jed did. Jed wasn't used to my being bold, and when I tried to change into a more assertive person, it caused friction in our relationship. Although he couldn't see any need to go to counseling, he went with me anyway. He couldn't see it because I had a hard time ever ruffling his feathers. To him, all was well, but to me I wanted him to see that I needed to feel free to speak my mind during an argument. I wanted him to see that although he was a better debater than I was, that didn't make him always right.

I wrote this on June 23, 2005: *"Today was as interesting a day as I ever dreamed of having in my married life. Jed came with me to a marriage therapy session with Marilyn and a man named Larry. This session was mainly for Jed to come to an understanding why a few sessions would be good for us. There was some very high tension as we both explained our points of view.…I appreciate Jed even coming once. The only hard part is convincing him he doesn't know everything.*

"Tonight after we put the kids in bed Jed and I went out and jumped on our new trampoline. We laughed and acted like kids. We had a 'bum war.' I won and then he did. We also lay there and enjoyed our beautiful yard (Jed has done a great job). The sunset was gorgeous. We didn't talk about the session. We didn't want any more intensity."

It wasn't two days after that that the Lord opened up a new path that Jed might learn the things he needed to. He woke up Saturday morning with what he thought was a kinked neck. He thought he could just rest and it would go away; however, it didn't go away. It got worse and worse. The pain spread and was more intense than he had ever experienced; it was the kind of pain that changes a person, for better or worse, forever.

CHAPTER 27

For Whom the Lord Loveth He Chasteneth

~

OVER THE NEXT two weeks I took him to four different emergency rooms hoping to find relief but no one had any answers. It wasn't until he was on his second hospitalization that his doctor found out what could help him by randomly putting different medicines in his IV. It was an anti-viral medicine that finally helped. The doctors figured that he had some kind of virus attacking his nerves. He was in so much pain that he couldn't sit up to even eat. I had to feed him, bathe him, etc. At one point he was in so much pain that he said, "Just cut off my arm." He would do anything if he could find a moment's respite. Even all of the narcotics that the doctors gave him didn't touch the pain. They only put him in some sort of psychedelic dream state.

During this whole event, I had never seen Jed so humble. He was in excruciating pain and he knew he needed God's help. One night our new bishop, came over with our home teacher to give him a blessing. He told Jed in the blessing that sometimes the Lord allows things like this to teach us our dependence on God and also to teach us other things.

I had suspected that Heavenly Father was using this experience to teach Jed, but in the end I had no doubt. During this horrific trial of pain, he learned what I hoped therapy would teach him. One night in particular I remember him crying as we talked and prayed together. He said he has realized that his worst fear is not fulfilling his mission in life and that he needed to work on our relationship and that would radiate into fulfilling all else the Lord wants from him. He said he wanted to go to therapy and to read books. He kept telling me how much he loves me. He said he didn't want therapy every week but I could see he was making a 180 degree turn.

He came home from his second hospitalization with an IV and a home-care nurse to teach him how to give himself the medicine. It took over a month more for him to recover as completely as the medicine could take him. He still had muscle loss in the affected shoulder and he still had pain. The doctors called that pain, "post-herpetic neuralgia." We were scared for a while because when we looked it up on the internet, it said that some people continue to have ghost pain for up to 30 years or so. Meaning that even though the virus was gone, the nerves had been damaged enough that there was a chance that he could continue in pain with nothing to do about it.

Ironically, that had a parallel to my emotional and mental trial. I looked fine, so did he. He had gotten help but didn't know how long the pain would last. I was getting help yet I didn't know exactly when I wouldn't feel the pain of OCD, depression, and anxiety anymore. This parallel helped Jed to empathize with me a little easier.

July 27, 2005, *"After we put the kids in bed…Jed and I sat on our bathroom floor and talked for almost two hours. We talked about the parallels we can draw between this painful trial of Jed's and my painful emotional trial. I cannot believe what a changed man Jed is. I am so amazed and so grateful. He says he feels changed and wants me to tell him if I even notice signs of him going back to the way he was. I talked to him about my struggle I've had with depression the last couple of weeks. He listened with so much more understanding and compassion. We kneeled together, hands intertwined with hands, and Jed prayed for us both. He prayed our pain would go away. That we would learn the lessons the Lord wants us to learn quickly and that we might afterwards humble ourselves without the pain compelling us. He cried. I cried. It was a lengthy prayer of both thanksgiving and pleading for healing. He thanked Heavenly Father for me and for putting us together. I felt his tears drop on my hands. Afterwards Jed said, 'This is the closest I have felt to my Heavenly Father in a long time.' This is the Jed I knew while he was on his mission when we were communicating through tapes. He has such a strong testimony that it is so wonderful to learn from him. He taught me this morning before I went walking. He hurried to get his scriptures to teach me what he learned last night. He was excited about it. He read the account of Nephi where Nephi says that he had been filled with the Spirit even to the 'consuming' of his flesh. Jed followed the footnotes and learned that it meant to renew. He taught me that the Lord has power to renew. He taught me that the Lord has power to change these bodies, to heal them. And that the Spirit, when He is with us, can renew us. He has all power over our physical bodies. I can't express my joy in witnessing Jed's hungering and thirsting for spiritual knowledge. I feel safe. I feel his priesthood protecting our family and especially our children. I don't think it's a coincidence that Sadie will now reach out for her dad to hold her whereas she used to just want me. She can sense his gentleness."*

It was so nice to have the Jed back that I loved and to have him listen to me with a newly found empathetic vibe. He was (and still is) such a confident and capable person, but in a way it became an Achilles heel for him. This huge trial came upon him less than two days after we went to our first therapy session. The session didn't go as well as I had hoped because I knew he didn't want to go back. I knew he thought that the therapists "were up in the night" and that he didn't need any coaching. It wasn't a coincidence that he had that horrible trial at that exact time. Not that I think the Lord was punishing him. That is not how He works. Maybe subconsciously Jed decided he would rather learn a different way besides therapy and the Lord allowed it. Some people don't learn from other people as well as they learn from experience. One day I will ask Heavenly Father exactly what or who caused Jed's illness. It really doesn't matter, I'm just curious. What did matter, though, was that Jed seemed to get everything out of that trial that the Lord wanted. Jed understood that he needed to be taught and that he was indeed taught through that experience. He was humbled. Not only did it help him see where he needed to repent in his life, but it also took him to a place where he could better see my pain and the trials I was going through. I was so grateful.

My trial had been hard for him to really understand without actually going through it, just like it would be hard for me to understand someone else that couldn't walk when walking comes so easily to me. I can imagine how it might feel to not be able to walk, just like Jed could imagine how I might have felt to have an emotional illness, but, unless you actually go through it, the only other one who literally knows how a person feels is the Savior.

I testify that He does know how we feel. He does have the power to heal us all. If we seek Him, He leads us to healing. Sometimes it's a short path and sometimes a longer one depending on His will.

Hebrews 12: 5–7 says, "My son, despise not thou the chastening of the Lord, nor faint when thou art rebuked of him: For whom the Lord loveth, he chasteneth, and scourgeth every son whom he receiveth. If ye endure chastening, God dealeth with you as with sons; for what son is he whom the father chasteneth not?"

I felt that the Lord must really love me! Oh how chastened I felt! Verse 11 says, "Now no chastening for the present seemeth to be joyous, but grievous; nevertheless afterward it yieldeth the peaceable fruit of righteousness unto them which are exercised thereby." Through Jed's trial I saw him obtain that peaceable fruit. I prayed that my chastening might one day yield to the peaceable fruit that I so desired.

CHAPTER 28

Recognizing Improvement

~

AROUND THIS TIME I received a letter from Sister Hughes of the General Relief Society presidency. She and I had kept in contact off and on. This is a letter that she wrote to me dated October 6, 2005.

> Dear Misti,
>
> Thank you for the note. I do love hearing about you and rejoice in the happiness you are experiencing in your life. You are a remarkable woman, and I feel so blessed that our lives have touched. Elder Maxwell often said that there are no coincidences in our lives; rather all things are of 'divine design.' I feel that way about our friendship.
>
> Give my love to your husband and children. Your little daughter must be a little toddler now. They grow so quickly, don't they?
>
> Please know that I think of you often and hope we'll soon be able to see one another again. Thank you for your thoughts and prayers for me.
>
> Love,
> Kathleen H. Hughes

Her letters meant a lot to me. I also believed our friendship was by divine design. I never saw her more than that first time, and after she was released as first counselor to the General Relief Society presidency, we lost contact with one another, yet she will always hold a special place in my heart.

As I came to the close of two years in therapy, I could see improvements in my thinking and thus in my life, but I wasn't healed. I still had OCD. I worked hard to combat it by quickly countering any negative thoughts I had. For an example, I wrote on November 24, 2005, *"I woke up early this morning and started feeling sorry for myself. 'I'm too heavy,' 'I exercise almost daily and it's just giving me bigger muscles,' 'I look big,' 'I don't look good in clothes,' etc."*

Now these thoughts are not very abnormal among women of today, but if I didn't counter even these simple negative thoughts right away, I would run the risk of falling into a deep emotional hole. What I understood about myself was this: When my brain became overwhelmed with a problem that it didn't like, then it would often resort to OCD because that was at least something that it was used to. It was familiar. The more that I focused on how much I hated that my brain wanted to focus on my eyes, tongue, etc., then the less I had to worry about whatever it was that was initially overwhelming me. As I began to understand this process about myself, I was able to counter-attack more.

When I had those thoughts about how I'm fat, things aren't perfect, etc., I immediately began writing down all the many things that I was grateful for. Manually changing those thoughts took away my need to resort to OCD. This is some of what I wrote (also on November 24, 2005):

"I am so thankful to Heavenly Father. He has given me my life back. I am able to feel the joy of everyday moments. I feel sad or other feelings when appropriate. When I get depressed or anxious I now have tools such as relaxation to help me stop the cycle immediately. Sometimes it takes

longer but I don't fear like I used to. I know I can do it. I now know how to stop my negative thinking cycle sometimes sooner and sometimes later. I am pretty okay with that. Like I said earlier this is an ongoing process, but I feel to sing praises to Jesus' name, for all good things come of Him and because of His Atonement. He has used and continues to use His power to heal me."

I went on and on about my children and all the other blessings in my life. The miracle wasn't in the blessings. I had always had them. The miracle was that I was beginning to really feel and enjoy them. That progress encouraged me to continue to strive and work up the ladder even further.

For the next year and a half, my stress came in several different forms. I pretty much had three full-time jobs. It ranged from building a new home, to being a full-time mother, to the work associated with all of the "brain changing" I was doing. I had the continual homework of writing irrational thoughts and practicing what I had learned at the one to two hours of therapy each week.

Stress is hard when a person is emotionally healthy. It's really hard when a person is prone to OCD. I worked arduously in order to not fall into OCD ruts. I couldn't help it sometimes. Marilyn helped talk me through it. We also practiced meditation and visualization. Those things coupled with a lot of prayer, putting my own name on the prayer roll in the temple, and journaling would help me get out of those ruts. Sometimes my OCD spells would last a couple of days and sometimes several weeks. It was hard but I was becoming increasingly less and less afraid of the actual OCD symptoms. There was still fear there, though. It wasn't easy to not be fearful of something that seemed to take over my thinking and then felt like it was taking over my life. When I was in an OCD rut, the everyday joys seemed to just zap away into a place that I could only see from behind a joy-proof window. I was glad the joy was there and would even laugh at all the right moments, but I was so sad that I couldn't feel them. At times, it felt like OCD was stealing my life.

As difficult as all that was, I could still see that I was making big strides of improvement. I wrote this on August 11, 2006, *"I finally feel like I've placed my ladder along the right wall. Now I work daily, even momentarily, to take a step up the next rung. I lose my footing and slip down sometimes but I keep going. The greatest part is that I know my efforts are taking me up and will continue to take me up and all because of Jesus Christ."*

The interesting part about all the work that I was doing was that no matter how high on the ladder I got, when I fell down a rung or two, it hurt just the same. Just like a knee scrape hurts the newly walking toddler as much as it does an Olympic runner. A fall is a fall. A scrape is a scrape. Even though the Olympic runner is a lot further in progression than the newly walking toddler is, it still hurts to get hurt.

Unfortunately I didn't understand this concept yet. When I fell down a rung or two it was easy to feel like maybe I wasn't making any progress. I have no doubt that Satan loved those moments. He didn't want me to keep working on my ladder. He would whisper, "Look how long and hard you have worked and to no avail. You aren't any better than you were when you started. You hurt just the same."

I will admit that sometimes I gave in to those thoughts. However, even when I wondered if I was making any progress at all, I knew that Marilyn was my God-given friend. I knew that the things she was teaching me were approved by God because I had constantly prayed and gotten the revelation that it was so. I also knew that she was helping me heal the other parts of my life that I didn't even know needed healing at first. My boundaries with my mother were getting healthier. My negative thinking habits were becoming more obvious to me. I was improving by using the tools that she had given me. I also knew that my relationships with my husband and kids were becoming increasingly healthier.

I couldn't deny that I was improving in all those areas and thus Satan didn't win. I knew that continuing to use the tools that Marilyn had taught me was what Heavenly Father wanted me to do even if I was still suffering at times from the OCD as much as I ever had. Again, I knew my ladder was on the right wall and so I continued on.

After about two and a half years of therapy, I was doing so well that Marilyn and I decided that I didn't need to see her every week anymore. I would just call her from time to time for a brush up. It had been several months since I had seen her when I called her needing a "Marilyn crash course" again.

December 22, 2006, *"Lately I have struggled emotionally again. It is because it's Christmas time. I have laughed at myself because I keep doing the same things every year and expect different, happier results. Marilyn called me yesterday morning and we chatted about it. I've realized that at Christmas time I feel coerced to do traditions I've always done. I feel trapped that I can't get out of them because either I will hurt my mom or I fear my kids won't have as much fun."*

At the time it was too late to kindly get out of that year's traditions so I talked with Marilyn about what I wanted for the next year. That in and of itself helped me deal with the present situation. I decided what I wanted to do and what I didn't want to do. One big change was that I wanted to stay home and celebrate Christmas Eve with just my little family. I couldn't wait to do that the next year!

Unfortunately, it took me four more years before I was finally strong enough to tell my mom that I was going to stay home on Christmas Eve. She didn't like it but she adjusted. It was the best change ever! My favorite part about being with just our little family was our pajama dance party. After we all opened our Christmas pajamas, (which, by the way, the girls all matched, including me), we had a dance party in the kitchen. Even Jed danced. We all laughed, twirled, and jammed. It was truly an unforgettable moment. I am sure we will continue that tradition. Looking back, I wish I had done it a lot earlier.

That Christmas of 2006 turned out okay. I prayed that night if there was anything Heavenly Father wanted me to know. There was. I wrote: *"I felt a surge of joy and felt that He loves me very much. I felt . . . I have an important mission to perform here that is so much more real (for lack of a better word) than all this superficial stuff that constantly surrounds me."*

Like always, He comforted me amid my affliction. I was going to need that because my mind was about to feel as if it had been set on fire.

CHAPTER 29

"Thy Dross to Consume and Thy Gold to Refine"

~

AFTER CHRISTMAS I was fine again. I even took a scuba diving course with my husband. I told Jed that I would take the course with him but that I reserved the right to back out at any time without any repercussions from him. He agreed. Step by step I kept moving forward. I surprised myself and became scuba certified. We were doing it for a Hawaii trip that we had coming up that March.

I had so much going on at the same time that I began struggling again. We were finishing building our new home. I wasn't completely sure I would like it as much as my old home. Plus, I was worried about moving ourselves from a ward and neighborhood that we loved and into a new one. To top it all off, we added a vacation.

That wasn't a smart thing to do knowing my history with change as well as with vacations. However, even though in the back of my mind I was worried, the thought of actually enjoying a well-deserved vacation sounded so nice that I conceded. It was poor timing. I was already struggling emotionally and to add a vacation the week before moving into our new home was a recipe for emotional disaster.

Some people might laugh at that and think, "Poor girl. A Hawaii vacation and a new home all in two weeks. How horrible." However, a person that has struggled emotionally knows full well what I am talking about. In fact, knowing how blessed I was and that I wasn't enjoying it was like adding fuel to the fire. It angered me. It saddened me. I wanted to enjoy my beautiful life yet I wasn't! When will my emotional past quit haunting me, I wondered?

The trip has very few good memories for me. We had to share a condo with other people and so I never felt like I had room to let my happy façade down. No one knew of my emotional problems. One of Satan's many tactics to destroy my peace came front and center on this trip. It was also one of the most horrific. He would put flash thoughts in my mind of me stabbing someone. It would make me nauseous at the thought. Those didn't happen very often but when they did, I thought for certain I was the worst person in the world and that I was, in fact, going crazy. I cried to Jed more than once. He was kind yet I am sure very sad that again we had another disappointing vacation. He gave me a blessing. While everyone else was at a beautiful beach, I was in the car on the phone with Marilyn trying to gain strength. I felt Jed's blessing helping. I did have some good moments; however, they were few and short lasting.

Right when we got home it was moving time. I was excited but not ready emotionally. I didn't want the moving-in process and memories to be tainted with what I was sick of by now—my mental hell. The OCD was out of hand. It took turns with anxiety and despair when I feared it would never go away. Would I ever be truly free? I had worked so hard for so long now. Why did it still feel like I was back to square one sometimes? Why did it have to hurt so badly?

During our last few days at our old house I had a breakdown. On March 23, 2007, I wrote, *"Today was very hard emotionally. I have been struggling off and on for one and a half months. I met with Marilyn last night at Jed's office. This morning I saw some pictures and remembered feeling low in all of them. I lost it. I went in my room and cried so hard. I prayed so hard. I called my bishop. Jed came home and they both gave me a priesthood blessing. Bishop was on his way home from the temple. I don't think that was a coincidence."*

Before Bishop gave me the blessing I told him all that was going on. He was a fairly new bishop; however, he did know a little bit already about me. I cried desperately to him. He was also emotional. He expressed his testimony of the mantle of a bishop. He said it wasn't until he was called as bishop did he fully realize that it's not the man, it's the mantle and that the Lord organized the position of bishop so He could use him to bless His children. He said, "God loves his children and He has used me to bless them. It doesn't work outside the ward. I've tried to give advice to people outside the ward and it doesn't work.'"

He told me that after a particularly hard day as a bishop, he received a special witness that the mantle of power that is bestowed on a bishop is real and that the Lord would lead and guide him. The Spirit bore testimony to me at that moment that what he was saying was true. My faith that God could help me through him increased.

Bishop then gave me a blessing after Jed anointed me with oil. At the first of the blessing he assured me that me asking for this blessing was very appropriate, and that God gave us this authority to give blessings for the sole purpose of blessing His children. I knew the blessing was from God. Privately, I had been very concerned that me asking for another blessing would be taking advantage of priesthood blessings. The Lord assured me He was glad I had asked to receive this one.

He told me that I was a choice and elect soul. That God was keenly aware of my anguish and that He could feel it with me. That God gives us weakness that we may be humble and if we turn to him those weak things will be made strong. I was weeping through it all. Bishop was as well.

He then said the words that I held onto for dear life. He said, "You will be made strong and you will be a strength to others. They will come to you with these same problems and you will help and strengthen them."

He told me afterwards, "I know that those were not my words. They came from Heavenly Father." I had no doubt at that moment that he was right. Those words were from Heavenly Father and I knew he couldn't lie. I was going to make it somehow, some way.

We moved into our new home the next week. I still had a hard time emotionally but because of Bishop's blessing, I was again given the stamina to keep going and keep hoping. As I moved in I listened to the hymn "How Firm a Foundation" on my iPod. I memorized most of it and those words gave me a lot of strength.

How firm a foundation ye saints of the Lord
Is laid for your faith in His excellent word!
What more can He say than to you He hath said,
Who unto the Savior for refuge have fled?

In every condition—in sickness, in health,
In poverty's vale, or abounding in wealth,
At home, and abroad, on the land, on the sea—
As thy days may demand so thy succor shall be.

Fear not, I am with thee; oh, be not dismayed,
For I am thy God, and will still give thee aid.
I'll strengthen thee, help thee, and cause thee to stand,
Upheld by My righteous, omnipotent hand.

When through the deep waters I call thee to go,
The rivers of sorrow shall not thee overflow,
For I will be with thee thy troubles to bless,
And sanctify to thee thy deepest distress.

When through fiery trials thy pathway shall lie,
My grace, all-sufficient, shall be thy supply.

Thy flames shall not hurt thee; I only design
Thy dross to consume and thy gold to refine.

E'en down to old age all my people shall prove
My sovereign, eternal, unchangeable love;
And when gray hair shall their temples adorn,
Like lambs they shall still in My bosom be borne.

The soul that on Jesus hath leaned for repose
I will not, I cannot, desert to his foes;
That soul, though all hell should endeavor to shake,
I'll never, no never, no never, forsake!

I sang that song as I cleaned and organized. I felt the power of those words as they reminded me that my suffering was for a purpose and that I shouldn't fear because the Lord was with me whether I was sick or healthy, rich or poor, and that He was the one that caused me to keep standing.

Why was I still suffering when I was living righteously? Why was I still in such pain when I had been working so hard on the path the Lord had opened up for me? How could the Lord ever make this go away? I did not know. In fact, I had no clue.

I found great comfort in the story of Alma the Elder in the Book of Mormon. He was a righteous man, yet he and his people were tried with much oppression and bondage. They, too, had no clue how they would be delivered.

Alma had been a priest of the wicked King Noah. God had sent a prophet to come testify against King Noah. Alma was the only priest who believed the prophet and repented of his sins. King Noah sought to kill him and yet Alma risked his life as he hid by the waters of Mormon to teach others the truth. He baptized over two hundred people there.

After awhile the Lord warned Alma and the new saints that the king was on to them and that they needed to flee for safety. They listened and escaped to a new and beautiful land. They worked hard there to keep the commandments. They were righteous so you would think that would be safe and happy, right? Nope. The Lord allowed trials to come upon them, too.

While they were working in their fields one day, the Lamanites happened upon them. They took possession of their land that they had righteously worked so hard to develop. They "exercised authority over them, and put tasks upon them, and put taskmasters over them" (Mosiah 24:9). They even caused that their children should persecute the people of Alma's children. Their afflictions became so great that they began to "cry mightily to God."

If you are ever tempted, like I was, to say to yourself, *"Why am I in this mental and emotional bondage? I am a good person. Why do I not then have peace?"* Remember the good people of Alma and also these words, "The Lord seeth fit to chasten his people; yea, he trieth their patience and their faith" (Mosiah 23:21).

Much like the people of Alma knew they would be killed if they didn't push themselves to finish their harsh tasks, my brain was my taskmaster. It was constantly constraining me to work harder to maintain equilibrium or I felt I would be crushed. I, too, cried mightily unto God almost constantly for deliverance. I took comfort in what the Lord told them. He said He would deliver them eventually but for now he would ease their burdens. He said, "And this I do that ye may stand as witnesses for me hereafter, and that ye may know of a surety that I, the Lord God, do visit my people *in* their afflictions" (Mosiah 24:14, emphasis added).

I, too, stand as a witness of the Lord's ability to carry our burdens even while they are still on our backs. Because of my prayers, the Lord in His mercy did grant me such relief that, at times, I even wondered if the OCD was gone. He visited me *in* my afflictions and I couldn't deny it. Those breathers always came in the nick of time and gave me the renewed strength to go on.

We don't know how long after the Lord comforted the people of Alma with the promise of deliverance they were still in bondage. However, we do know that He did fulfill His promise.

Mosiah 24:16 says, "And it came to pass that so great was their faith and their patience that the voice of the Lord came unto them again, saying: Be of good comfort, for on the morrow I will deliver you out of bondage."

I love the part where we learn how exactly the Lord finally delivered them. It was simple. No fireworks. He caused the Lamanites to be in a profound sleep one night and they just walked out of bondage.

When it comes right down to it, deliverance is easy for the Lord. He is all-powerful. When tempted to be angry with Him because it would be so easy for Him to deliver you and you question why He doesn't do it now, remember—His loving kindness never departs from us. He knows our pains perfectly. Perfectly means that He knows exactly how bad it hurts and how hard it is. Nevertheless, because of His love, He withholds Himself from delivering us until in His omniscience he knows we are finally what He wanted us to become by experiencing the trial of our faith in the first place.

How hard it was for Alma's people to escape by themselves. Yet, how easy it was for the Lord!

I was surprised at how quickly our new house felt like home. We felt like we were meant to live there. However, no matter the goodness in my life, no matter that everything physically was working out great, no matter it all—I still struggled emotionally. I started meeting with Marilyn again. This time I was even more serious. We began meeting twice a week again.

A couple weeks after we moved in I woke up one morning and immediately felt bombarded with irrational and hopeless thinking.

The thoughts that were in my mind were terrible. I had again in my mind thoughts of stabbing someone. I was full of despair. I had thoughts of doubt in those blessings of a future healing that I had received. I felt like all was black; that I had worked so hard and yet was no better. Because of the evil thoughts that were circling in my head, I thought that I must be the most horrible person and not deserving of God's love and power.

Thankfully, I remembered Bishop telling me of an experience he had where he had to command Satan to leave. He said that a couple of months previous he couldn't sleep and a prayer wasn't helping so he sat up and put his arm to the square. He commanded Satan to depart. He said that it worked.

I don't think that I had ever put my arm to the square before to cast out Satan and his followers. It was a very scary thing for me to do, yet I did it. I kneeled up on my bed, raised my arm to the square, and with confidence in my voice I said, *"I command you to depart in the name of Jesus Christ and by the power which I have been given."* I immediately felt peace.

I knew then, more than I have ever known, of the reality of Satan and his angels. I felt peace all that day. The relief I felt after all that darkness left me, compared to the way I felt right before, taught me a huge lesson—Satan is real. He really does make "war with the saints of God, and encompasseth them round about" (D&C 76:29).

In Moroni 7:17, Moroni writes what his father Mormon had taught him about the devil. He says, "But whatsoever thing persuadeth men to do evil, and believe not in Christ, and deny him, and serve not God, then ye may know with a perfect knowledge it is of the devil; for after this manner doth the devil work, for he persuadeth no man to do good, no, not one; neither do his angels; neither do they who subject themselves unto him."

Never again would I doubt the reality of Satan and his purpose here on the earth. He really does want God's children to be as miserable as he is. Although I feared putting my arm to the square, I felt so thankful to a Heavenly Father who provided us with a way in which we can rid ourselves of evil's company when all other endeavors fail to do so.

CHAPTER 30

New Ward, New Bishop

~

BEFORE WE MOVED into our new ward, my old bishop asked if he could talk to my new bishop and tell him what had been going on with me and my trial. At first I was reluctant. My pride was kicking in. I wanted a fresh start in a new ward with no baggage. I was worried about what he would think of me. An old habit of thinking came knocking. If no one knew of my trial, maybe I could just pretend my way out of it. My old bishop helped me see reality. After talking to me for a while I could see what he was trying to teach me. He said that we don't go to church to pretend we are perfect. We go to church to be helped along that path. Even though I didn't want to, I knew it was in my best interest and so I gave him permission to talk to my new bishop for me.

A few weeks after moving in, our new bishop called Jed and me to his office. We talked to him and he really understood. He got teary eyed and truly meant it when he said that he was sorry. He knew how hard depression can be. Someone close to him had struggled with depression before. I instantly had a new friend; a liaison with the Lord that I trusted would be there when I needed him in the future. I was so grateful that my old bishop had opened the door for me to talk with my new bishop.

I found out I was pregnant with our fifth child on June 15, 2007. I was so excited! That very day we went with our friends rock climbing and rappelling. It had been planned for several weeks and I didn't feel like I could cancel so the day I found out I was pregnant, I went rappelling down a 45 foot cliff for the first time ever! I did it twice. It was exhilarating and scary all at the same time. I was so proud of myself and I thought my kids, especially the one in my belly, would think I was a pretty cool mom.

Pretty soon the excitement of being pregnant took a backseat to the nausea of being pregnant. I was sicker with this pregnancy than I had ever been before. One day while writing in my journal I recognized a parallel.

On July 17, 2007, I wrote, *"I felt very sick today. I barely made it to the kitchen sink before I vomited. I feel discouraged like I will never feel better again or enjoy food again. It is really hard feeling like I have the flu every day yet still having to live and work and love as though I'm fine. As I wrote that I just realized I have experience with that although in a different way."*

My emotional trial that I had was like being sick with the emotional flu yet "still having to live and work and love as though I'm fine."

In that same entry I wrote, *"I feel bad that I wasn't very loving or patient with my kids today. I want to show my love for them more than I discipline, but lately with my lack of energy and wellness I seem to use my energy on disciplining only. I asked Heavenly Father to forgive me tonight. I immediately felt forgiven. It almost seemed that He was too quick to forgive me—that I deserve more punishment. I am so grateful for the real cleansing power of the Savior's atonement."*

CHAPTER 31

Book of Mormon Pride Cycle = Misti Cycle

~

I DID NOTICE THAT when I was physically sick, the OCD seemed to take a back seat. If OCD itself,had a brain, I'm sure it would've said, "She's miserable enough, I think I'll take a break until the second she is over her morning sickness."

That is exactly what happened. As soon as I started feeling the tiniest bit better, OCD poked its ugly head back in my life. I also noticed another cycle. It kind of felt similar to that of the Book of Mormon pride cycle except this one was the "Misti pride cycle."

I recognized it, got inspiration on it, and wrote about it all on the same day. On September 2, 2007, I wrote, *"I haven't felt as well emotionally since yesterday morning but overall I haven't been really happy for quite awhile. I have been really crabby with everyone. I thought to myself, 'This cycle is so predictable. I go through hard times, I lean on the Lord more, I'm more humble, then I'm blessed and my troubles seem to go away. Then I begin to casually read scriptures (still daily but not loving it) and casually pray and then even though I'm emotionally fine, I'm still not happy. Instead, I'm negative and crabby about the imperfections in my family and me. I wondered how to escape this cycle so that I'm not just heavenward when trouble comes, so that I can be happy almost all the time.*

"I feel like Heavenly Father heard my thoughts because on the BYU Channel today I listened to Henry B. Erying give me a flat out answer. He said he noticed this cycle in himself so he decided to do something about it. The mists of darkness are temptations of the devil but the word of God is a clear light that pierces the darkness. Elder Erying says that he chooses to remind himself what the prophets say about the peace and happiness of those who have the Holy Ghost. He chooses to remember what the companionship of the Holy Ghost does to him. That way he is not waiting for troubles before he pleads for the Holy Ghost. He set a higher standard for his prayers. In 3 Nephi they prayed for that which they most desired—the Holy Ghost. Angels speak by the power of the Holy Ghost, so feast upon the words of Christ. Elder Erying's scriptures are more worn out where Christ's own words are written, like in the New Testament, 3 Nephi, and Doctrine and Covenants. He said that casual prayer, a few verses of scripture, etc. are not enough—only steady, increasing effort will allow the Lord to get us to higher ground.

"He said to not set our expectations to what we think we can become, but to what God sees and expects us to become (or something like that). That really hit me. I set limits for myself but Heavenly Father sees above what I think. As I pray for and obtain the Holy Ghost, the ebb and flow of happiness will be more of a flow. Through the Spirit and, thus, joy, the Atonement will change my very being, talents, and limitations to a higher place. Elder Erying said, 'Set your expectations of yourself high and then higher…Heavenly power lifting me above where I am now.' (Eyring, 2005).

"I want to implement this knowledge."

I needed to hear that talk. He not only answered my question on how to avoid the pride cycle but He put an idea in my mind that I had never thought of before. I had never thought that God had higher expectations of me than I had for myself. After hearing that, it was like I could see myself in my mind's eye going so much higher through God's power than I had ever before imagined. It broke an invisible barrier for me—the barrier I had unknowingly set for myself. At that moment I desired to set my sights on becoming what God could see me becoming instead of the little that I had envisioned for myself. That was an important moment for me.

Recognizing that sometimes the Lord immediately answered my questions was a powerful faith promoter in my life. He heard my inner plea for more truth and He gave it to me. I was so thankful when the Lord reminded me that although I hadn't completely gotten what I wanted yet, He was still there and He was still listening. My prayers were being answered in stages. The next stage of healing came in recognizing my false beliefs.

October 24, 2007, *"Tonight while talking with Marilyn the Lord bestowed a tender mercy upon me. He brought to light a mystery. The mystery is why I've been afraid to heal all the way. I allow OCD, depression, and anxiety to slip in and stay in my life because my irrational fear is that if I'm whole then I might become like my mom and be too worldly, forget my Savior, and not get me or my family to heaven.... The purpose it is serving in my false belief system is that it's getting me to heaven, or at least protecting me from hell."*

At this point in time it had almost been four years since I had begun my journey on the right ladder. I knew my ladder was leaning on the right wall. I knew that all I had to do was keep climbing. So why was I still finding myself slipping down the ladder? What was holding me back? I learned this night that it was because of some of my false belief systems. Deep down I believed that the OCD was serving me. I believed that it was keeping me humble, but what it was really doing was hiding the fear I had of actually blossoming into what the Lord wanted me to be.

This quote from Marianne Williamson's book, *A Return to Love*, explains what I feared perfectly. Marilyn read this quote to me one day.

"Our deepest fear is not that we are inadequate. Our deepest fear is that we are powerful beyond measure. It is our light, not our darkness that most frightens us. We ask ourselves, Who am I to be brilliant, gorgeous, talented, fabulous? Actually, who are you not to be? You are a child of God. Your playing small does not serve the world. There is nothing enlightened about shrinking so that other people won't feel insecure around you. We are all meant to shine as children do. We were born to make manifest the glory of God that is within us. It's not just in some of us; it's in everyone. And as we let our own light shine, we unconsciously give other people permission to do the same. As we are liberated from our own fear, our presence automatically liberates others."

I did sense greatness in me, we all should. However I now understood a profound truth: I was afraid of that greatness coming out. I allowed OCD to squash any success I was having because I was afraid, deep down, that if I didn't have these emotional issues, I would, in fact, become great and then I would become worldly and prideful and lose my salvation. What a horrible weight on one's shoulders to want to be happy and successful yet believe that having those very things will make you end up in hell! O the power of the adversary to trap those that believe in the Savior! He can even take our good and true beliefs, like the importance of being humble, and use it to make us miserable! Truly, we must heed the Lord's counsel in D&C 10:5 where He says, "Pray always, that you may come off conqueror; yea, that you may conquer Satan, and that you may escape the hands of the servants of Satan that do uphold his work."

Recognizing our false beliefs is a huge step in the right direction but not the only step. We need to retrain ourselves to not automatically respond in the false way that we always had while in the grasp of that false belief. In other words, our minds work on autopilot most of the time and unless we consciously work to change our autopilot, we will still run on those same false beliefs even when we know they are there and untrue. It takes real work, but, it is oh so worth it!

My next false belief that I was working on was the belief that I had to be nearly perfect in order for the Atonement to work in my life. Like the Pharisees, I thought I had to do it all myself, and then the Atonement would kick in when I was good enough. The problem with this false belief was that I had no idea how to manifest the true belief. How do I trust in the Savior more? I needed Heaven's help for this one.

One morning I received a witness of Heaven's power to bring me peace without me doing a single thing besides being quiet enough to hear it. November 3, 2007, *"I woke up this morning while still dark. I came in the living room to meditate. While meditating I felt an over-whelming feeling of love, joy, and peace cover my whole body. I thought to myself that this must be what you feel like in heaven all the time. I am not sure why the Lord let me feel that for those brief few minutes but I believe it's because I was praying for more faith and hope....I don't know how to rely on my Lord enough.*

"I don't think it was a coincidence that I heard Elder Richard G. Scott of the Quorum of the Twelve Apostles give me an answer to this on the BYU Channel.

"He said, 'There will always be a need for you to walk to the edge of your knowledge...into the twilight of faith. You will be asked to exercise faith in truths that you've not yet come to prove through your own experience or through the sacred witness of the Holy Ghost. Exercise faith in Jesus Christ and His infinite capacity to bless. Faith leads one to action to achieve goals even when there is little evidence of any hope of success. Faith is abiding trust, and truth therefore is the source of power to know simple but pro-foundly important truths and to have the faith to live them. Enduring happiness is rooted in unchangeable truth, lived in faith....As you center your lives in truth you are assured of success and happiness'" (Scott, 2001).

His last sentence summed up why living with false beliefs even while living righteously does not produce happiness. We must center our lives *in* truth. I had been confused about faith. How do I get it? Fear of not being able to find enough faith in order to be healed actually sapped the faith I had. I felt so blessed to hear the word of the Lord through His trusted servant. Through him, I felt the Lord was aware of me—even keenly aware.

I was learning so many important truths at that time. I hoped that just learning them and having the Holy Ghost witness the truth of those things to me would alleviate the symptoms of my emotional trial. I was sorely disappointed.

November 10, 2007, *"This morning I lost it. I cried and cried in the mud bathroom. I feel discouraged with my emotional troubles. I need the Atonement but I feel like I don't have the faith and hope necessary to tap into that."*

I remember that moment well. I was in the bathroom just off of our mudroom. I cried so hard as I curled up in a ball against the wall. I wanted my pain to stop. I felt that I couldn't take it anymore. I couldn't take the constant barrage of repeated thoughts and over-awareness of my eyes or tongue anymore. I couldn't take the thought of having to deal with the debilitating anxiety and depression and hopelessness one more day let alone who knows how much longer the Lord wanted me to suffer so. I felt true despair in that moment. My hope was depleted.

That night was the adult session for stake conference. I wrote, *"It was written for me. Faith and hope were the topics."* I had a hard time not crying through it. Jed squeezed my hand in silent communication that the talks were meant for me. I knew they were too.

Earlier that day I had written in my thought journal, *"What if I exert faith and hope, get better, then get sick again? What if that makes me lose all faith and hope?"*

The answer came to me that night during the session. *"Joseph Smith and the pioneers in extreme poverty were asked to build the Kirkland Temple. When they finally did it, they enjoyed it for a time then the same trial came again when the Lord told them to leave, go to Nauvoo, (which was in another wilderness) and build another temple."*

What faith it must have taken the pioneers to pick themselves up, move on, and built yet another difficult temple! If they could do it and not lose faith, then I would try to do the same. I was much like them only I was building emotional temples instead of physical ones.

The next day after stake conference, Jed and I met with the bishop. He calmed my fears. Through him I learned that I am not at fault when symptoms come back. I am doing all I can and the Lord will heal me in His time. He gave me a blessing. He said, "Like other blessings have said, you will be healed all the way when the time is right." I left there feeling so grateful for the office of the bishop and for the love of a very faithful husband.

However, even after all of those wonderful spiritual answers, Satan didn't want to leave me so easily. That very night I could not sleep peacefully. The next morning I wrote, *"I wrestled with the thought that if it's not my fault when I begin struggling again then I must have no control over it, and if I have no control over it then why see Marilyn, journal, or do anything but wait for something that is out of my control to leave?"*

I prayed for understanding in our couple prayer that morning. The answer came to me while blow-drying my hair. I wrote it down: *"I am to do something. I am to work as I have been working while being as joyful and serviceable as I can while I wait for healing. This is part of my mission."*

I read in my scriptures right after that and received further light.

"And now, verily, verily, I say unto thee, put your trust in that Spirit which leadeth to do good yea, to do justly, to walk humbly, to judge righteously; and this is my Spirit.

241

"Verily, verily, I say unto you I will impart unto you of my Spirit which shall enlighten your mind which shall fill your soul with joy.

"And then shall ye know, or by this shall you know, all things whatsoever you desire of me, which are pertaining unto things of righteousness, in faith believing in me that you shall receive.

"Behold, this is your work, to keep my commandments, yea, with all your might, mind, and strength" (D&C 11:12–14, 20).

That was the answer that I needed for that day. I was to do something. I was to keep God's commandments as well as do my part to overcome my weaknesses until it was the right time for Him to heal me. He helped me avoid a pitfall of Satan that day.

Satan had tried to send me off the path of progress and onto the detour of despair and idleness. He wanted me to think that I could do nothing to help my situation so why try? Thankfully the Lord quickly and gently guided me back on the path of work, self-respect, and stamina to keep hoping for future healing. Was it over just because I received His divine help? Absolutely not! I wished it was so but it wasn't. It was, however, another step up the ladder.

A few days after that, on November 15th, I needed help up the next step on my ladder. I wrote, *This morning I felt annoyed with my eyes for a moment then fear and anxiety. I worked through it as best I could. I prayed and I challenged irrational thinking. I did think, 'Well, this is annoying,' and tried to go on but I thought, 'Do I welcome it in and really think about it or do I try to brush it under the rug?' The answer came and it is, 'Let it come or not come. I'm going to do 'all things cheerfully that lie in my power.' I am grateful for the opportunity to practice this skill of taking the fear out of my weakness."*

The full scripture is in D&C 123:17, "Therefore, dearly beloved brethren, let us cheerfully do all things that lie in our power; and then may we stand still, with the utmost assurance, to see the salvation of God, and for his arm to be revealed."

When the adversary whispers, "Why try then? If it's all up to the Savior, why even try?" Douse his flames with that scripture. Verse 17 is a powerful mantra. It is simple truth. It takes power away from the trial and back into your hands, where it rightfully belongs. When you cheerfully accomplish your goals, you are not giving the trial, whatever it is, control over whether or not you become who you want to be.

I learned that the Savior himself practiced this very concept. In D&C 20:22, it says, "He suffered temptations but gave no heed unto them." I found strength in that. He didn't wait for the temptations to leave before He fulfilled His mission. He "heeded them not" and fulfilled it anyway.

I tried to do exactly what I had learned. I did more acts of service and even volunteered at the nearby tabernacle where they displayed hundreds of nativity sets. I was set in a lonely hallway to direct performers to their various places. It wasn't quite what I had in mind.

I wrote, *"It was boring. I began ruminating over my trials, my fears, and my lack of faith (or so I condemn myself). I prayed and I wrote in my notebook. I had the thought that Jesus was peaceful even though He knew that He had an awful, painful experience of both body and mind in His future. He knew He'd carry everyone's pains and sicknesses, sins and burdens in the future, yet He was peaceful. I can be peaceful even though I probably will go through this again in the future and maybe even soon."*

November 25, the very next day, the Spirit gave me another example to follow. *"I read in 1 Nephi this morning. I realized that Lehi could've despaired about Jerusalem being destroyed. He could've despaired that his only two options were 1) stay and die or 2) go through tremendous trials in a wilderness. The easier route would've been to stay in Jerusalem, but he wanted the Promised Land so he chose the wilderness with faith that he would then obtain the Promised Land."*

The easier route for me would have been to stay in my trials, suffer all my days, and then at the end of my life "curse God and die" (Job 2:9). Easier doesn't mean better.

I took comfort in Lehi's story. He, like me, chose the wilderness route. I sometimes felt embarrassed that I had been fighting my way through my wilderness for almost four years and still had not found my promised land yet. What was wrong with me? Why was it taking so long? Would I ever get there? Lehi gave me the perfect example to follow. His journey took much longer than mine had thus far. He took it a day at a time and in righteousness followed the Liahona this direction and then that direction until he made it to the promised land.

Even after that spiritual epiphany where the truth hit me smack in the face, the very next day was still hard emotionally. I was still sick. A person may know without a doubt that there is hot water in their bathtub but unless they are actually in it they are still cold and dirty. I was learning truths, but I was still outside the tub, so to speak.

November 26, 2007, *"It was a harder day emotionally. I felt fat and ugly and my sins seemed like scarlet. I called Jed's sister for him and asked if they wanted to come to dinner and watch her husband's team play Jed's team. I hate TV sports on Sunday. Why did I do that? Why didn't I prepare my lesson earlier? I began feeling depressed."*

I tortured myself for sinning against the light I knew. I could only accept myself when, seemingly, I was doing things perfectly, which wasn't very often. I felt weak. That night the Lord gave me a boost. I wrote, *"Tonight as I lay in bed, I felt the whisperings of the Spirit tell me I am getting stronger and it wouldn't be long before I feel strong."*

CHAPTER 32

Finding Lights in the Dark

~

W E TOOK OUR kids on our first big vacation with just our little family. We went to Maui, Hawaii, for a week in early December 2007. Our kids were so excited. It was fun watching them anticipate such an adventure; however, I was scared. Last time I went to Hawaii just the previous March, it was a disaster for me emotionally. I was scared that I would leave there with scarred memories from yet another vacation. This one meant even more to me since it would be a memory with my children. I wanted it to be full of good memories.

Mother Nature was against us. We were gone for six days and saw the sun for maybe two hours total!

December 2–8, 2007, *"It rained and rained and rained some more. They had flash flood warnings and even the power went out one night. Everything we had planned, like the submarine ride and luau, was all cancelled because of the rain. Even the beaches were closed because of contamination!"*

Our kids didn't mind, though. It was still 80 degrees. Our condo was on the bottom floor, which went right out onto a ton of green grass and the swimming pool.

Even though I remember having one moment of crying because I wasn't feeling well emotionally, I didn't want to remember the trip that way and so I kept notes of all the things that I loved. Here are a few of them:

Hannah and Jeren frolicking in the ocean. They laughed and had so much fun with Jed as the waves pushed them over while trying to reach for seashells and coral. I couldn't believe Hannah's bravery—I thought she'd be afraid of the ocean.

Me, Kate, and Sadie making a sand castle the shape of Maui.

Jed reaching back and holding my hand on the airplane ride there.

Watching Hannah skip.

Jed, Jeren, and Kate playing football in the rain.

Jeren said, "Just think, I would've been in school, but instead I'm here having 20 times more fun."

Sadie not testing the hot tub before running and jumping in—ouch! It was hot!

Hannah finding a newfound talent—a squeaky cartoon voice.

Sadie and Kate laughed, imagined, and played so well together and it showed when Kate boldly declared, "I'm just so happy that Sadie is my sister. She is so much fun."

Kate was afraid of the whale at the bottom of the pool. It was made out of tiles.

Going to Bubba Gumps to eat. Jeren, eating a ton of shrimp, said, "I'm in heaven."

Kate and Sadie screamed in delight as they followed the waves in the ocean and then pretended they were chasing them on the way out of the ocean.

Our breakfast adventure in a tropical storm. We ended up at a breakfast place that we now fondly call "psycho Barbie place." Jeren covered his eyes because of the drawings of naked people in there.

Swimming with so much rain falling down that you could open your mouth to the sky and get a good swallow.

Kate and I got laughing so hard while swimming in the pool. "Runny Babbit" was part of it.

Sadie taking one arm and shoulder out of her shirt and saying, "I look like Jesus.

Jeren running or walking right into the glass sliding door (thinking it was open, of course).

Okay, so I wrote most of them down. They were all good memories so it was hard to cut any out. The interesting thing is that if I hadn't written down all these wonderful and genuinely good memories, I am almost certain that I would look back at that trip and would think it was a failure since I had to work really hard to not crash emotionally. I did this by writing in my thought journal to counter irrational and negative thinking and I also prayed a ton for heaven's help. Had I not done this, as well as write down all of the good, I probably would have only remembered the parts when I felt like an emotional failure. I would have missed all the wonder and goodness of it—rain and all.

It is an interesting dichotomy how I could find such fleeting moments of joy, yet still be in such unrelenting suffering. A week after Hawaii I wrote of yet another breakdown.

December 17, 2007, *"I had an all-out bawl session. I don't know if I have ever cried that hard."*

I was sad that I wasn't perfectly happy still after what I considered more than enough time in therapy. I knew that I was going to have my fifth child in just six or seven weeks and I was fearful that I wouldn't feel happy by then. I felt that I deserved to have this baby in complete peace and joy. I wanted it so deeply. I was willing to do anything—to go even further.

Marilyn suggested I go to some group therapy at LDS Family Services. I had always been so extremely private with my trial that she and I both hoped group therapy would help. At the very least, it would open up an avenue for talking about it to others and hopefully receive their acceptance anyway. I only went about three times before Brinn was born. I did not allow myself to be too specific with what my OCD entailed. I was too embarrassed. It seemed too stupid and too crazy. I feared they would think, *"What weird woman is this that blinking and her tongue bothers her? That would never bother me. She is crazier than I am!"*

I did learn at group therapy, however, that there are a myriad of situations and trials in people's lives that cause anxiety and depression. However, I still felt hopeless because I could see how their troubles could be fixed but I couldn't see how my memory could be erased. I felt unfixable. I wrote, *"I have realized that I suppress anger and I am just plain angry at a lot of things (even at Heavenly Father)."*

It was hard to admit to myself when I was angry with Heavenly Father. It seemed unforgivable. I knew He loved me and that He did what was best for His children, but how could this be best? I was wasting my life in pain! That can't be best! Why was He allowing me to still suffer when I had done *everything* He had asked of me thus far? I was confused. What could I do more?

I didn't like those feelings at all so I asked for forgiveness and tried to work through them as fast as I could. I needed God. I needed to be on His side so that I could hear His voice leading me along.

I studied and gave the Sunday School Christmas lesson that next week. I wrote, *"My faith has grown. I have been doubting God's omni-science, omnipotence, love, and mercy."* After the lesson I concluded that, "If He knows all things, loves me perfectly, and has all power, then my trials are for my eternal salvation. He wants me to overcome them, and He will take it all away when it's best for me."

As I write this book by going through my journals, I am even amazed at how quickly the Lord answered my questions. I don't think

I realized it then, but now it's like I can see Him right by my side, leading me to answers to my questions. He did it far more quickly and consistently than I realized at the time.

Another example of the Lord being right with me occurred just days after the previous one. I had been feeling like I should get what I want, which was peace, without having to work so hard for it. I learned in sacrament meeting one Sunday that the opposite is true. I wrote, *"I learned it is good to first visualize ourselves overcoming what it is we want to overcome and then work daily to get it. I learned it's okay to have to work hard in order to get what we want."*

The Lord taught me through that speaker in sacrament meeting. I was able to give myself permission to work hard for my emotional health and to not feel "weird" in doing so. It was my happiness and my family's happiness that was at stake! What could be more important than that?

January 13, 2008, Sunday, *"Today was a wonderfully normal and joyful day. Church was good. My testimony of Joseph Smith was strengthened, I like my new 12-year-old's Sunday School class, and I enjoyed holding Sadie in sacrament meeting. I made a yummy meal and then the best apple pie for dessert. After we all cleaned up, I went down to play house with Hannah, Kate, and Sadie. I actually had fun. We pretended a lot— like the pizza man came to the door and Sadie paid him with her fake money in her purse. I even went to the pretend pet store to buy Kate (she was a kitty). Hannah made pretend cookies. I then played the Wii with Jeren. He beat me. After that . . . we went to visit Jed's sister. We went a new route to get there and it was obvious we confused Jeren when we sent him to the door to see if anyone was home and he ran across the street to ring the wrong doorbell! I laughed pretty hard at that one. I have struggled lately but today has been beautiful. I'm so thankful!"*

I added that seemingly benign journal entry to show that the tender mercies of the Lord were upon me. Oh how I loved my children!

How I loved the moments I could feel the joy that I knew was around me! The Lord gave me breathers once in a while and just like the people of Alma, He lifted the burdens on my back even while I was still in bondage.

There were many days and moments like the one above, even amid the trial. I just had to look for them. I also noticed the days that I extended myself to "fake it 'til I make it" were the days I felt better. I felt that my life wasn't a waste. It brought with it the joy of being who I wanted to be, even if it was just for a moment. It brought a sense of accomplishment and a sense of control, like my life and legacy wasn't a victim of my emotions. I realized I was in control of what I became and what I accomplished no matter how my body was feeling. When I was feeling really low, I knew that if I made a list of what I wanted to do and just did it no matter how much my body wanted to just do the bare necessities, that I would inevitably feel better, even if only a little. It was because of the greater control I felt over my life. For example, I loved to cook great meals for my family and always felt very accomplished when I did so.

Work was my antidote. Yet even when I found myself feeling slightly better, I knew the race wasn't over. I knew they were, indeed, just breathers!

The race I was running included a lot of work in the spiritual, physical, and emotional realms. The spiritual included a lot of scripture study, prayer, meditation, temple work, etc. On top of the spiritual I was also keeping up with the physical—as much as I could with being almost nine months pregnant. I had gotten into yoga soon after Sadie was born and had been converted ever since. I did yoga as well as went walking with friends up to the day Brinn was born. Staying physically strong is good for everyone but especially if you have a brain that is not quite on its A game.

On top of the spiritual and physical, I was also working hard on the emotional in therapy. I saw or talked to Marilyn almost weekly.

Although I had gone quite a while without needing her before, at this time I needed her very much. My goal was a peaceful delivery and first few weeks with my fifth baby. Like I said earlier, I even went to a few group therapy sessions until Brinn was born.

I wrote of one of those sessions. January 22, 2008, *"I went to group therapy tonight. I was assigned the opening thought. I used some thoughts from Elder Maxwell's CD I just got called 'All These Things Shall Give Thee Experience.' It went so well that the rest of the discussion was based on that. When I left I felt shame that I was that good and that insightful. 'I'm not healed yet. I don't deserve to help others yet. I'm a fake.'*

"I then remembered that Elder Maxwell said, 'Sometimes we are tutoring others while being tutored' (2007). That made me feel a little better."

I sensed that day that I might have a gift to help others. That scared me. I was tired of seeming like I had it all together on the outside while feeling like a mess on the inside. When would my Reality #1 and Reality #2 finally mesh into one? When would I feel like the person others thought that I already was? I wanted to be her.

CHAPTER 33

Willing to Submit

~

A S THE DAYS dwindled down before my due date, I began to feel more and more sad. I could tell that my time was running out to get on top of myself emotionally so that I could be truly present and happy during the delivery.

January 24, 2008, I wrote, *"Today I hurt. I felt depressed and depressed because I felt depressed. I think I am just so worried about not enjoying my delivery that it makes it worse.*

"I talked to Marilyn tonight. She told me something that I'm not sure if she has ever told me before. She said that 'studies show that OCD needs to be medicated.' I feel a bit relieved and a bit confused. Maybe that's why it's been so hard to do it alone.... I don't know but Marilyn and I are going to try and find a psychiatrist (even the name makes me cringe) for after I have the baby.

"She told me to just know I might or might not have a good experience (emotionally) having my baby but to remember that it is okay because I have a lifetime to enjoy her and love her and that I can go back in meditation and relive it in joy.

"I am grateful for the Lord's omniscience, for my patriarchal blessing, and my own strivings for righteousness. With that combination and the Lord's ability to never lie, I know I will make the changes that I want."

When Marilyn told me that studies show that OCD needs to be medicated, I was a bit shocked for two reasons. Marilyn wasn't a huge advocate of medicine, for one (unless it was coupled with therapy), but mostly I was a bit taken back because it was a new idea for me that I might actually have a "condition" that could be helped with medicine. I knew from the therapist I went to see in Salt Lake in 2002 that I had OCD, but she taught me that I could unlearn my OCD symptoms with practice. Since then I had vacillated between two different ideas about my OCD. Did I have an actual illness or was it just a learned behavior?

At the time I believed that I just had some bad habits of thought to break. Going to a psychiatrist was taking it to a new level and not an idea I necessarily liked. I even hated the word "psychiatrist." It reminded me of how it must feel to be on death row—a death sentence. Nevertheless, I conceded. Any new option sounded like a good one. At least it gave me hope.

I later learned the truth at the psychiatrist. I did have a condition called OCD, not just a bad habit of OCD. Knowing that a lot earlier could have alleviated a lot of guilt. I thought that if nothing was technically wrong with my brain, then I, alone, should have the ability to change it. When I couldn't do it, at least not to the degree that I wanted, I felt guilty and defective in some way. Marilyn gave me hope that day that maybe, after Brinn was born, medicine could be my key to freedom.

It is important to note that even though after four years of therapy I hadn't been healed of the actual OCD, I had learned invaluable tools to cope with and lessen the hold OCD had on me, and I had received the greatest education I could've received on how to live. Marilyn didn't preach life, she lived it, and through hours and hours of talking, listening, and practicing, I began to see myself emulating her and growing in strength in every other aspect of my life. It was a priceless education that I so desperately needed. She re-mothered me in confidence. I will be in debt to her forever for that. Had the OCD gone away quickly, I probably would've quit going to therapy and thus I would've missed out on the years of education that I received from her. I am thankful for that.

The last week before Brinn was born seemed to go on forever. Thank goodness for the comic relief that children bring. Just five days before the big day I wrote, *"When me and the kids were eating lunch we were talking about how the world thinks we are animals. I said that the world may label us as mammals but the Lord never thinks of us as animals. 'Yes he does!' Kate said, 'He thinks of us as sheep!'"*

Finally, in February we met the newest and last member of our little family. We named her Brinn. It was a very special day. We treated this day like we did when Sadie was born and we didn't invite anyone to the hospital except our own children. They were extremely excited. Even though, again, it was very hard for me to tell my parents and Jed's parents that they couldn't see her until day two, it was well worth it. I felt the Lord blessing me because in spite of my trial, I was able to take it all in and enjoy it! It was as quiet and sacred a day as you can get while in a hospital. Being alone as a family bonded us together.

Getting used to having a baby around wasn't as hard as I anticipated. Brinn was a beautiful and very happy baby. We couldn't believe how easy she was. All she brought to our family was joy. However, no matter the good in my life, I was still sick and still struggling to stay on top of my emotions.

I followed through with what Marilyn and I had talked about and went to see a psychiatrist for the first and only time. It wasn't as weird as I thought it would be. I did leave confused, though. He thought that I could have a separate problem on top of the OCD. He said I could have a type of rolling in and out of depression that I just blame on OCD. He wanted to put me on Cymbalta, the anti-depressant, but I was nursing and didn't know if I felt good about that.

Marilyn also wanted me to get tested by another doctor that was supposed to be number one in the state for this particular test. I had to go in and answer all sorts of questions. He then showed me several different pictures. I responded with the first thing that came to my mind when I saw the abstract pictures. I felt like a nut case in there. It was like something I had seen out of the movies. "Okay, now what does this picture remind you of?" I hated it and didn't have much faith that those tests could actually tell anything of a truth about me.

When the tests came back, Marilyn said she wasn't that surprised by most of it. She did say that the next step is for me to be more honest with myself and also with her. I needed to learn to accept all parts of me—the good, bad, and ugly.

How do I do that? I didn't know, but I was ready to try.

Meanwhile, I was still happy Misti while living in Reality #1 according to what my family and Jed's family thought of me. I went about my daily Reality #1 business with my mom and Jed's mom whether it was going shopping, going to lunch, or just talking on the phone about what I deemed to be very superficial. The most important thing to me was getting well and they knew nothing about that. My mom had had the opportunity to know several years earlier but put up her blinders, and so I let her run about blind. She didn't want to know I was hurting and so I didn't tell her.

In many ways, I was getting more and more emotionally healthy. I was, at the very least, getting more emotionally smart. Marilyn had taught me so much about life. She re-mothered me in the lessons I should have learned as a child. She not only taught me about what *assertive* meant but she helped me practice how to be assertive. She helped me become a woman of confidence and control. She taught me that it is right to honor myself as well as others instead of just others. She helped me work out the kinks in all of my relationships especially my relationship with Jed. She helped me see that I put him on a pedestal and me below him. She helped me practice seeing us as the equal partners that we really are. She helped me practice making myself equal to him by changing how I thought, spoke, and interacted with him. So although I wasn't healed yet, I most surely was on the right track to becoming the powerful woman I wanted to be. Unfortunately, all of that education and practice wasn't enough to give me an emotional break.

April 27, 2008, I wrote, *"I feel depressed. I am so tired of fighting it. I want to try medicine but I'm scared that the meds might hurt my nursing Brinn, yet I don't want to quit. Jed and I are going to pray about it."*

A week later I stumbled onto a website that I really don't know how I found. It talked specifically about what meds are good for nursing moms. It said Zoloft was okay. It said that some studies show it not even being in the milk at all. I believed that was an answer to our prayers and so I went ahead and started on Zoloft. I didn't like how I felt on it but was determined to give it a full six weeks to see if I felt a difference.

Two weeks into taking the Zoloft, I was still struggling. I hated how it seemed to numb my good feelings too. I felt like a zombie. May 11th was Mother's Day. My kids were so darling to me yet I couldn't enjoy it fully because I was hurting. They brought me breakfast in bed and then they took me downstairs to the theater room where they had been working the whole day before. They made me a banner and stuck it on the wall. They wrote all kinds of nice things on it. They had a balloon finding game and Hannah gave me a flowerpot with a growing plant. Kate and Sadie drew me pictures and it was all so cute. But sometimes, "cute," and "nice," and "fun" were like emotions hanging around me and not in me. It was like the emotions were mocking me because I couldn't feel them. I could only feel sorry for myself and sorry for my kids that although I was saying all the right things, I couldn't really receive the gifts they were giving me.

We went to sacrament meeting that day at my brother's church because they were blessing their baby. I wrote, *"While at sacrament meeting I had a hard time keeping my emotions in check. I wanted to all-out bawl. I get so tired of fighting to feel peace and happiness. What do I need to do next? I've been in therapy on and off for over four years now, plus I've tried some meds, and I'm almost two weeks into trying Zoloft. What to do? I hate to burden Jed yet I feel alone if I don't. Is this a physical or a spiritual malady I have? The answer is faith. I need more faith—real faith that is the bridge to access God's power."*

If faith could move mountains then that was the only thing that could help me, and even that was iffy. I often wondered how God would follow through with His promise to me that I would be healed. I really couldn't think of anything that could take away my obsessive thoughts except an outright miracle. In order to get a miracle, I knew I needed greater faith.

D&C 46:19 says, "And again, to some it is given to have faith to be healed." I was coveting a gift of the Spirit…is that wrong? Oh how I desperately wanted enough faith to be healed!

I was feeling so hopeless that day. It seemed as if I were in a race against time. I didn't want my kids to grow one more day older without me feeling the joy I knew I could have with them, if only I were well. It was Mother's Day, a reminder that one more year had gone by where I still feared my emotions almost daily. One more year that I didn't feel as present with my children as I wanted. Yes, there had been tons of progress, but I still feared. I still felt trapped in my emotional prison. I still felt like I was at the mercy of my brain.

While at my brother's sacrament meeting, I think it was only by the grace of God that I didn't break down and bawl. That and the fact that there was a 10-year-old blonde boy that sat in front of us that must've had his mom's permission to do his own hair that day. He had a huge goop of blue gel still sitting on the crown of his blonde head.

It made me laugh. Jeren laughed with me. Thankfully even depression couldn't take away my funny bone.

I wanted the gift of faith. I prayed for the gift of faith. I didn't know if Heavenly Father was just teasing me, but it seemed He was constantly showing me examples of how He works in the lives of His other children. Of course He wasn't teasing me. He doesn't work that way. I'm sure He was showing me these small miracles so that my faith might increase.

One such example happened just a day before Mother's Day. In our old ward they had a terrible tragedy. Our old bishop's daughter suddenly died while on her mission. She was just jogging when she collapsed. She was a wonderful girl. Jed and I taught her in our young single adult class when we lived in our house on this hill. It felt like a horrible loss, even to us.

That Monday for family night we, and a couple families, went to their home to plant a tree in memory of their daughter in their yard. When we told them that we brought a beech tree to plant she said, "My daughter loved a beech tree that is on the Logan temple grounds." My friend, who had chosen the tree, said, "No way! Really? I called my dad on Saturday and asked him what kind of live plant to give you and he said, 'I went to the temple (Logan temple) this morning and I saw a really pretty beech tree—get her a beech tree.'"

As many times as we constantly hear that God knows everything, you would think that we wouldn't be surprised when we get a clear cut example of how He does. That wasn't a coincidence. It was the Lord, in His tender mercy, showing that He cares for them and for their loss. I also felt like He was saying, "Misti, I also know your life and your pain and I am taking care of you, too."

At her funeral, her dad—our old bishop—spoke. He quoted a senior missionary couple from their ward that struck me to the core. He said, "God is too wise to err and too good to be unkind."

The Spirit bore testimony to me that that was true. If He was too wise to make a mistake and too good to be unkind then I could conclude that I was meant to grow up in the family that I did. We were meant to be together and learn from one another's mistakes. I was meant to suffer and learn from my sufferings. If God was too good to be unkind then surely all of my suffering would ultimately pay off with equal amounts of joy. It comforted me to know this.

CHAPTER 34

Fearing the Good

~

LIFE BEGAN GETTING better. July 5, 2008, I wrote, "*The meds I just started two months ago, coupled with the things I learned in therapy are working. I feel joy, peace, and more confidence and hope for each day....Life isn't perfect, my emotional health isn't perfect, but it's so much better. I am grateful.*"

I was so relieved to have an emotional breather in my life that I thought I would share the good news with my bishop. July 5, 2008, I told him, "You probably don't hear a lot of good news, so I thought I would share with you some of mine." I told him how good I was feeling emotionally. He asked why and I told him it was probably a combination of all I learned in therapy and the meds I was taking. I told him I wasn't in therapy anymore at that time because Marilyn and I felt I had learned what I needed to and staying with the therapy would just keep me in it.

He thanked me for sharing the good news. Knowing that I have never been able to count on good feelings for too long I warned Bishop with a smile, "I may be back in a month crying," and he laughed and said, "And that's okay."

Two weeks later we took my parents and our little family camping at Downata Hot Springs in Idaho. The first night I battled anxious and despairing feelings. I couldn't sleep soundly that night. I basically meditated all night long while in and out of some degree of sleep. I visualized emotional success seemingly all night. It worked. The Lord helped me recover fully and I really had joy with my family the rest of the time. I learned the power of visualization from Marilyn. Sometimes it worked better than others. When I found myself struggling, and when journaling my negative thoughts wasn't enough, I would try to find a moment to visualize. It was best for me if I were lying down on my back. I would visualize myself doing exactly what I was doing at the time or what I wanted to do that day with the exact feelings I wanted to feel. I visualized doing those things in peace. Sometimes it was enough to get me going on the right emotional track and I could ride that train for a while with ease. It basically got me in the right frame of mind. Sometimes I would visualize several times a day. I even did it, when necessary, on our way to dinner on date nights. Jed soon understood what I meant when I said I was going to lay my seat down for a few minutes. Visualization had immense power to redirect me in a positive direction.

That summer I deemed as one of my best in many years. I had many good days and I experienced many good moments. I took turns taking the kids out at night to sit on the porch and look at the stars. One night I took Sadie out front and we lay on the grass as we looked at the stars. They were beautiful. Sadie asked how come the stars were circles and then she would laugh so hard that I just had to tickle her (which she loves). Sadie's profound statement of the summer was, *"If you want to keep living, you got to keep breathing."* At age four she was almost always laughing unless she was screaming, which she did readily if she didn't get her way. She was always up to something and always leaving a mess. Jed called her "a one-man wrecking crew."

That summer was so wonderful that I didn't want it to end. I took kids on long bike rides, went on kid dates, and enjoyed Brinn immensely. I wrote, *"This has been the best summer. I have enjoyed my family so much. I am not looking forward to them being at school all day."*

I had felt so good lately that I freely spoke of my happiness to Jed one day. Just talking about the good really scared me and threw me for a loop.

That was another prison (made out of a false belief) that I put around myself—don't talk about the good times or you might start feeling depressed again. If I talked about the good, I would start questioning myself. What if I can't rely on the medicine? What if it quits working? What if Jed expects me to be healed now that I told him I am doing better? I started to feel myself going down.

On August 20, 2008, I wrote, *"I have struggled on and off for four days now. I am still concluding what to do about it. Where I am now is that this medicine is the right medicine for me for now, that Marilyn's teachings were the right teachings for me and with this thorn in my flesh I must keep practicing what she taught me until the Lord heals me and makes me strong as he has promised.*

"The Olympics in Beijing have been on TV and as I watched a gymnast get her long awaited gold medal I thought of myself. I am not in a gym working on my body day in and day out, but I am working on my mind, body, and spirit day in and day out. Even when I want to quit and wallow in self-pity a while, I don't stay sitting. I struggle to stand and while enduring the pain, I work hard and I exercise hope and trust and faith. My gold medal is every time I get peace for days, weeks, or months, but my ultimate gold medal will be when I am resting in my Heavenly Father's arms knowing that through it all I did everything my Heavenly Father wanted me to."

Jed took Jeren, Hannah, and Kate to Lake Powell with his family the last week in August. I stayed home with Sadie and baby Brinn. We went to the material store, bought material to make a blanket for each kid, and then went to Jed's grandma's house to sew around the edges of all the blankets. I remember feeling a lot of anxiety the whole time, but felt good that at least I was doing something productive.

While Jed was gone, on August 25, 2008, I wrote, *"I struggled emotionally today. I know why I've digressed. It is stress—the stress of being home without Jed and all my kids with me, the stress of 'are they okay?', the stress of school starting, am I a good enough school mom, how about piano mom?, the stress of homework and running around in the car all the time, the stress of feeling like I have no control over my schedule and what I do, and the stress of feeling inadequate to get better at dealing with stress!"*

I recognized that stress of any kind could throw me for a loop if I wasn't careful. Life for me really was like trying to walk on an emotional tight rope. As long as I could stay calm and focused on my every step or emotional thought, I was okay. Just a few stresses, or wiggles of the rope, could send me down holding on for dear emotional life.

Two days later I canned salsa all day with my mom. I wrote, *"I really had to work at staying in the right frame of mind today. I would say a quick prayer or a quick meditation. It's hard work getting back to where it is easy to stay peaceful. Tonight I was feeling anxious. I knelt in the kitchen to say my night prayers. I testify that I felt the Holy Ghost enter me and bring me peace."*

Oh what an understatement to say that I was grateful for the gift of the Holy Ghost! Although I still struggled, the Holy Ghost brought me hope that everything was going to be okay. That was a powerful antidote to the despair that was ever ready to take me down the second that I would give in to even the smallest pity party. The most important thing was being worthy of the Spirit and striving to keep Him with me. It was this very Spirit that inspired my next move in the healing process. A move that was absolutely necessary.

Chapter 35

Quest to Heal All The Way

~

W HEN I FOUND myself struggling yet again after a wonderful reprieve of a summer, I asked myself, "When would this have a final end?" For four and a half years I had been working on and off in counseling. Marilyn and I both felt that she had taken me as far as she could. I was doing tons better and had learned so much from her, yet it wasn't enough. I didn't feel I was at the top of the ladder and on safe ground yet. I felt so close to being whole that I said I could almost taste it. I was just done. I felt done with this whole trial. I didn't want to do it anymore. I had just experienced my most wonderful summer yet, however, it ended sourly. Just before Jed went to Lake Powell with the older kids and definitely while he was gone I felt as bad as ever. No matter how much I had learned and improved, when it hurt, it hurt. Sometimes it hurt worse because of self-pity. I listened to Satan say, "Look at all you have done to get over this and you are still no better off. You will never escape this hole."

Shortly after they returned from Lake Powell, I decided I had had enough. Jed was on the couch watching TV when I came in, sat on the arm of the chair and unapologetically said, "I want to be healed. And if it is not the Lord's time to heal me then I want to know. Either way, just knowing His will for me, will give me strength."

Jed had a blank look on his face and just listened. I said, "I want to know if you will come with me to see Bishop so I can ask both of you to fast for me on this next fast Sunday."

As much as I know Jed, I know he thought I was out of my mind, but he dutifully said he would. He went with me to see Bishop the Sunday before fast Sunday. He agreed that he would fast with us. This is an excerpt from my journal entry on August 31, 2008.

"I met with Bishop after church. I asked him if he, along with Jed and I, would fast for me. I asked if we could end our fast with a priesthood blessing on Sunday. The purpose of the fast and blessing of course is that I want to be healed all the way. I'm doing better now than I ever have, but I still don't feel emotionally safe. I explained to Bishop that I feel that there are two major neural pathways in my brain (neural pathways are where automatic thoughts flow fast and subconsciously and thus cause good or bad feelings). For me, the biggest pathway is the one that causes bad feelings because since I was eleven that's the one that has been used and formed. The other one is what I've been working so hard on for 4 ½ years in and out of therapy, prayer, meditation, journaling, and so forth. I feel fabulous when my automatic thoughts are flowing down that one. The problem I have now is that I feel like I'm always one negative thought from being pulled down into the negative neural pathway. It's so easy to step off the cliff, so to speak, and just fall down and then it takes so much emotional energy to get back to where I want to be. I feel so close to being healed enough to where I can truly feel safe. Where I could maybe even go a year or two without a relapse or maybe more. I feel like I'm almost there but that I need or want the Lord to heal those neural pathways that are so easy to slip into for me. I know He can if it is His will. He blessed the three Nephites that they would not feel sorrow except for the sins of the world (3 Nephi 28:9). I want to not feel emotional pain unless the situation calls for it. But if it is not the Lord's will, I want to know. If he wants me to continue to struggle and learn line upon line and precept upon precept then that is obviously what

is best for me and I will do that. I am just seeking for healing and to know His will concerning my cross that I have carried for so long."

The next Sunday, Bishop gave me a beautiful blessing. This is my journal entry on Sunday, September 7, 2008.

"I am shaking. I haven't eaten in over 24 hours. Jed and I just got back from Bishop's office where he and Jed gave me a Priesthood blessing for the healing of the sick and afflicted. This was done to conclude our fast together. I feel so emotional, so grateful, and awestruck. I finally know. This is what I have wanted for so long now. We petitioned the Lord through fasting, prayer, and temple worship and He responded. Jed anointed me with the oil and Bishop gave me the blessing. It was beautiful because I felt Heavenly Father's Spirit near. Through the blessing I know that one day I will have peace that doesn't go away and the way he worded it was so poetic and filled me with assurance and hope....He said, 'Peace that will fill your days, the kind of peace that doesn't end.' He assured me I am going to be healed but not yet, that I would in the Lord's time....He blessed me that as I have depressing, hopeless, and helpless thoughts that I might be able to overcome that and be happy in my mind. He told me I am 'a marvelous mother' and 'the Lord has compassion' on me and loves me. He told me that specifically there is one sister that as I open up to her she will be a strength to me such as I have not known before; that we will have a bond and a love. I am so grateful and excited about that. I wonder which sister it is and pray I will have that blessing soon.

"After the blessing both Bishop and I were crying. I told Bishop sincerely that I am not disappointed. I know it is His will and that is all I want. Of course I want to be healed now, but it is so wonderful to know it will happen gloriously in the future. Bishop said he wanted to be disappointed but he's not. He wanted to bless me with healing but the Spirit directed otherwise....

"When I pulled into my garage the song, 'Be Still My Soul' came on the radio. That was not a coincidence. It is beautiful and full of truth. I stayed in the car and listened and cried and even sobbed for a myriad of reasons."

After receiving that blessing, I felt immensely grateful to know the will of the Lord. It lifted the guilt that I sometimes had. What if the Lord wants me to be healed by now, but I'm not because I'm lacking in some way? What if I am just defective and I don't have the inner strength to overcome? What if every time I fall into my emotional pits I am letting the Lord down? What if He is disappointed in me when I am hurting and have a hard time being happy? These and many other questions had been weighing on me, but after the blessing I knew that it wasn't the will of the Lord that I be healed yet. I still had something else to learn. He was okay with me still struggling and learning by experience. There was nothing wrong with me, meaning my spirit, but my body was still imperfect. He assured me that I would feel the peace that I so desperately wanted, sometime in the future. I trusted that. It brought me much joy and happy anticipation.

However, OCD is still OCD and I still had it. It wasn't fun to experience it even after the blessing but at least I then knew it was okay. It was the Lord's will. The constant Tourette's of my brain, at times, was enough to make me feel crazy. It still hurt, but the guilt was gone. For that, I was very grateful.

The very next morning after the blessing when the realities of life and motherhood set in, when piano practice, homework, and other daily stresses were staring me in the face along with the reality that I was still brain-sick, I recognized exactly where the adversary would attack me. He would whisper in my ear, *"God said you weren't supposed to be healed yet and so you shouldn't even try to get better. You should just wallow in your misery because it is what God wants. He wants you to suffer. That's how you will learn. Don't even try."* I knew these whispers would be a temptation for me. I prayed fervently for help. This was my prayer. I wrote it down right after I felt the Spirit confirm its truth.

September 8, 2008, *"I thank thee for the blessing I received and I am so thankful to know that one day I will have 'peace that doesn't end.'*

Please help me now as I go day to day to not allow myself to give in to my weakness and listen to the adversary say, 'It's what God wants.' Help me to remember that thou wants me to strive and struggle and gain strength and to derive strength from the valiant spirit and the elect daughter that I am (according to Heavenly Father's words in my Patriarchal blessing). That thou wants me to get stronger each day.'"

As I prayed, the Holy Ghost filled my heart. What I prayed for was truth and I knew it would help me in the hard days ahead.

I still had good and bad days, but overall it was a more secure and hopeful time. I finally knew what the Lord's will was for me and I had hope in what the future would bring. However, there were times when the pain was as hard as ever to bear.

I remember one night in particular that Jed and I were out on a date but I was so depressed that I could hardly stand it. What made it worse was that Jed is human, too. He was sick of helping me and didn't even want to talk about it. I sobbed and sobbed. I felt so alone. Even Jed was tired of it. I felt I had no one to turn to. It was a dark night. One of the darkest.

However, with never ending prayers, the Lord continued to help me understand my own strength. I was in the temple one day and in my mind the Lord told me to be "big, bold, and beautiful." I had never allowed myself to be too big or bold and deep down I thought that being beautiful was some kind of sin. So, this pronouncement of the Spirit was somewhat of a surprise to me. However, it rang true. I knew heeding that counsel would be a must for me.

Also, once while in the Ogden Temple, the Lord gave me a present. For a few seconds I sensed my own power and strength from before I came here. It is hard to describe, other than for just a moment the valiant spirit daughter I was before I was born overpowered me in the present and gave me a moment's heavenly perspective of all that I truly am and can be. That feeling sustained me many times since. When I remember that experience, I can somehow feel it again and again.

Have you ever thought of how strong and resolute you were before you came here? We are not just an accumulation of all of our earthly experiences. We are literal children of God who lived with Him for eons of time. We are so much more than what we know of our earthly selves. Sometimes we don't even know much about our earthly selves. As we try to figure out who we are here on earth, we often make the mistake of comparing our weaknesses with other people's strengths. We forget how strong and valiant we were before we came here. Instead, we just feel our mortality so keenly that we compare our trials in our Reality #2 with what we see on the outside of others (their Reality #1). We forget that every person has weaknesses to overcome. We can't always see past the Reality #1 of others. What a tool of the devil it is to compare ourselves to others! How dangerous to our very souls that can be!

One date night Jed and I invited another couple to go to dinner with us. We had a nice dinner with a lot of catching up to do since we didn't see them all that often. After dinner, my friend and I had a moment to talk alone. She confided in me her frustrations about her weight and her friend issues. She looked at me and said, "I look at you and think 'if only.'"

What? She looks at me and thinks, "if only"? I almost laughed out loud! I surprised myself by saying, "I have things that I don't tell everybody that I struggle with, too." She said, "Well, one day tell me, why don't you." I said, "Okay" and I told her of my struggle with depression and anxiety. I didn't go into detail. I didn't need to. She immediately cried and said she just got diagnosed with depression too. She no longer felt alone and neither did I. Often I had looked at her and thought, "If only I had a healthy brain like she does." Satan had had his way with the both of us. He said, "Compare yourself to her," and we both listened.

As life went on, nothing new occurred; I continued to go in and out of good and hard times. I had a new motto. "I can be happy and live life fully even amid my 'brain issues.'" I didn't want to feel like I was wasting my life away. I wanted to live with purpose.

I tried to incorporate this new motto in my life. I had known for some time of a lady in my ward that was struggling deeply with depression. I don't know if it was my pride that kept me from calling her or if it was my false belief that I couldn't help someone else while I was still struggling myself on and off. Nonetheless, I had been thinking of her for some time. The Spirit kept nudging me to go to her. I kept putting it off until one night I was making soup and I accidentally started doubling the recipe. I thought, "Who can I give the extra to?" Immediately I thought of this sister and her husband. I knew that I should do it and I finally had the strength to follow through. I called and told them I was coming. When I brought the food to the door I asked if I could talk to them. We sat in their living room and in going against all of the pretense I had become accustomed to, I told them that I too had struggled with depression and anxiety. I told them I had OCD but that I had been taught by a wonderful counselor and that she had helped me a lot. As I talked she smiled and said that I was an answer to her prayers that day. She had been struggling with the idea of going to see a therapist. Her husband had been urging her to go for some time. I gave her Marilyn's phone number.

I left there feeling so incredibly privileged to have been an instrument in the Lord's hands. However, I struggled the next day because of it. I called Marilyn for a "reality check" as she called it. I asked her how she did it. How does she help other people without getting down herself? She said, "I have hope for them. It's kind of like someone going to a hospital and the doctor knowing certain things can help them. I think that since the Lord wants you to help others that He will strengthen and sustain you." She also told me to give myself permission to go slowly and only help other people as I feel strong enough to do so. I felt better after talking to her.

Ever since the September blessing, seven months previous, I continually asked to be shown who this sister was that the Lord promised me would be a strength to me like I had "not known before." Once in a while I would wonder if it was this person or that person. I even wondered if I would receive strength from a sister by giving help to her. It wasn't until I was sick physically that I finally found her.

CHAPTER 36

Meeting My "Special Sister"

~

I BEGAN HAVING REOCCURRING yeast infections. My OB would always give me the same prescription over and over. Through a friend I found a new doctor, who along with modern medicine, also used natural herbs and vitamins for healing. It felt right. I found out I had low thyroid, high cholesterol, low white blood cell count, low vitamins, almost no progesterone. On top of all that and worst of all, I had systemic Candida (yeast that spreads throughout the body). I learned that I needed to go on the Candida diet to get rid of it. I needed to starve the yeast in my body. No sugar, no bread, no carbs at all. Basically, no fun. I could only eat protein and vegetables. It was so hard.

I remember one night crying to Jed. "I know I shouldn't complain," I said, "but I have dealt with really hard emotional issues almost my whole life. Why do I have to go through this now? This is so hard too. I don't feel good. I want to nap twice a day and now I can't eat anything satisfying."

I wouldn't have been crying had I known that the issue I was complaining about having was the exact issue that would lead me on the path I had been praying to find! It would lead me to the sister that would be "a strength to me such as I had not known before." And if anyone needed strength, I did. At that time, I needed it in both body and mind. I was literally worn down, inside and out.

A few weeks after I started the diet, I had a neighbor who knew I had Candida tell me of a lady who helped her daughter get rid of mono very quickly and thought that maybe she could help me. I learned her name was Janice. I called her and told her I had Candida. I asked if she could help me, she said she could. I was excited and a bit nervous to meet her. I think deep down I knew she could help me. I also knew that Jed would not approve of natural healers. I wondered if God would approve.

The first time I drove to her home I was surprised and grateful to see that she wasn't in some dark shack with purple velvet curtains with candles in it. She lived in a normal, affluent part of town. Her house was big and nice and had beautiful rock on the outside. I was told to walk down a steep driveway on the left side of the house and knock on the door down there. She had her own office down there. I was nervous and excited the first time I went. Again, I was surprised that she looked so normal. She had on nice, not out-dated clothes, and her toes looked like she got pedicures quite frequently. She had short but not really short auburn hair. Much to my surprise, Janice seemed normal. She welcomed me in and had me take a seat in a very bright, naturally lit room that overlooked the valley. I felt comfortable yet still a bit nervous.

She asked me to tell her about my symptoms. While I was talking, it seemed she was both here and there. She seemed to be listening to me while she was listening, or paying attention, to something else. It was the weirdest thing I had ever seen a Latter-day Saint do. By my 'energy' she could tell me what supplements to take and how much. She said she was just testing and asking my body. Right away she told me that I was "sick because of emotional stuff." She said that if I could get rid of the emotional toxins I would be able to eat normally. Otherwise I would have to eat the Candida diet almost all of the time.

I had never really correlated physical symptoms with the emotional. I always thought they were totally separate; however, it made complete sense. Considering the years I spent in emotional distress, it was no wonder my body was finally a wreck!

She felt impressed to tell me, "You have a journey to be on and probably because of this you aren't on that journey yet. It's something you are supposed to do." Then she paused a bit and said, "It is a giant thing or a really big mission you are to do. Does that ring a bell to you?"

When she asked me that I was surprised. I felt grateful, a little weirded out, and agreeing all at the same time. Was I supposed to be here? Why did I feel so comfortable when it felt like this might be wrong? How could she know that about me? I had felt like I had a giant journey to be on but of course never knew how.

Interestingly, just three weeks earlier, after hearing a woman speak who overcame MS, I wrote this in my journal, *"A lady with MS... said that through trial you find your voice. I believe my voice on the subject of my trial will be heard by many."*

I did believe that, yet at the time, I had no idea how I would first get through my trial.

Janice, a woman I had known for an hour, confirmed what the Spirit had whispered to me just a few weeks previous and again it rang true; but how did she know that?

I didn't fully understand what I had learned all of my life in church; that God really does give some of His children the gift of healing in order to benefit His other children. I had learned about gifts of the Spirit (in D&C 46); however, I had never really understood it, and seeing it in action bewildered me. The gift that Janice and people like her have is not the same as the priesthood. The priesthood is the power to act in the name of God on the earth. That is *very* different from the gift of healing that I witnessed in Janice. Hers is a gift of intuitiveness. She is blessed with a knowing of what people need

275

physically or what they need to let go of emotionally in order to heal. It was fascinating to me, yet I wanted to make sure that it was what Heavenly Father wanted me to go forward with.

May 27, 2009, *"This morning I went to Janice a second time, but this time it was for emotional work. I prayed that I would know if Heavenly Father approves of me going to her for more healing. I think he does."*

Since the way Janice did emotional work was so different from conventional therapists, I was concerned about making sure it was sanctioned by God for me to do. If it wasn't, I would have quit, but I kept getting the feeling that it was right. It went against my natural inclination. She knew what I needed to release, forgive, and heal by listening to the Spirit direct her. She says she has her own angels and my angels helping her. The scriptures say that there are different gifts of the Spirit and that one is the gift of healing. I prayed a lot to know if her gift was from God.

It was strange and totally against my own grain to accept her when on the surface I wondered if it was against my religion. Through much prayer I realized that she was the "sister" that Bishop mentioned during the blessing that he gave to me in September of 2008. He said, "There is one sister that as you open up to her will be a strength to you such as you have not known before."

Could there be anything further from what I have "not known before" than the gift that she has? For her help in my healing journey I will love her through all eternity. She has been my other angel. I have since learned that other people claim to have the same gifts to help others that Janice does, but many are listening to the wrong spirit. Jesus gave us a sure way to judge. He said, "Ye shall know them by their fruits.... Every good tree bringeth forth good fruit; but a corrupt tree bringeth forth evil fruit. A good tree cannot bring forth evil fruit, neither can a corrupt tree bring forth good fruit" (Matthew 7: 16–18). I learned through much prayer and experience that she was, in fact, "a good tree." Knowing this helped me move forward with what she outlined for me.

Not only did we work on my emotional toxins, but we worked very hard to get rid of the Candida in my body. I stayed on the horrible Candida diet, took the natural supplements she gave me, and I used her SOQI Bed. I nicknamed it the "redbed" because it emits infrared rays into the body for healing. It feels like a tanning bed but without the bad cancer-causing rays; and unfortunately, no tan.

In between the time that I first went to see her and the third or fourth time, I had a mothering breakdown. How could I possibly do all that I need to do for each child? I wrote, *"I feel like I'm failing, that I'm trapped in what I can do for my children because of my limitations."*

I literally felt like I was failing every one of my children. That is not an easy false belief to overcome, nor is it comfortable to believe. It took so much work to keep myself on my emotional balance beam as well as staying on the Candida diet that I felt torn. I knew I needed to take care of myself so that I could be a good parent, but I felt terribly guilty not being with my kids every second. I had no idea how to solve that.

I always made sure I had something to be uncomfortable about. I was good at that. I needed something to keep me "humble." Another false belief hard at work!

Because of the overwhelming stress I was feeling, I once again took advantage of the priesthood holders in my life—Jed and my bishop.

Sunday, June 7th I asked Jed and Bishop to give me a blessing. Jed was the mouthpiece. This is what I wrote on that day—*"Jed gave the blessing. He told me to be assured that the words he would speak are from Heavenly Father. He blessed me that all the blessings I had been given concerning this trial would work together or that I will understand how they will work together. He blessed me to come to understand the gift of healing which is the gift of the Spirit and to pray for it—to pray for the gift to be healed. He also said that the time I spend away from the kids getting better is actually indirectly strengthening them as they see my strength. (That is a relief since I do spend a lot of time and energy in getting better and stronger from my trial.) He blessed me with faith that during the times of ebb and flow I would remember how much I have progressed. He told me through the blessing that our kids would continue to make right decisions as I work hard to provide a safe environment for them. He told me to take the time to take care of me and that it's not time away from the kids. I cried during the whole blessing. Afterwards I hugged him so fervently with gratitude for a worthy husband. I felt the Spirit during the blessing and I knew that it was from God. Yet, the funny thing was that most of Jed's talk and advice after (while still with Bishop) bugged me. I realized, even more, that the blessing was from Heaven because when he talked outside of the blessing, it didn't feel as right."*

I was learning to discern between man and God.

CHAPTER 37

Gifts of the Spirit at Work

~

AT THIS POINT in my own healing journey a whole new world was opening up to me. Since I didn't usually write while I was in a session with Janice, as soon as I could when I got home I got out my journal and wrote all that I could remember.

On June 9, 2009, I wrote, *"Janice said I have abandonment issues with Jed because of my dad. My dad abandoned me emotionally when I needed help as a teenager when he told me what I should be worrying about. Instead of helping me, he forced me to pretend all was well. Today we did some emotional work to let go and forgive him as well as myself for not standing up and taking care of me or demanding they take care of me when I needed it. She also included Jed in having me release worry that he would abandon me. Then...she went through some 'DNA releasing.' It all seemed very new and weird but strangely right. Here are a few reasons why I think she has a real gift and Heavenly Father uses her to heal others. With the DNA thing—as she went through her book of ailments, she was silently writing down which things in my DNA we needed to heal. She says she knows this through the Spirit and my energy. She was going along fine and then I started thinking how Jed and Marilyn (my old and some-times present therapist) would think this is so weird and wrong. Just then Janice stopped, had me say something (can't remember) and then going back to her book with a smile and a sigh she said, 'There was one on that page but you wouldn't let me have it.'*

"When we were going through my DNA stuff (which is still confusing to me), one was my fingernails and how I'm worried I would hit someone and as she did the affirmation, which is not a script, she talked about how it's okay for me to reach out and that I won't hurt them. I never told her that at times, because of what my mom told me as a kid, I've had some disturbing thoughts of stabbing someone. How could she have known that?

"She also said this, 'Your children are your very own.' I never told her that I feel like my mom steps on my toes and I feel less like my children are mine. There was much more but it's late and unfortunately I can't remember it all. She talked of letting go of control—'no one can control anyway', she said.

"I asked her about my mission. She said she could only help me heal so that I'd be free to feel the Spirit and be guided myself."

It made me trust Janice even more when she said that she couldn't tell me what my mission was or what I needed to do. She made it clear that her only job was to help me heal and that in doing so, I would be able to feel the Spirit easier. She called it "mud." She was helping me get rid of all the mud on me that had built up over the years so that I would then have greater power to find and fulfill my own mission.

It was exactly what the Spirit taught me that very day. I felt it so profoundly that I quickly wrote it down. I wrote, *"Heavenly Father wants us to use the Atonement to free ourselves of all guilt, anxiety, fears, grudges, etc., because after taking that action, however many times needed, we are freeing ourselves up for the Spirit to speak to us and allowing us to find and fulfill our missions in life."*

Looking back I can see what a truth that is! Guilt, anxiety, fears, grudges, etc., confuse us and can easily distract us from all the power and goodness inside us. The Lord is the giver of our power and goodness. He intends for us to use that power to benefit His other children until they can do the same. Goodness and power can spread and grow just as evil and bondage can. However, before we can access that power, we need the Atonement to help us clear all the excess garbage off of us (i.e., guilt, anxiety, fears, grudges, etc.). It isn't easy, but when, through the Savior, we have our rocks lifted out of our backpack and feel the lightness of soul, we will realize that it was worth every sacrifice it took to get there. It takes both parties to make it complete even though our part is minuscule compared to His grand contribution.

After these sessions, I was beginning to recognize how much lighter and better I was feeling. When something is wonderful you want to share it, but I had no one. I tried to talk to Jed about it but quickly realized that he had a huge wall in front of him made out of critical, skeptical, and immovable bricks. He didn't believe that Janice had a gift to help me, but to his beautiful credit, he never tried to discourage me to go nor did he try to control the amount of money I spent there. There was just an unspoken rule of don't talk don't tell.

On June 24, 2009, I wrote of an interesting experience just trying to get to Janice's. Heaven was definitely on my side that day. Someone from the other side wanted me to make that appointment!

I wrote, *"On my way there, my car wasn't reacting when I pushed on the gas. I realized I was running out of gas—in fact—out of gas. I was literally coasting. I was praying out loud, 'Heavenly Father, Pease help me get to the gas station.' I kept repeating it. I was going so slow. I pulled over a bit so cars could pass me. I went up a little hill, barely made it, and coasted around the corner on Shepard Lane, and barely—I mean barely—coasted into a gas stall to refuel at Smith's. My car literally died right there where I needed to be! I said a few prayers of thanks.*

"I made it to my appointment with Janice a bit late. It was a good session. It's still weird but it gets a little less so each time. She told me to look

in the mirror each morning and as I'm looking right in my own eyes say 'I love you' over and over again until I laugh or cry. I'm supposed to do this for a month.

"*She told me to pray for the Lord to change some of my genetics or DNA that got passed down to me that I don't like (behavioral tendencies, etc.). This made me think of Jed's blessing where he counseled me to pray for the gift of faith to be healed. I'm not sure why, but it did.*

"*She felt impressed that I feel I can't live up to some of my neighbors—so true. We worked through that.*

"*She felt that I need to go to the library and find three books on the goodness in womanhood and mothering—not what I should be doing. She said, 'I feel that you don't need a book on what you should be doing—that you are doing 98% of all those things anyway.'*

"*She said, 'I'm hearing that you are so pure. You are the most beautiful woman I've seen and you are so pure with so many spiritual gifts.'*"

Well, that solidified it! With a compliment like that, she must be the real thing!

On a much more serious note, words will never describe the water that Janice was to my thirsty soul. I was beginning to heal in a deeper way than ever before and that hope was delicious.

As the summer wore on and as I continued to see Janice every couple of weeks or so, I could feel myself go in and out of actually feeling the joy in my life. And to my surprise, I was feeling it more than I wasn't, although I still didn't feel healed yet or "safe," as I liked to put it. I was still doing all that I could do to not fall off the OCD cliff, so to speak. I took my vitamins, said my affirmations (i.e., "I love myself"), meditated, prayed, and as always I studied my scriptures.

Through this time I was noticing how much fun I was having with my family. One Sunday in particular I made a yummy peppered roast and horseradish sauce that I was so proud of because my family loved it. We went outside and played kickball as a family in our backyard.

Later that night, we laughed and laughed together as we played charades with Taboo cards. Our 5-year-old Sadie had a creative way of charading an "apple tree." She stood all solemn-faced with legs tight together and teardrop hands at the end of her straight out "T" arms. For a little girl who had never played charades before, we knew right what she was depicting. As parents often do, we thought she was brilliant! We laughed over that one.

I felt it! I not only saw the joy I should be feeling but I felt it! This was happening more and more and I was beginning to realize something was happening…I was healing. I was healing above and beyond the healing I had received from my hard work in therapy. That's not to say that the work wasn't necessary. The therapy I received from Marilyn was crucial. I needed that education, but even she said at the end that I could learn nothing more from her. She and I both knew that the part she was to play in my life was done. It was accomplished. The Lord then led me to the next person who could help me take that next step in healing. I knew that person was Janice.

July 13, 2009, *"Wow. All I can say is 'wow.' I just got back from Janice's. I feel so much better now. When I first got there she said, 'You have a tight right hip' and something about a block or tightness in my midsection. She had me lie down and she showed me how my right hip really felt tighter than my left. She wiggled it and some small adjustments and it felt better. But what was more astonishing was that just this morning while lying on my back, I noticed a big knot in my gut and Janice knew about it before I even lay down. She asked if she could massage my stomach and she got rid of the knot! Then she threw the built up negative energy away from me and I felt a definite relaxing after all that.*

"She then did some 'tapping' with me (EFT—emotional frequency technique). That's where I tap some part of my face, head, chest, or hand while I repeat what she has me say. Today it had to do with forgiving my parents, my aunt, and some childhood things. After all the emotional work,

283

my head hurt. I didn't say anything and she just came over and started putting pressure at the base of my head and such, and after a few minutes she laid my head back down and the headache or tension was gone. Janice told me what vitamins and medicine (from the doctor) to keep or quit taking. She said that after doing all that releasing, I didn't need as much. She said we all have seven layers and we got through to your second layer, which is really good. I am to tell myself I love myself 40 times a day. She said it's all about retraining the brain. When deciding when I should come back she said, 'I feel like you should come back in two weeks. You want to move faster than most.' Isn't that the truth!

"As weird as this all is, I'm beginning to feel better—a lot better.

"She said, 'I get that you had OCD last year but not this year.' I said, 'Well, just lately I've had OCD 'triggers' that have sent me down that path and she smiled and said, 'We've done a lot of work and this is a new week. We still have 2 layers and that's what we need to release next time (in 2 weeks).' She said if OCD tempters come, say, 'I am strong and powerful.' She said that those words are for me."

When Janice told me that I had OCD last year but not this year, my heart took courage. I wanted to believe it, but at the same time I dared not believe it. How wonderful that would be, I could hardly imagine. I pondered it a lot and prayed for it to be true. Later that very day, I had a sacred experience that confirmed what she said. It was my greatest desire.

July 14, 2009, *"I hesitate in writing this, however, it has presented itself in my heart three times since yesterday. While meditating yesterday afternoon I felt a whisper that I now have the gift of faith to be healed. I asked over and over in my mind and kept feeling the Spirit. Elder Oaks once said that if you get a 'yes' answer to something you want, then ask again, so I did last night and again this morning and I felt the peace of the Spirit both times.... I am so grateful and admittedly a little scared, but I'm pushing it with faith."*

That right there was one of my most treasured and sacred experiences. I remember that the thought that came to my mind that I had "the gift of faith to be healed" was very unsolicited and quite surprising like, "Where did that come from?"

Obviously, I liked it very much, since that is what I have wanted ever since I was little. Ever since Jed had told me in a blessing to seek for the gift of faith to be healed, I had done just that. I studied it and prayed for it. I specifically asked Heavenly Father if He might grant me that gift by July. So, after I felt that impression, I immediately asked Heavenly Father in my mind if that was for real. "Did that come from you?" I felt the Spirit powerfully. Everyone feels the Spirit differently. For me, it is this feeling in my heart like a butterfly is taking over the pumping. Of course, the universal feeling is the same. It is a feeling of peace and joy. Two more times the same thought came to me: "You have the gift of faith to be healed." Each time I asked if it was for real. My faith and my hope increased as I received the same spiritual confirmation: "Yes."

I was hesitant to tell Jed of my impressions. What if he thought that I was crazy? What if he wouldn't support me in it? I felt vulnerable and wanted my experience to be validated by him. I trusted my spiritual instincts but I had no proof yet. I still wasn't healed. It was still an act of faith.

It was the next morning when I finally had the courage to tell him. When I said I needed to talk to him I'm sure his heart sunk. Historically that meant I was falling emotionally and I needed him to lean on. He sat on the hearth of the fireplace in our room. I knelt on the ground in front of him. I said that I had felt several times in the last 24 hours that I have been blessed with the gift of faith to be healed. To my relief, Jed smiled really big and said, "That is great news." As we knelt down to say our morning prayers, I was a little emotional, but with happy anticipation this time.

Even though Jed said the right thing, I'm not sure how much he really believed me. However, this much I knew; he was getting as tired of helping me as I was of experiencing the pain and daily uncertainty. We both exercised hope that this was finally the real deal. We both looked forward to my being healed.

CHAPTER 38

Is This For Real?

∽

JULY 15, 2009, *"I went to the temple by myself. It was very crowded and quite warm—not good if you are tired. Glad I went. Yes, I believe and may even dare say 'I know' I have been granted the gift of faith to be healed.... The Lord answered my prayers that I would be blessed with the gift of faith to be healed…and I am so grateful. It almost doesn't seem real—but it is—I have been assured it is by the Spirit at least five times."*

Here I had been given assurance that I now had the faith to be healed, yet I wasn't healed. I had made some real progress with Janice but I still had some very hard days. It was awkward and wonderful at the same time. Never before had hope and pain battled so fiercely inside me. I had great hope, almost an assurance, that I would be healed soon, yet I wasn't. I struggled, I hurt, I obsessed, and I hoped all at the same time.

July 24, 2009, *"Just now I had one of my most sacred moments. I've had a hard OCD day. I just knelt down and prayed, thanking Heavenly Father that though in pain 'my table is spread.' Then I asked, 'Will thou heal me of my OCD, depression, and anxiety problems and my tendency to worry and fear a lot?' As I asked that or right after, I felt the most power-ful spirit come over me. I didn't want to move. At first I was surprised that I could get an answer like that after having such a normal day (I just finished watching a princess movie with my girls). I asked what it meant and I thought of a verse in D&C section 6 that says, 'What greater witness can you have than from God.' My eyes are wet with tears of gratitude that I am blessed to tangibly feel the Spirit and know that Heavenly Father is very real and He cares about me and hears me. After all this time He is promising to heal me. I don't know how or exactly when but I'm praying for August—maybe even a blessing on fast Sunday. The power of the Spirit I felt is still lingering in my heart. I don't want it to ever leave. It almost seems unreal that this manifestation of the Spirit happened to me. I am so grateful. I pray that my untalented words don't cheapen this special experience."*

The very next day I went to see Janice. After the session I hugged her and I meant it. It was absolutely solid in my mind—she was the sister Bishop had talked about the year previous that would help me. I had prayed about it and received confirmation. I wrote, *"I am so grateful for the strength unwrapping in me—she is literally helping me shed layers of fears so that I am free to be me. It is amazing. I never knew someone with gifts like hers existed. It was necessary for me to do all I did beforehand, but this is the final touch.... During the session she said, 'No matter what all those doctors said that you would have OCD all your life, God tells you that you won't.' I never told her about my special experience last night."*

I didn't tell anyone about that experience, but God knew and I knew and I rejoiced. Oh how I secretly rejoiced, yet inwardly wondered how it could be. As I contemplated being healed, I wondered how my mind could not just go back to being sick. With this question on my mind I opened up my scriptures and they literally opened up to my answer. The three Nephites, like John in the New Testament, were blessed with a change in their bodies so they wouldn't suffer pain or sorrow except for the sins of the world. I was reminded that morning of the Savior's power to heal me in such a way that I would not have the power to override it or go back to being sick.

I began to realize that what I had learned from latter-day prophets and apostles was, in fact, true—the scriptures can be my own Urim and Thummim if led by the Spirit. I found myself receiving answers to my deepest concerns in a book that I had read over and over again my whole life.

While at the Oquirrh Mountain Utah Temple dedication a few weeks later, which was broadcast to our chapel, I learned even more about healing. When I first got there I was a bit uncomfortable thinking that I was stuck there for a long time. I feared, like I often did in a regular temple session, that OCD would set in. I prayed in my heart that I would learn something that I could only learn by being there. The Lord heard my prayer.

Elder Spencer Jones of the Seventy spoke. He said Christ didn't heal the blind man's eyes by some magical spittle and clay, but by being able to control and move the molecules of the eye to restore perfect eyesight. The Spirit witnessed to me that that is what the Lord will do for my brain. That He has the power to align the molecules in my brain to the health I desire. I got emotional.

After receiving assurance after assurance that I would, in fact, be healed very soon, I started to wonder, "Why me?" I hadn't even been healed yet, yet I wondered about all the other people I knew that struggled with mental and emotional issues. What about them? Is that fair that I be healed and not them? I had never even voiced this concern, yet I was led to Mosiah 29:20 where my concerns were laid to rest. The verses seemed to pop right out of the page: "But behold, he did deliver them because they did humble themselves before him; and because they cried mightily unto him he did deliver them out of bondage; and thus doth the Lord work with his power in *all* cases among the children of men, extending the arm of mercy towards them that put their trust in him" (emphasis added).

The Spirit taught me. Heavenly Father is perfectly just. He extends His arm of mercy to *all* who put their trust in Him. Other people can be healed too, because this is how God works and He cannot change. Everyone who trusts Him and follows Him faithfully will, on His timetable, be delivered just as I was told I would be soon.

He relieved my unspoken fears. What a glorious, all-loving, perfectly just God we have! No one is exempt from His power of deliverance!

I feel like rejoicing when I think of all the times the Lord's voice was given to me through various means to confirm my hope that I would indeed be restored to full emotional capacity and peace. He gave me these inklings "line upon line, precept upon precept; here a little, and there a little" (D&C 128: 21). They had come to me throughout my life, but nothing like the fast and furious pace they came that summer.

After all of the spiritual witnesses that I was to be healed, it was hard to not be concerned with when it would take place. I felt like a child anticipating a birthday present who couldn't quit asking how many days left. After much praying, I felt impressed that Tuesday, September 1st was the day.

August 30, 2009, I wrote, *"At 4:30 today Jed and I met with our bishop to share with him some of my experiences I've had and ask him to help Jed give me a healing blessing—a final one in this matter. I knew it would be awkward. I knew I sounded a bit presumptuous to come to him and tell him, 'I've had all these revelations, I'm supposed to be healed, and I want you to do it.' Obviously, I didn't say it like that.*

"Bishop asked what has happened to make me feel like I am to be healed. I had just read my journals before I had come and so I shared most of my stories from the last two and a half months. Bishop was non-emotional, which wasn't like him, and so I felt uncomfortable like he was wondering if I was playing with a full deck. He did tell me he appreciated my feelings about wanting to be healed.... Bishop expressed some concerns he has about whether or not he is capable of giving me a healing blessing.

"Afterwards Jed and I sat in the car in the garage and talked. He expressed similar concerns as Bishop's, yet also expressed that he believes me."

I left Bishop's office and then mine and Jed's conversation in the car feeling immensely embarrassed and like I had just asked the world of them. I started questioning all of my spiritual experiences I had had. What if it was all in my mind because I wanted it so badly? What if Jed and Bishop didn't have the faith to do what I was asking them to do? It sure didn't seem like either one of them did. Why was Bishop non-emotional when I told him of such sacred experiences? What had I gotten myself into? What if the blessing didn't work? Would all my experiences be chalked up to more craziness? Would I be left feeling more alone and more out of my mind than ever before?

These questions were swirling around me like tangible mists of darkness. I went in my room and prayed. I felt assured by the Spirit that I had experienced all that I said I had. I felt peace and that all would be well. I prayed for Bishop and Jed that they would feel the same thing.

The next two days were filled with both glorious anticipation as well as doubt. Deep down I knew I was right, yet it all seemed so far fetched, like this story couldn't actually be mine.

Jed and I fasted on the much-anticipated day of Tuesday, September 1st. We did all that we could in order to have the Spirit with us. We went to the Bountiful temple to attend a session before heading to the church to meet with Bishop. I had vacillated back and forth on whom I would ask to give me the blessing. I wanted Bishop to give it, only because I feared that Jed was too close to the situation and might not hear the words of the Lord because of his own emotional involvement. I also felt like both he and Bishop had some doubt in their ability to heal me as well as doubt in the experiences I had had. I could almost hear what they were saying to themselves by the look on their faces. "Did Misti really get revelation that now was her time to be healed? What if she didn't? How can I do what the Lord doesn't want yet?"

I ultimately decided that after all Jed had been through with me, I wanted him to be the one to pronounce the words that I had been healed. It was an act of faith on my part but also an act of love towards Jed, the one that I had more than leaned on for strength all of those long hard years.

There wasn't a lot said once we got into Bishop's office before the actual blessing. It was a bit awkward and again strangely unemotional. Bishop anointed the oil and Jed pronounced the blessing that I had been waiting to hear all of my life. He seemed a bit nervous. He paused a bit at the first of the blessing. He told me at first that the Lord is very aware of what I have gone through and that He wants me to be healed. Then he said that I'd be healed according to my faith and then he said, "You have been healed."

I sighed in absolute relief. I didn't understand what he meant by using the past tense, "You have been healed," but the meaning was the same. I was healed. That was all that mattered.

I listened as intently as I could to the rest of the blessing. He said to read my patriarchal blessing in a new light, to help others, and that others will come to me that have dealt with my same trial. He said that I will lift up the hands that hang down. He told me how special I am to the Lord and that He loves me. It's funny how we sometimes let those words that the Lord loves us just brush us by because the devil on our shoulder says, He loves everyone so it doesn't mean that much. That night it didn't matter how many children He had, He loved me and I felt it.

I stood up from having the blessing and hugged both Jed and Bishop. Again, we were all strangely non-emotional. I always envisioned us crying in relief and joy but instead there was just joy and a feeling of, "Was that for real?"

"We all sat down and talked for a while. Jed shared his own sacred experience that he had early that morning. He opened up his scriptures to where he was reading and then he thought, 'Wait a minute, Misti says she can open up her scriptures just anywhere and get answers. I am going to try it.' He said, 'I first turned to Matthew and thought, 'It's not there. Misti likes the Doctrine and Covenants,' so the next place I opened to I started to read. I read the heading first and then I read right where it says, 'require not miracles except . . . the healing of the sick . . . And these things ye shall not do except it be required of you by them who desire it' (D&C 24: 13–14).' He bore testimony to Bishop and I that the Lord had answered his concerns by leading him there."

After Jed bore his witness to us, I couldn't resist asking Bishop what he thought since it seemed he was so out of character. He was usually so emotional and the last two times we had met with him, he wasn't. He said, "I felt really uncomfortable Sunday until that night when I got home and prayed about it. Then I felt calm and peaceful and just kept having the feeling that you need to be willing to share with other people and help them. And I know you will."

Bishop kept saying, "It's a new day. It's a new day." I felt its truth, yet I wanted to part the veil for just a second, stick my head through and ask, "Tell me again, Heavenly Father, how is this supposed to feel exactly? Am I supposed to feel differently? Because I don't. How am I not going to go back to old habits of thinking?"

Right when we got home I wrote, *"I am not as emotional as I thought I'd be. I'm just happy. I came in my dark room, saw the bright moon, knelt down and said out loud, 'Thank you. Thank you so much.' Then I said another prayer of thanks and here I am. These next few days are going to be weird and testing for me but I am so excited and so grateful. Several times today I have asked if I was doing the right thing by asking for this blessing and every time the peaceful Spirit entered my heart. Even after the blessing I asked, 'Is this for real? Am I healed?' and again that same peaceful Spirit testified 'Yes!' and again the words, 'What greater witness can you have than from God?' came to my mind" (D&C 6:23).*

In my perfect world this would have been the end of my story, except of course, the words, "And she lived happily ever after." However, the Lord had taken my finish line and moved it up one more very tall mountain.

CHAPTER 39

The Unforeseen Battle— The Fiercest Yet

~

I WAS RIGHT THAT the next few days would be weird and a testing period for me. I felt a bit stressed about how the Lord would make my mind not have obsessive hyperawareness about my tongue or eyes. So the second I had a thought about either of them, my heart would race and I would wonder, "Am I healed?" I would immediately go to the Lord in prayer and ask, "Am I healed?" and literally every time I would feel the reassurance of the Spirit saying, "Yes, you are healed." What was all of this about? It didn't make sense. Why was my stomach in knots? This was supposed to be the easy part. Why wasn't it?

I felt like an athlete that had prepared for the Olympic games for years and was expected to come away with a gold medal, yet didn't even place at all. I expected to come out of Bishop's office after the healing blessing and never feel OCD fears again. And the second I felt OCD fears when I thought they were gone forever, I was susceptible to the deepest despair.

I am sure Satan was laughing as he whispered, "Misti, all of that was in your mind. You never received any revelation that you could be healed. That healing blessing didn't work and thus you will never be free from OCD. Ever!"

I allowed myself just a moment of listening to his lies and I fell in a heap of sobs. I resisted telling Jed any of my feelings because I feared that he too might begin to lose faith in the experience we had. I feared he would think I am crazy. After a while I couldn't keep it to myself any longer and I had to tell him. I needed his rational mind.

We spoke to Bishop about it as well. That was a very humbling experience for me. A few weeks earlier I had come to him in confidence and in just a short time later my confidence was being sorely tested. Bishop asked if my pride was getting in my way of using the tools I had learned in the past to combat my OCD, depression, and anxiety. It absolutely was. I had resisted really working on my thoughts as hard as I could because I had been blessed to be healed, and as a stubborn child I thought that meant no more work. I can almost see how I must have looked back then to the Lord, with my foot stomped on the floor, arms folded, nose in the air and all. I wasn't about to use any tools on a job that was supposed to be done! That would be admitting that the job had more work to do. What I didn't want to recognize was that even though the Lord had, in fact, healed me, there was a bit more work to be done on my own.

I wrote on September 25, 2009, "*I am feeling hope again that if the Lord says I'm healed then I will feel it, and if the Lord is testing and trying my faith and patience, I refuse to fail. I listened to a BYU talk tonight by Gene R. Cook from February 1, 2005 on 'The Love of God: Suffering Tribulation in the Redeemer's Name.' I really believe that I listened to that by design and not by chance. I felt the Spirit so strongly. I felt a renewed desire to press on and not only to press on but to even thank the Lord for my suffering. Even at this time as I write, my tongue and jaw and mouth are very tight and bothersome and I could easily be discouraged, ask why me, or why still, and cry, but after that talk I recognize why I must suffer a bit longer, that this is and will be my true test of faith and patience, and the desire in me is to conquer and not let the devil win by being discouraged.*"

At that time I felt a renewed strength to not be discouraged although that strength waxed and waned as the days went by and I wasn't feeling safe yet. I wanted to feel a safe distance between myself and my past struggles. They still felt too close.

September 26, 2009, I wrote, *"I, again, feel as if the Lord has spoken to me personally through the scriptures as I read last night. It is in D&C 105:19, 'I have heard [your] prayers, and will accept [your] offering; and it is expedient in me that [you] should be brought thus far for a trial of [your] faith.'"*

It was as if the Lord was right there by me telling me why He had dealt with me in this very disappointing way. I was brought thus far as a trial of my faith. Just knowing that there was a reason for this madness I was feeling gave me a challenge that I wasn't about to fail on now.

I learned what the Lord was talking specifically about in D&C 109. He was talking about Zion's Camp. When there was much persecution of the Saints in Missouri, the Prophet, while in Kirkland, received revelation to gather 500 men and in the very least 100 men to go to Kirkland and help the Saints there. By the time the band of men got to Missouri they had 200 men, but it wasn't enough to fight against the mobs so Zion's Camp was disbanded. Some men were bitter that they were asked to go that far just to turn around and go back home. Many left the Church because they couldn't see why the Lord would command them to go that far for nothing. Those that left couldn't see that everything the Lord does has a purpose even if we can't see it.

Elder Delbert L. Stapley said, "Zion's Camp was disbanded on June 24, 1834. It had furnished the know-how and experience which made possible the subsequent exodus of more than 20,000 men, women, and children from Nauvoo to the Rocky Mountains, and prepared leaders for the great exodus. It also provided a proving ground—some 1,000 miles of it—for the future Church leaders. This is evidenced by the fact that when the Quorum of the Twelve Apostles was 'searched out' by the three witnesses to the Book of Mormon, [most of these] chosen had been members of Zion's Camp. These men had demonstrated their willingness to sacrifice everything, even life itself, when commanded by the Lord. The First Quorum of the Seventy was likewise made up of the men who followed the Prophet to Missouri in Zion's Camp" (Stapley, 1970).

The Lord sometimes leads us on hard journeys not necessarily for the outcome, but for the lessons we learn along the long, hard way. I also learned that things that make us question our faith, when pulled through, actually increase our faith, make us stronger, and allow us the opportunity to teach others. Many of those members of Zion's Camp became leaders in the Lord's church because they didn't become bitter about the outcome. I wondered if there was something I was yet supposed to learn that I could teach others. I hoped I would learn it fast because I felt I was beyond my max when it came to dealing with this same trial.

Out of the mouth of babes, my 5-year-old, Sadie, taught me a great lesson. I was taking Sadie and baby Brinn on a walk when Sadie asked me, "Why do you have your exercise shoes on?" I said, "Because I'm exercising." She thought for a moment before she said, "So, is exercise when you walk until you don't want to walk anymore and then you walk anyways?"

That was the best description of exercise that I had ever heard! The best part about her description of exercise is that it pertains to so many other things as well. For example, fasting is when you don't eat until you want to eat and then you don't eat anyway. It also defines a hard worker. You work until you don't want to work anymore and then you work anyway. As pertaining to suffering, a faithful sufferer is one that works so hard to fight the pain until they don't want to fight anymore and then they fight anyway. I knew that was exactly where I was at that point in my life. I did not want to fight anymore. I thought that when the Lord did His part that I was done. When I realized there was still more work to do, I realized I only had one choice—work.

I was healed but I was still mentally hanging on to the OCD. My brain had scars. It still had mental patterns that needed to be retrained. For some reason still unknown to me, God let me have the experience of retraining my own mind even after being healed. It could be likened to an accident victim that needs to go through physical therapy to learn to walk again. Even though the accident was over and done with, the person still has the residual effect of needing to retrain the body in order to regain full health. My mental injuries that were sustained from 23 years of sickness were in definite need of rehabilitation, and the Lord wanted me to go through the process of clearing them myself. Even though the actual OCD causes in my brain were healed, I still had work to do to fully recover. I needed to retrain my mind to understand a new way. It needed to feel safe in its new environment.

Because my old OCD symptoms were hyperawareness of my actual body, and being healed couldn't change the fact that I blink, close my eyes, and have a tongue, I had to work the mind until it understood that the brain was healed. The mind and the actual physical brain are two different things. My physical brain was healed but the habits of my mind didn't know it yet. Because of that discrepancy, which I didn't understand at the time, I was wholly confused. I knew from the strong Spirit in my heart that I was healed, yet I didn't feel safe from the OCD symptoms as I had imagined and dreamed that I would.

I believed that the Lord had put Janice in my life to help me through all of this. Unfortunately for me, all while I was going through this really hard time post-blessing, Janice was in California for over a month. She was attending healing classes that she felt she was led to learn more about. We talked on the phone once in a while. On October 2, 2009, she told me that she had just learned of a new technique to help heal the body. I wrote in my journal about it. *"It has something to do with clearing your energy all around you and then putting colors and light into you through visualization."*

Right when I hung up the phone, I opened the scriptures with the question on my mind as to whether or not Janice was talking of a truth and whether or not the Lord approved. I opened my scriptures to Alma 19:6 where it talks of Lamoni's experience with light. It says, "Yea, this light had infused such joy into his soul, the cloud of darkness having been dispelled, and that the light of everlasting life was lit up in his soul...." The Spirit witnessed to me that I was led to this scripture in direct answer to my question. I understood that day that "light" wasn't just a nice word but that light is real and tangible and can dispel darkness in our souls. I couldn't wait for Janice to get home so that I could start my emotional "rehabilitation."

Meanwhile, I did my best to stay positive. I stayed as close to the Spirit as possible. I prayed a ton. Yet, I felt the devil on my shoulder saying, "Look at all the life you have wasted. Look at all the good times that you could have had with your kids. Now the Lord has healed you but you are still wasting your life."

I had a hard time combating that one. I did feel like I had wasted precious time being sick and now that I was healed and even felt the Spirit testify that I was healed, I was still fighting the despairing thought of how much more time would I "waste" until I felt whole and safe from the scars of the past.

Jed and I went for a weekend to our houseboat in Page, Arizona, and while in a sacrament meeting there, the Spirit taught me a humbling lesson. We sang hymn number 195, "How Great the Wisdom and the Love." I wrote this while singing that song, *"I realized a parallel (that isn't even close, yet still parallel) from the life of the Savior and mine. I often mourn that when I'm struggling I'm missing out on my own life (i.e., losing my own life) and I feel sorry for myself. The Lord on the other hand freely gave His own life. He didn't live the 'normal' life that I often covet. We don't even know if He married."*

I realized at that moment that the Savior understood. He freely gave up the life He could've had in order to do the will of our Father. During that sacred moment, I was given greater power to do as Neil A. Maxwell used to preach, to give my will to the will of the Father. I knew that I was on His path and so could thus conclude that what was happening to me was His will for some reason or another.

When the Savior was at that unbelievably heavy moment in the Garden of Gethsemane, He, the Lord of all, "fell on His face, and prayed, saying, O my Father, if it be possible, let this cup pass from me: nevertheless not as I will, but as thou wilt" (Matthew 26:39). I, too, wanted my cup to pass from me. I had believed and hoped that the healing blessing meant emotionally happily ever after for me. Realizing that I still had a heavy burden to overcome was almost more disappointment than I could bear. Figuratively I felt like I had fallen flat on my face.

I realized I still had scar tissue to remove after the refiner's fire that I had been through, a refiner's fire that had lasted 23 years. I was through the fire, but the scars still had to be removed. Who knew how long that would take. That was the biggest disappointment of my life. I felt like I was as low as I could go, yet the Savior's example gave me strength, "Nevertheless, not as I will, but as thou wilt." He freely gave His life and then at the end of it was asked to bear so much pain that it astonished even Him, the creator of all things. Yet, He being the perfect example let the Father's will override what He would've chosen for Himself. Yes, in my self pity, my life seemed harder than anyone else's at that moment, but the Spirit gave me strength in those moments to venture off my self-pity path and onto His path and, at least for the moment, relax and let the Father take the lead. If He had more work for me to do to heal the scars then I would do it. I had come this far, so surely the end couldn't be far off.

The funny thing about having spiritual experiences is that it was like a good meal. I needed one almost every day in order to stay strong. I desperately needed to know that God was still there for me.

I went in and out of peace over the next several months. It's hard to explain how I felt literally healed yet I still had OCD fears and scars. I still found myself from time to time ruminating over how I was feeling, yet every time I asked if I was healed or thanked Heavenly Father for healing me, I felt the light of His love resting on me. It was a fact that I was healed, yet I still hadn't fully recovered.

I continued to work hard by seeing Janice once or twice a week. She helped me work on those scars. We worked on ridding myself of old ways of thinking that didn't need to be there anymore now that I had been healed. We also continued to work on my relationship with my parents. I did this weekly with Janice and sometimes daily by myself, by forgiving them for the way they continued to try and control my life. She helped me release those things within me that wanted to judge them. I wanted to enjoy and love them, but still found it hard while I was trying to overcome the scars of my past. It was all intertwined—my OCD scars, my judgments, and my inability to divinely forgive those who unknowingly but decidedly hurt me and continued to do so.

I had days when I would kneel down and with tears of joy thank Heavenly Father for blessing me to really feel for the first time the joy of being in my body having my experiences. Those were glorious feelings, and they began to happen more and more often. However often they were occurring, I still prayed very hard that I would feel safe in those feelings, meaning that I would trust that they weren't just another ride at the top of the roller coaster but that it was finally the peace I was promised—the kind that doesn't end.

I fasted and I prayed and I prayed and I fasted that all the fear that I had developed over the years about my emotions would all depart. I read one day in Job. It said it perfectly, "Thou shalt be stedfast, and shalt not fear: Because thou shalt forget thy misery, and remember it as waters that pass away" (Job 11:15–16). I knew I would always remember my trial, yet I prayed that it would soon be as the waters that passed away.

Christmas had historically been really hard for me. Probably because I wanted to enjoy it so much and when I didn't because of OCD, anxiety, or depression, I really felt like life was unfair. However, this first Christmas after being healed was indeed a beautiful gift from Heavenly Father. On December 25, 2009, I wrote:

"It is nap time after having had the most peaceful, wonderful, fun Christmas that I have ever had! Why? Because the Lord has rescued, delivered, and healed me. I lay awake in bed after a nap and I thanked the Lord in my head and pondered. I felt that the Lord had something to say to me and so I opened my scriptures and they literally opened straight to Alma 38: 4–5.

"It says, 'For I know that thou wast in bonds: yea, and I also know that thou wast stoned for the word's sake; and thou didst bear all these things with patience because the Lord was with thee; and now thou knowest that the Lord did deliver thee. And now my son, Shiblon, I know that ye should remember, that as much as ye shall put your trust in God, even so much ye shall be delivered out of your trials, and your troubles, and your afflictions, and ye shall be lifted up at the last day.' I read the whole chapter and feel like it was meant for me to read and even to own in some small way. As much as I know and have experienced, I am still amazed when the Lord reaches out to even me in such a literal way. Thank you, Heavenly Father!

Thank you so much my Savior and brother Jesus Christ for delivering me and then for the promise that thou always will if I always trust in thee."

I went on to say that although I did everything that Christmas that I had done in years past, this time I was living in vivid color! I wasn't outside the window looking in at my wonderful life—I got to feel it! My heart poured out in thanksgiving that day. It was proof that I was healed. I knew that Christmas Day was a gift and that I still had work to do to become stronger and stronger; however, my hope had become knowledge that day just like I had prayed for. I was healed. I wanted more days of "proof" until I feared no more.

CHAPTER 40

Claiming the Blessing

∾

CHRISTMAS THAT YEAR was proof to me that I had indeed been healed. I labeled it "Christmas Proof" in my journal and it became a pattern. Over the next several months, whenever I did or experienced anything that in days past were full of emotional misery, but this time were peaceful, it also became proof to me and so thus I labeled it.

My next proof was "Snowboarding Proof." During Christmas vacation, I wanted to go snowboarding but Jed didn't, so I took Jeren and Hannah and went without him. We went to Ogden to rent snowboards for them first, then I found my way up to Snow Basin, bought the tickets, and went snowboarding without Jed for the first time. I know that it almost sounds silly to someone who has never experienced emotional illness, but in days past, doing those same things wouldn't have produced the peaceful, fun result that it did that day. It was further proof that I was healed and that my scars were healing. Jed ended up coming up that day a little later. He must have been as shocked to see me leave without him as I was in doing it. He probably had to come see it for himself.

I next had "Temple Proof." Going to the temple had historically been very hard for me. My OCD and anxiety would act up in there for some reason, which actually made me feel awful and more ashamed of myself because everyone else always said that it was a peaceful place. Thankfully, no matter the emotional battle I almost always felt in the temple, I still chose obedience. I chose it because I had hope that in so doing I would be worthy of Heaven's continued help. Jed and I went there almost every month in spite of its being a challenge. However, on January 5, 2010, I now had "Temple Proof." I felt healed while in the temple for the first time.

I wrote, *"I feel like shouting hallelujah, but part of me is hesitant and wants more time and more days of 'proof,' but I know that the 'hallelujah' day is coming."*

I then had "Vacation Proof." We took our kids on a Disney vacation and cruise for a family Christmas present. It was January 7–14, 2010. I wrote, *"Wow! I just experienced my first completely wonderful vacation ever! Meaning, it was my first vacation that I was emotionally healthy. I was pretty confident I would be, but our first evening in Florida I started to feel a bit off kilter. When back at the hotel I went in my room alone and I prayed. I really don't know how to explain this, but I've noticed in the last couple of months that whenever I find myself feeling the tiniest bit like I used to that this distinct but fairly new feeling of peace hits my heart and bursts and spreads its peace throughout me. The Lord is there and He is keeping His promise."*

I felt assured that I was healed. The Spirit testified this to me as well as the testimony of my experiences. I was given greater power to overcome the ghost pains from the past. Nevertheless, I still didn't feel safe. Why? I asked myself. Why wouldn't I feel safe yet? I struggled, studied, meditated, and still did a lot of praying. I wanted to feel safe. On February 5, 2010, I asked Jed to give me a blessing. He told me that I was "to know that this is all part of the learning curve to further healing."

Instinctively, I was tempted to think, "Why a learning curve? I have been healed. Haven't I suffered enough?" But I decided, as I often chose to do everyday, that if this was the path the Lord wanted me to take, then I would take it. Really, the only other choice I felt I had was to give up, and I couldn't do that, not after I had come so far. So, I fasted again for more strength and further answers and continued to work with Janice.

Ironically, I received some of those answers while at yoga. The Lord works in mysterious ways! On February 9, 2010, Robin, my yoga instructor said, "Don't just hang out in a pose and stay there. Keep going further, stretching more even if it's imperceptible." I thought, "No matter where I get to on life's ladder, never just hang out there, keep reaching upward and improving even if it's imperceptible."

The second lesson was even more applicable to me at the time. I had been allowing myself to ruminate over how I was feeling. I let myself feel a bit of self-pity that I was still thinking about it. I wanted to just get lost in life and not think about it *anymore* but I didn't know how. While in a straddle stretch, Robin said, "Tighten your quads and it will relax your hamstrings. It is called reciprocal inhibition." I thought, "Lately, I've been miserable because I have been too concerned with when I won't have to think about my emotional state, and that has made my emotional hamstrings too tight. Wow! If I just tighten my quads or, in other words, accomplish a bunch of other things that I want done, then my emotional hamstrings will have to loosen up. It's a law of physics."

The Spirit helped me learn a basic law in life: what we give attention to grows. I was sick of giving attention to my emotional state; I was giving it more attention in order to try and rid myself of it. Instead, I learned that if I give attention to, or tighten up opposite muscles, then the one that was uncomfortably tight would have to relax. It is the law, and what is law in nature is truth and there is no changing it.

I gave it a try and although not easy, and not comfortable at first, I did it! It worked! I made a list of my goals, other than my emotional ones, and I went to work. Work really is a great antidote to our problems. President Hinckley used to say, "The best antidote I know for worry is work" (Hinckley, 2001).

It wasn't easy though, because unfortunately we have unseen enemies out there. Satan is real. He wants us to focus on what is wrong in our lives. He knows our problems will keep growing and wreaking havoc in our lives if we keep focusing on them. We can't force ourselves to not think of something because then we are thinking of it. But we can, like in yoga, choose to focus on tightening other muscles, and natural laws will come into play and loosen the hold our tight hamstrings (or problems) had on us.

Learning or relearning this concept and then practicing it really got me back to a good place in my life. For several months my emotional hamstrings felt loose. At first it was from genuinely concentrating on fulfilling other goals, but then, unfortunately, I got sick physically with something that nobody could quite pinpoint. Being sick was an equal distraction, though not a welcome one.

I never did know exactly what I had. I went to several doctors and had a lot of blood work done as well as a biopsy, to not much avail. What did work was a lot of Janice's natural herbs. I got better after several months. That's not to say that it wasn't really frustrating and discouraging. It felt a bit like a déjà vu. I found myself not knowing what was wrong, how long it would last, or if I would ever get over it. It was a bit like the emotional questions that I had about myself seemingly my whole life, except this time it was physical.

I don't know why I went through it, but I now have a greater appreciation of the emotional strain that can come along with physical ailments. I used to almost be jealous of someone who had "just physical issues." At least others could see it. At least it wasn't in their head. At least no one would think they were crazy. At least they would get sympathy from others. At least it was socially acceptable to seek for help with a physical ailment. I thought all those things, but after going through my very minuscule physical ailment experience, I think otherwise. Even though all those things that I thought about physical verses emotional illness are still true, I had always left out the fact that emotional pain, discomfort, and fear also accompany physical sicknesses. That is where the most hurtful pain comes from—our emotions.

As with all trials, whether physical or emotional, laughter can really be the lubricant that gets you through the tight spots. Jed had and still has this amazing ability to make me laugh at even the most stressful or worrisome things.

On March 30, 2010, we took our little family to dinner at Red Lobster for Jeren's 12th birthday. He got to pick where we ate. On our kids' birthday it has become a tradition to retell the story of the actual day of their birth. My favorite birthday story about Jeren is the one I already told earlier. After delivering Jeren and while up late one night nursing him, I told him I loved him. He immediately quit nursing, looked up at me, and gave me the biggest, toothless grin you have ever seen a newborn baby give. That has always been really special to me.

As I retold that story to Jeren and our family over dinner, I tried to make it as serious and special as possible when Jed interjected. He tried to pull the same face that baby Jeren did and with the breathiest, sweetest, baby-like voice that he could make he said, "Ya Jeren, you smiled and said, 'Ahhh, I'm not going to do my homework when I'm in the sixth grade. Ahhh, I won't want to take a shower when I'm in the sixth grade." I got laughing so hard—all of us did! Jeren had been giving us a run for our money when it came to getting him to do his homework, and as stated, getting him to take a shower was also a challenge. Laughter really is the best medicine. Maybe Jed's humor did more than just make us laugh. Maybe it clicked something within Jeren, because that was his last really hard year with homework and showers!

That spring we took the kids out of school the last week and went to San Diego for a vacation. I felt safer and happier than I ever had and because of that, I wanted time to stop so that I could soak in all of my wonderful children fully. I wanted to savor each moment together. I knew I still had more work to do, but wow, was I ever enjoying the moment! It was joy! We experienced San Diego in every way possible that week and my whole self was a part of it all!

We took our kids to the Padres baseball game. I was a bit worried that all our little girls would be terribly bored and so I let them bring their stuffed animals. Sadie brought her San Diego Zoo giraffe. I started making them laugh with it. I was the voice of the giraffe. I was just being silly but they got laughing so hard that we unknowingly got on the Jumbotron! I entertained them and myself with that little giraffe seemingly the whole time. I don't think they ever quit laughing. I'm sure we must've got on the nerves of the people sitting around us, but at that point it was too wonderful to care. That is a super fun memory and one that I experienced in only one reality—the real one.

That summer I had a bit of a bump in my emotional road. My old triggers were still scaring me. I was still letting them take away some of my peace. One day I wrote these two lessons down that I had learned over the years. I wrote it as if to someone else going through similar circumstance:

Lesson #1: Get all the help you can: Priesthood blessings, pray constantly, therapist if needed or people gifted like Janice, and then the rest is up to you. Counter your negative thoughts with hope and truth. Your mind believes what you tell it. Be determined to conquer. It is a mindset; even a degree of anger is needed to be mad enough to fight the battle constantly *until it's gone. Lots of countering negative thoughts. Do it because you love yourself enough to fight for yourself. It's like being under the water and you're trying to get on top where it's easy to breathe again. It's hard work clear until you are only a centimeter under water, and then "air" and relief comes and then you ride the wave and wonder why 'air' was ever hard to come by—until it is gone again. But then you've learned how to swim faster and which direction to go to get to the air and catch the wave faster.*

Lesson #2: If it is OCD or hyperawareness of something completely bothersome and even silly (so silly that it is bothersome) and all your mind wants to do is focus on it, the best weapon you have is to not ignore but acknowledge what is bothering you and then say, "Oh well, I guess that's going to be my constant companion for a while, but I'm not going to quit laughing and living while it's here." And then busy yourself with work. Do service if possible, and then pretty soon your "little companion" will get bored watching you live and will slip offstage. Life will flow easily, or at least "normally," for a little while or maybe a long while. Your "little companion" may try and get back to center stage (usually at a time of stress or worry). Again, you love yourself so much that you deserve the work you will do for yourself no matter how many times a day, a week, a year, or a lifetime you do it. No matter how many times you cut yourself in your life, you will always work to find yourself some antiseptic and bandage. Remember God does nothing for us that we can do for ourselves. It would be contrary to His plan of happiness (ironic, I know). I believe the Lord allows us to learn to take care of ourselves when we can so that we can learn to trust in ourselves and thus always feel safe wherever we are. A result of "safe" is peace, love, and happiness. You are worth that!"

As I found myself again having to practice what I just preached (although not sure if you can say it was preaching if there was no audience), in humility I turned to the Lord for strength. And yet again He was there to provide.

I went along with life for the next couple of years happier than I had ever been, by far. I continued to enjoy my family and my life in a heightened and wonderful way. My confidence grew and grew with each passing day from the joyous moments as well as each trial of my faith. I was still somewhat afraid of all of my old trigger words because of the emotional work it caused me if I was caught off guard. Satan would wait until I was tired or frustrated and then BAM—a trigger word like "eyes," "blinking," or "tongue" or an object such as a knife would send my heart in a lurch. They had much less power than they used to; nonetheless, I still hadn't overcome my fear completely. Satan would say, "See, you aren't strong. You aren't even healed. You will never have peace that doesn't end." I believed him sometimes.

One particularly hard day I felt the need to ask specifically for divine help to "claim" the full measure of the healing blessing that I had received in September of 2009. For over 24 hours I used the word "claim" in all of my pleadings to Heavenly Father. "Help me, Father, claim *all* of the healing blessing." I asked for knowledge to know how. I then prayed to be led to a scripture that would show me that this is what God wanted me to do or to show me that He was listening. I felt the Spirit confirm that He had a scripture to share with me. I turned right to D&C 101:99. It says, "It is my will that my people should *claim*, and hold *claim* upon that which I have appointed unto them" (emphasis added). I almost couldn't believe it and probably wouldn't have had the Spirit not been burning within me. I was led to the exact word, "claim," that I had been using in all of my prayers for the past day. Not only was God still listening to my pleas, but He was telling me that it *was* His will that I "claim" this final blessing of protection against all objects, thoughts, or trigger words the adversary had been using to try and confuse and hinder my mission. I knew then that Heavenly Father wanted me to feel as powerful and free as I did!

Knowing this gave me courage, but I knew I still had to find a way to do it. I had tried for so long that I felt I was all out of tricks. I went to see Janice with a prayer in my heart that both she and I would be inspired and that I would receive the help I desired. I felt so weak. For a few weeks previous I had been feeling Satan on my shoulder telling me I would never be as strong as I wanted to be. I wanted her to help me fix my problem, but to my dismay she told me she couldn't. She told me that the healing blessing I received in 2009 was all that I needed and that I just needed to believe it. She quoted, "Ask and ye shall receive."

Incredulous, I asked her, "You mean to tell me that I could've claimed the blessing of not fearing all of my triggers way back then?" When she said, "Yes," I lost it emotionally. I felt like I had failed. What was wrong with me? I started crying. I went in her bathroom, knelt on the floor and sobbed. I felt so humbled and so weak. How do I ever claim this blessing of no longer heeding Satan's attempts to throw trigger words and objects at me to confuse me? How do I do that? I felt so alone, so weak, and so unable to do what the Lord expected me to do. He had healed me, but He expected me to trust Him more. He expected me to do something that I didn't know how to do. He wanted me to claim all the blessings that He had already given me. It seemed impossible.

When I gained enough strength to quit crying I went back in the room where Janice was. She hugged me and let me cry some more. Even though I had only been there 15 minutes she suggested that I go home and spend some quiet time with Heavenly Father. I left and did just that. I lay on my bed. I cried, I prayed, and I slept. I felt peace.

After a couple of hours, I felt the Spirit forcefully hit my heart and I finally heard the words that I had been waiting for ever since my physical healing blessing: "I will do for you what you can't do for yourself. You will be given strength to step over Satan's temptations...things are going to change." With renewed hope and energy, I went about my day as a mom. Doing normal daily activities seemed awkward after having such a divine experience.

The next morning I got up early for some quiet hours by the living room fire to write my experiences down in my journal. As I did so, the Spirit quickly filled me. I asked Heavenly Father if He would give me a message from the scriptures. Because of the Spirit within me, I trusted that He would. I opened right up to 1 Timothy 4:14–16. "Neglect not the gift that is in thee, which was given thee by prophecy, with the laying on of the hands of the presbytery [elders]. Meditate upon these things; give thyself wholly to them; that thy profiting may appear to all. Take heed unto thyself, and unto the doctrine; continue in them: for in doing this thou shalt both save thyself, and them that hear thee."

I knew that the Lord was telling me to not discount the "gift" that He had given me the day before as well as the physical healing blessing I had already received. I was to accept all that had happened to heal me and then to tell all others that would need to hear my message. He was telling me to share my experience so that His other children in need would also be helped. Isn't it amazing how the Lord doesn't waste any time after helping one of His children before He is commanding them to help others?

I sat in awe as I pondered that scripture. That, combined with the Spirit in my heart, I felt as close to my Heavenly Father as I ever had. It felt like we were having a conversation person to person through the scriptures. He was proving to me yet again that His love is intimate, all-knowing, and all-caring. He is indeed a Father. More importantly, He was my Father.

I then heard in my mind and in my heart the most precious words confirming what I had been told the day before. "It is granted you now even as you have always desired it. You are made stronger even as we speak. Satan can no longer derail you in those old ways. Your peace is just beginning. Enjoy, my daughter. You deserve all of it. You have ever been faithful and will be to the end of time and forever. You will never be the same again from this time forward, my daughter."

No sweeter words had ever been spoken to me. I was experiencing, in live action, the redeeming power of the Atonement. He was ransoming me from Satan's grasp; He was setting me free (see "I Believe in Christ," hymn #134).

I knew that I had heard correctly from the strong feeling of the Spirit in my heart. However, I still wanted another witness so that I wouldn't be tempted to doubt later on when the Spirit left. I asked that He would help me open up to a scripture that could testify that these things I had heard and felt were true.

I then opened my scriptures randomly and the first verses I read were D&C 46:30–32. "He that asketh in the Spirit asketh according to the will of God; wherefore it is done even as he asketh.... And ye must give thanks unto God in the Spirit for whatsoever blessing ye are blessed with."

The Lord couldn't have solidified this experience more perfectly. I immediately heeded His counsel to "give thanks" in prayer. Afterwards I found myself singing *Amazing Grace* all day long, but it was more my heart than my voice that I could feel praising Him.

> "My chains are gone. I've been set free.
> My God my Savior has ransomed me.
> And like a fire His mercy reigns.
> Unending love. Amazing Grace."

I can testify that from that moment on I have been 100 percent healed in every single way that I dreamed of. I am absolutely "safe" with my thoughts, my feelings, and myself. What a miracle! I am finally free and it feels every bit as good as I ever imagined it would. The peace inside me is real and tangible. In the end, God did for me what I couldn't do for myself: He took away all of my former "triggers." They are there, yes, but they no longer affect me. I now understand why the angels of God never cease praising His name. Having experienced the redeeming power of the Atonement and having been carried across the great abyss of my life and into His divine peace causes such deep gratitude in my heart that I, too, feel like endlessly praising Him.

CHAPTER 41

Summary of Learnings

~

I WANT TO REITERATE and emphasize that although the Lord helped, blessed, encouraged, and finally healed me, I worked very, very hard for it both physically and spiritually. It took several years of therapy, a couple more of natural healing work, a priesthood healing blessing, and then more years of stretching, natural healing work, and building faith until He finally took me the rest of the way. I sacrificed myself, my time, and my money to relearn life and relationships, and then I sacrificed the same in order to pull out the trapped negative energy, false beliefs, and negative emotions that haunted me. Although I put the effort in, it was the Lord that led the way. He still gets every ounce of the credit. However, like a calf to the stall, I let Him lead me, and even that took effort.

I don't want those who read this to think, "Well, I can't feel the Savior in my life and so I can never be led by Him and heal the way that she did." Remember that we are all climbing our own unique Mount Everest. The Savior knows your path as well. I testify that He will guide you on your specific journey just as He did me, if you let Him.

It might be that before you can feel the Savior guiding you, you may need to do some prep work. If you have major sins, it can be a big barrier to personal revelation, so repentance can remedy that. Some of us may need to unload some of our baggage before we can even begin climbing. Meaning, some of us may need to start by shedding our false beliefs that are the chains of the adversary that hold us down. Paul said, "Let us lay aside every weight, and the sin which doth so easily beset us, and let us run with patience the race that is set before us" (Hebrews 12:1).

You can lay aside your weight in several different ways. You could start by seeing your bishop or other ecclesiastical leader. Or you may have a friend that can direct you to a trusted counselor. Marilyn was my trusted counselor. She helped me see my many false beliefs that were holding me back. I worked tirelessly (although I was very tired) to retrain my thinking. As I said earlier, I even tied notebooks around my neck so I could quickly catch and bring to light the false or irrational beliefs that were swirling around in my head. I have a stack of notebooks at least a foot high that are filled with the notes that I took while in her office. I hungered and thirsted for the knowledge that she was giving me. I met with her anywhere from one to four hours a week. I worked with her off and on for over five years until she and I both knew that she could teach me no more.

After all that, I still struggled with OCD. I still hurt. Even after all that work, it hurt just the same. However, underneath the sickness I was stronger, more assertive, and more capable than I had ever been to deal with life and as well as the OCD.

After my work with Marilyn was over, the Lord led me to my next station. It was to Janice, whom He had given the gift of healing to. I spent hours and hours in her office. We did energy work, inner-child work, and other techniques such as Emotional Frequency Technique (EFT), and Pranic healing. I spent hours shedding layers of the "mud" that was all over me. I forgave and forgave—time and time again—everyone in my life, but especially my parents, until my soul felt clean.

I took herbs and vitamins, especially B-complex to also help heal my body from all the stress it had been under over the years. Each time I left her office I felt lighter, literally. I could feel the rocks being lifted out of my backpack with each session.

Yes, her techniques were much stranger to me at first than just the talking that I did in therapy, but I humbled myself enough to recognize that just as Christ healed blindness and leprosy in a myriad of ways, Janice's techniques might be one of those ways for me. That proved to be true. Her gifts were like the clay and spittle the Lord made for me (see John 9:6).

I love Janice and Marilyn. They are both my angels. They both used the gifts that God has given them to mentor, to teach, and to help me heal. Be careful who you choose to mentor you. Do your homework and make sure they are led by the Spirit. In Moroni 7:17, Mormon tells us how to do that. "I show unto you the way to judge; for every thing which inviteth to do good, and to persuade to believe in Christ, is sent forth by the power and gift of Christ; wherefore ye may know with a perfect knowledge it is of God."

I want you, the reader, to know that the Lord trusts us. He knows what we are capable of. He knows that He has poured enough knowledge down upon the earth in these latter days to get us started on our own. He knows that He has given his children gifts that they might be a benefit to one another. He wants us to search out those people prayerfully and do all that we can on our own before He will finally step in. Why does He wait? He knows the power that often lies dormant within us. He knows that muscles will come from struggling seemingly on our own. We are like caterpillars that have to work and work—not to just get out of our cocoons but to gain the strength necessary to be able to flap our wings and fly once we are out.

In this book I have written a lot about the reprieves and the direction I was given from the Comforter. Those experiences were but 10 percent of the total sum. My path has been laced with 90 percent tremendous struggle. If you, the reader, are searching for answers, it's my prayer that you won't let Satan mislead you. He may try and tell you what he tried to tell me at times: "Why try? Why work? You just need to wait for God to do it all for you. You are weak. Your power is nothing compared to His." If you are tempted in this way, remember what Nephi taught us. He said, "We know that it is by grace that we are saved, *after all we can do*" (2 Nephi 25:23, emphasis added).

It is His grace that ultimately saves us, but let's not forget the second half of the recipe. Healing is a lot of work. It takes a lot of stretching, a lot of time in developing the faith necessary, a lot of study, a lot of practicing what you learn, and a lot of exercising hope that God can do what He says He can. This may seem daunting, but for me, as soon as I felt like my ladder was on the right wall, I felt an almost insatiable desire and energy to keep climbing. It felt so good to know that finally the effort I was putting in was getting me a little closer with each step to where I wanted to be. Like an irritating itch on your back that has been there for years, when you finally find a stick long enough to reach it, it is worth all the effort it takes to scratch it. The work itself brings relief, hope, and joy.

When it gets tough to keep going, which it usually does at some point, envision Jesus and the vision of joy He must've had in order to endure the cross. We, too, can envision the fruits of our labors that will surely come if we keep working and faint not. The journey getting there may be hard, but it is exciting and invigorating all at the same time. It is not only worth it in the end, it is worth it all the way through.

During those years after being healed physically, although it was tremendously disappointing to encounter setbacks, I learned some important truths. I learned that my heart can know I am healed through the power of God, yet my mind could still be too weak in faith to be able to claim all that God had already bestowed upon me. Thus, I was left with scars or habits of thinking that still needed some rehabilitation. I learned that Heavenly Father doesn't waste divine energy. He only does what we can't do ourselves. He leaves all else to us. I learned when you make a covenant with the Lord that you shouldn't waste any time to fulfill it or He will "help" us remember in sometimes very painful ways. I learned, like Nephi, that there are things that can easily "beset us" even after we have had profound spiritual experiences. I learned that Satan doesn't waste any time in using our weaknesses against us, especially when it destroys our peace and our confidence in the divine.

I learned, like the Willie and Martin Handcart Companies did, that I can go further and endure far more than I ever thought possible. I have come away, like they did, with a confidence in the Lord that I could've learned in no other way. I have learned that my way is not God's way, and thankfully so. If I would've had it my way, I would've missed out on several years worth of spiritual experiences and first-hand learning. My way would have been, "She was healed and lived happily ever after." Instead, God said, "She was healed and continually learned ever after."

I learned that feeling forsaken by God at the very hardest time will one day be looked at through the eternities as the time that the Lord lovingly turned up the heat in my refiner's fire so as to purify me the very most. One of the hardest things for me was being healed and then unexpectedly finding out I still had scars left to heal. I was so tired yet still had further to go.

Christ, too, felt forsaken at the pinnacle of His suffering. Why should I be any different? To feel forsaken is to feel a bit like our Savior did as He carried the hardest burden of all—a consummation of all our burdens at once while in the greatest of mortal pain. I learned that if the Lord of All can't get out of this life without feeling completely and utterly alone, then why should I be the exception? If I want to become like Him, I must be willing to submit like He did. I learned a lot that year but mostly I learned that Heaven's angels are much nearer than we think. We are never alone. I know that for certain.

In summary of this 26-year grand adventure that the Lord has led me both on and through, I will record one more journal entry. The Spirit helped me see yet another parallel between the experiences of those in the Book of Mormon and my own. This story is in the book of Alma. It is a story about Moroni, Helaman, and others as they were in the middle of fighting a long and awful war with King Amalickiah and the Lamanites.

I wrote, *"Early this morning I was reading in the book of Mormon when some verses really stuck out to me. It was Alma 58: 9–12.*

"'We were grieved and also filled with fear, lest by any means the judgments of God should come upon our land, to our overthrow and utter destruction.'

"This is how I felt many times while dealing with my huge emotional and mental trial. I was almost always filled with the fear of a complete emotional destruction and thus everything that I loved in my life would come crashing down.

"Verse 10, 'Therefore we did pour out our souls in prayer to God, that he would strengthen us and deliver us out of the hands of our enemies, yea and also give us strength that we might retain our cities, and our lands, and our possessions, for the support of our people.'

"I, too, poured out my heart many more times than I could ever remember for deliverance from the bondage I was in. When I felt that I had made some progress, I prayed for the strength to 'retain' those cities, or progress, I had made.

"Verse 11, 'Yea, and it came to pass that the Lord our God did visit us with assurances that he would deliver us; yea, insomuch that he did speak peace to our souls, and did grant unto us great faith and did cause us that we should hope for our deliverance in him.'

"This same assurance came to me several times over the years but nothing like the summer of 2009 when I was given the assurance that I then had the gift of faith to be healed. What hope I then had of deliverance in Him!

"Verse 12, 'And we did take courage with our small force which we had received, and were fixed with a determination to conquer our enemies, . . . and [maintain] the cause of our liberty.'

"I, too, took courage with what small confirmations I had received for strength, and I too went to work with Janice, and with a planned priesthood blessing, with a fixed determination to conquer my enemies and maintain the cause of my liberty or freedom from bondage. And that is exactly what happened. The Lord finally gave me the strength to conquer, but not without a great test of faith and a lot of tears.

"I love these verses of scripture! It gives us an outline of what to do when all seems lost. We pour out our souls to Heavenly Father, we continue to do so until His sweet assurance comes (no matter how long), and then with courage we get to work with a fixed determination to conquer."

I never even dreamed of telling anyone of my deepest darkest secrets, let alone write a book about them! I really did think that I would take these secrets with me to the grave. At least I thought that before I began to feel the little inklings of the Spirit telling me that I needed to share these experiences. Oh how I fought those feelings. "No way," I thought "I can hardly even talk to Jed about this!" But, little by little, I knew what Heavenly Father wanted me to do. And if God wanted me to do it, well, like I said in the beginning, I've always been that sort of girl. And thus I began this journey of writing my story.

I knew the Lord had answered many of my prayers before I wrote this book. After writing it, I really know.

I now have a bird's eye view of what used to be me lost in a deep, dark forest and seeing no way to get out. I can see the beginning to the end now, at least to the end of this journey. Life isn't over and there are many more mountains and valleys yet to traverse. However, the light of Christ that has come into my life through my many struggles now lights my path, and although there are mountains yet to climb, I know His light will keep illuminating the path all along the way. His yoke is easy and His burden is light (see Matthew 11:30).

I know that at the end of this book I can't honestly say, "And she lived happily ever after." I still live in the same dangerous and stressful world that we all do. I still must endure to the end. Yes, I have been delivered from my deepest abyss, yet mortal life is still mortal. I still, at times, expect too much of my kids, get frustrated with my husband, bemoan all the laundry I have to do, and most especially have a keen sense of all my inadequacies. My journey has not ended, yet the journey is exciting now. Yes, I am still a human who is a little too keenly aware of all my weaknesses, who desperately needs repentance and to take the sacrament each week, yet I am living life in full color now. Everything is more gorgeous and vivid than it has ever been. I feel, in many ways, like I have been born again. Life is amazing! It is delicious to me! It is all because of the Savior's patience, His tutoring, His chastening, and ultimately because of His grace and love. I feel like Alma when he said, "Nevertheless, after much tribulation, the Lord did hear my cries, and did answer my prayers . . ." (Mosiah 23:10). I, too, can see that the Lord did hear all of my cries. He heard every one of them, all of those long, painful, and confusing years. He answered my prayers. He fulfilled *all* of His words.

Alma 37:16 says, "God is powerful to the fulfilling of *all* his words. For he will fulfill *all* his promises which he shall make unto you" (emphasis added). I add my personal testimony to his. I know Alma's words are true.

I will leave you with my favorite scripture, Mosiah 29:20—"He did deliver them because they did humble themselves before him; and because they cried mightily unto him he did deliver them out of bondage; and thus doth the Lord work with his power in *all* cases among the children of men, extending the arm of mercy towards them that put their trust in him."

He delivered e*ven me*. He will deliver *even you*.

About the Author

Misti J. Stevenson lives near Salt Lake City, Utah, with her husband and five children. She loves being a dance teacher, and is known for her canned salsa, blackberry jam, and homemade rolls. She is a huge fan of yoga and walking early in the morning with her friends—and she plans on doing both forever. She has always been an avid journal writer, but this is her first book. She loves hearing from readers and can be contacted at evenmeevenyou@gmail.com or through evenmeevenyou.com.

MY ANGELS

MARILYN STEPHENS-BURTON is a licensed marriage and family therapist, and has worked in this field for 15 years. She specializes in working with children.

JANICE ERICKSON has an intuitive gift to help people and has been a counselor in the health field for over 20 years. If you would like to get ahold of Janice, she can be reached at janicererickson@gmail.com.

Reference List

Adams, Sarah F. "Nearer, My God, to Thee." *LDS Hymn Book.* (1985). The Church of Jesus Christ of Latter-day Saints. Salt Lake City, Utah. 100.

Beck, Daniel. (2008). *EFY Hymns.* "Amazing Grace."

Blake, Leon. (n.d.). Director of LDS Family Services in a Codependency workshop as reported to author by Marilyn Stephens Burton.

Clark, D., & Gale, M. (1997). *Puppies for Sale.* Florida: HCI.

Codependency. (n.d.) In Wikipedia: The Free Encyclopedia. Retrieved from http://en.wikipedia.org/wiki/Codependency

Codependent. (n.d.). In The Free Dictionary by Farlex. Retrieved from http://www.thefreedictionary.com/codependent

Cook, Gene R. (2005, February 1). "The Love of God. Suffering Tribulation in the Redeemer's Name." Retrieved from http://speeches.byu.edu/?act=viewitem&id=1418

Eyring, Henry B. (2005, January 25). "Raise the Bar." In Brigham Young Univeristy–Idaho devotional. Retrieved from http://www2.byui.edu/Presentations/Transcripts/Devotionals/2005_01_25_Eyring.htm

Groberg, John H. (October 1994). *In the Eye of the Storm.* Bookcraft: Salt Lake City, Utah.

Hinckley, Gordon B. (2001). *Standing for Something: 10 Neglected Virtues That Will Heal Our Hearts and Homes.* Three Rivers Press: New York, New York.

Hinckley, Gordon B. (n.d.). Retrieved from http://quotingquotes.com/40771/

Keen, Robert. "How Firm a Foundation." *LDS Hymn Book.* (1985). The Church of Jesus Christ of Latter-day Saints. Salt Lake City, Utah. 85.

Maxwell, Neal A. (September 2007). "All These Things Shall Give Thee Experience." Deseret Book: Salt Lake City, Utah.

McConkie, Bruce R. (1972). "I Believe in Christ." *LDS Hymn Book.* The Church of Jesus Christ of Latter-day Saints. Salt Lake City, Utah. 134.

Palmer, William R. (n.d.) "Writings of William R. Palmer." Retrieved from http://mormontrekkers.com/Martin_company. htm

Poems of Ella Wheeler Wilcox. (1910). "Gethsemane." W.P. Nimmo, Hay, and Mitchell: Edinburgh. Accessed through http://www. litscape.com/author/Ella_Wheeler_Wilcox/Gethsemane.html

Preach My Gospel. (2004) The Church of Jesus Christ of Latter-day Saints. Salt Lake City, Utah. 52.

Restless Legs Syndrome. (n.d.). In The Free Dictionary by Farlex. Retrieved from http://www.thefreedictionary.com/ restless+leg+syndrome

Scott, Richard G. (2001, January 23). "To Acquire Knowledge and the Strength to Use It Wisely." In Brigham Young University devotional. Retrieved from http://speeches.byu. edu/?act=viewitem&id=274

Scott, Richard G. (November 2010). "The Transforming Power of Faith and Character." Retrieved from https://www.lds. org/ensign/2010/11/the-transforming-power-of-faith-and-character?lang=eng

Stapley, Robert L. (1970, April 15). "The Importance of Church History." In *Brigham Young University Speeches of the Year*. Provo, Utah. 3.

Talmage, James E. (2004, November). *Jesus the Christ*. Deseret Book: Salt Lake City, Utah.

Tourette's Syndrome. (n.d.). In Merriam-Webster Online Dictionary. Retrieved from http://www.merriam-webster.com/dictionary/tourette%27s%20syndrome

Williamson, Marianne. (1992). *A Return to Love*. HarperCollins: New York, New York.

Wilson, Larry Y. (May 2012). "Only upon the Principles of Righteousness." Retrieved from https://www.lds.org/ensign/2012/05/only-upon-the-principles-of-righteousness?lang=eng

Wirtlin, Joseph B. 2000, April. "Finding a Safe Harbor." Retrieved from https://www.lds.org/general-conference/2000/04/finding-a-safe-harbor?lang=eng&query=finding+safe+harbor